EMI

VOLUME TV

…IS STORY TAKES PLACE I…
…HE WEEKS JUST PRIOR TO…
…ND DURING THE EVENTS I…
…TAR WARS: A NEW HOPE…

WARS: EMPIRE VOLU…

…s © 2004 LUCASFILM LTD. & ™. A…
… USED UNDER AUTHORIZATION. ™…
…ONS FOR STAR WARS ARE © 2004 L…
… HORSE BOOKS™ IS A TRADEMARK…
…OMICS, INC.DARK HORSE COMIC…
…K OF DARK HORSE COMICS, INC.,…
…S CATEGORIES AND COUNTRIES. AL…
… NO PORTION OF THIS PUBLICATIO…
…ED OR TRANSMITTED, IN ANY FORM O…
…THOUT THE EXPRESS WRITTEN PERM…
…SE COMICS, INC. NAMES, CHARACTER…
…ENTS FEATURED IN THIS PUBLICATIO…
…PRODUCT OF THE AUTHOR'S IMAGIN…
… FICTITIOUSLY. ANY RESEMBLANCE T…
…LIVING OR DEAD), EVENTS, INSTITU…
…WITHOUT SATIRIC INTENT, IS COIN…

…UME COLLECTS ISSUES #8-12 A…
…OMIC-BOOK SERIES STAR WARS:…

PUBLISHED BY
DARK HORSE BOOKS
…SION OF DARK HORSE COMICS…
10956 SE MAIN STREET
MILWAUKIE, OR 97222

WWW.DARKHORSE.COM
WWW.STARWARS.COM

…O FIND A COMICS SHOP IN YOU…
AREA, CALL THE COMIC SHOP
LOCATOR SERVICE TOLL-FREE
AT 1-888-266-4226

FIRST EDITION
ISBN: 978-1-56971-975-6

3   5   7   9   10   8   6   4

…D BY MIDAS PRINTING INTERNA…
…LTD., HUIZHOU, CHINA…

VOLUME TWO: DARKLIGHTER

WRITTEN BY PAUL CHADWICK

ART BY DOUG WHEATLEY
AND TOMÁS GIORELLO

COLORED BY CHRIS CHUCKRY
AND BRAD ANDERSON

LETTERED BY SNO CONE STUDIOS

FRONT COVER ART BY KILIAN PLUNKETT

BACK COVER ART BY DOUG WHEATLEY

PUBLISHER
MIKE RICHARDSON

COLLECTION DESIGNER
LANI SCHREIBSTEIN

ART DIRECTORS
MARK COX
LIA RIBACCHI

ASSISTANT EDITOR
JEREMY BARLOW

EDITOR
RANDY STRADLEY

SPECIAL THANKS TO
SUE ROSTONI, AMY GARY,
CHRIS CERASI, AND LUCY AUTREY
WILSON AT LUCAS LICENSING

IN THE COURSE OF TELLING THIS STORY, IT WAS DECIDED TO USE DRAMATIC LICENSE
AND SHOW THE FACES OF TIE FIGHTER PILOTS. IN REALITY, TIE FIGHTERS ARE NOT
EQUIPPED WITH LIFE-SUPPORT SYSTEMS. PLEASE DO NOT ATTEMPT TO PILOT YOUR OW
TIE FIGHTER WITHOUT FIRST DONNING A PROPER PRESSURE SUIT.

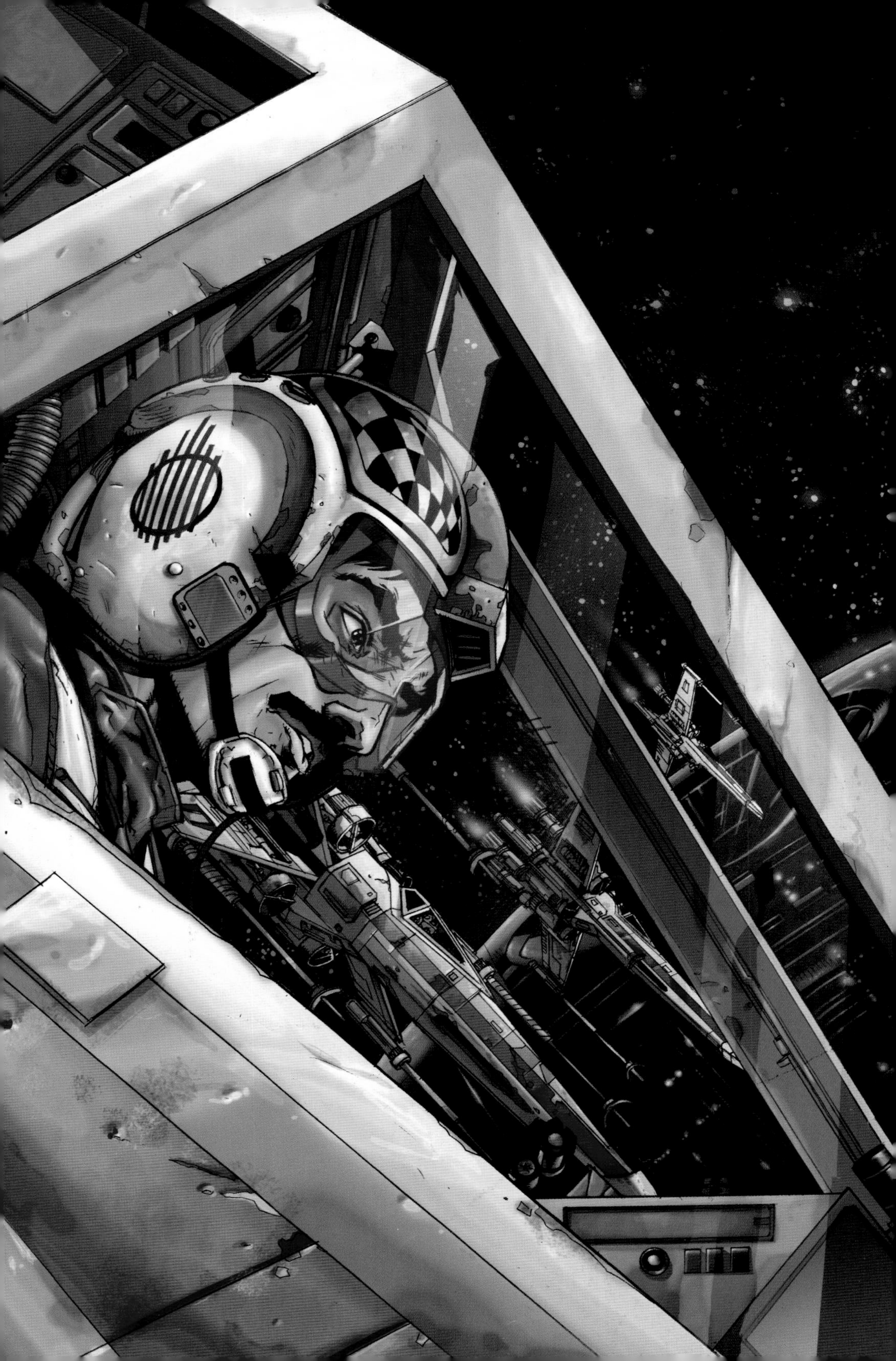

THE SAGA OF
BIGGS DARKLIGHTER

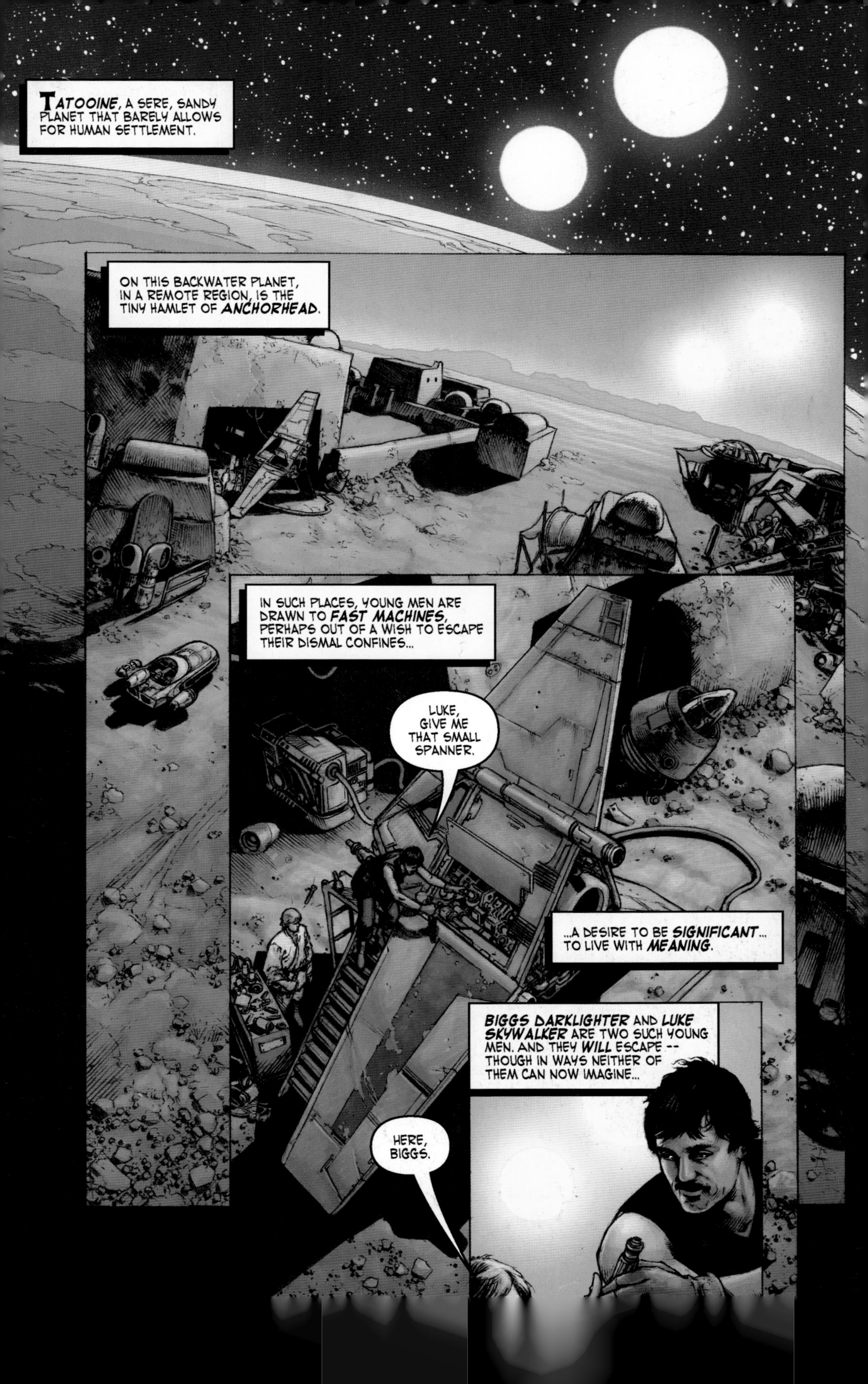
TATOOINE, A SERE, SANDY PLANET THAT BARELY ALLOWS FOR HUMAN SETTLEMENT.
ON THIS BACKWATER PLANET, IN A REMOTE REGION, IS THE TINY HAMLET OF ANCHORHEAD.
IN SUCH PLACES, YOUNG MEN ARE DRAWN TO FAST MACHINES, PERHAPS OUT OF A WISH TO ESCAPE THEIR DISMAL CONFINES...
LUKE, GIVE ME THAT SMALL SPANNER.
...A DESIRE TO BE SIGNIFICANT... TO LIVE WITH MEANING.
BIGGS DARKLIGHTER AND LUKE SKYWALKER ARE TWO SUCH YOUNG MEN. AND THEY WILL ESCAPE -- THOUGH IN WAYS NEITHER OF THEM CAN NOW IMAGINE...
HERE, BIGGS.

YOU AND WORMIE GOT THAT THING SO IT'LL FLY AGAIN, BIGGS BOY?

YEAH, FIXER. I THINK *LUKE* AND I *HAVE*.

THINK I'LL GIVE HER A SHAKEDOWN RUN IN BEGGAR'S CANYON.

OKAY IF I COME TOO? IN CASE IT BREAKS DOWN, I MEAN.

YOU'D BETTER NOT. SUNDOWN'S COMING, AND YOU HAVE A LONG TRIP BACK TO YOUR UNCLE'S SPREAD.

YEAH. BESIDES, YOU MIGHT WRECK THE SKYHOPPER.

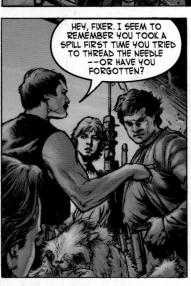

HEY, FIXER. I SEEM TO REMEMBER YOU TOOK A SPILL FIRST TIME YOU TRIED TO THREAD THE NEEDLE --OR HAVE YOU FORGOTTEN?

HA HA!

THAT'S RIGHT, STICK UP FOR YOUR LITTLE SIDEKICK!

WHAT'S HE GOING TO DO WHEN YOU'RE GONE?

I'LL DO JUST *FINE*.

BUT THAT ISN'T HOW LUKE SKYWALKER FEELS.

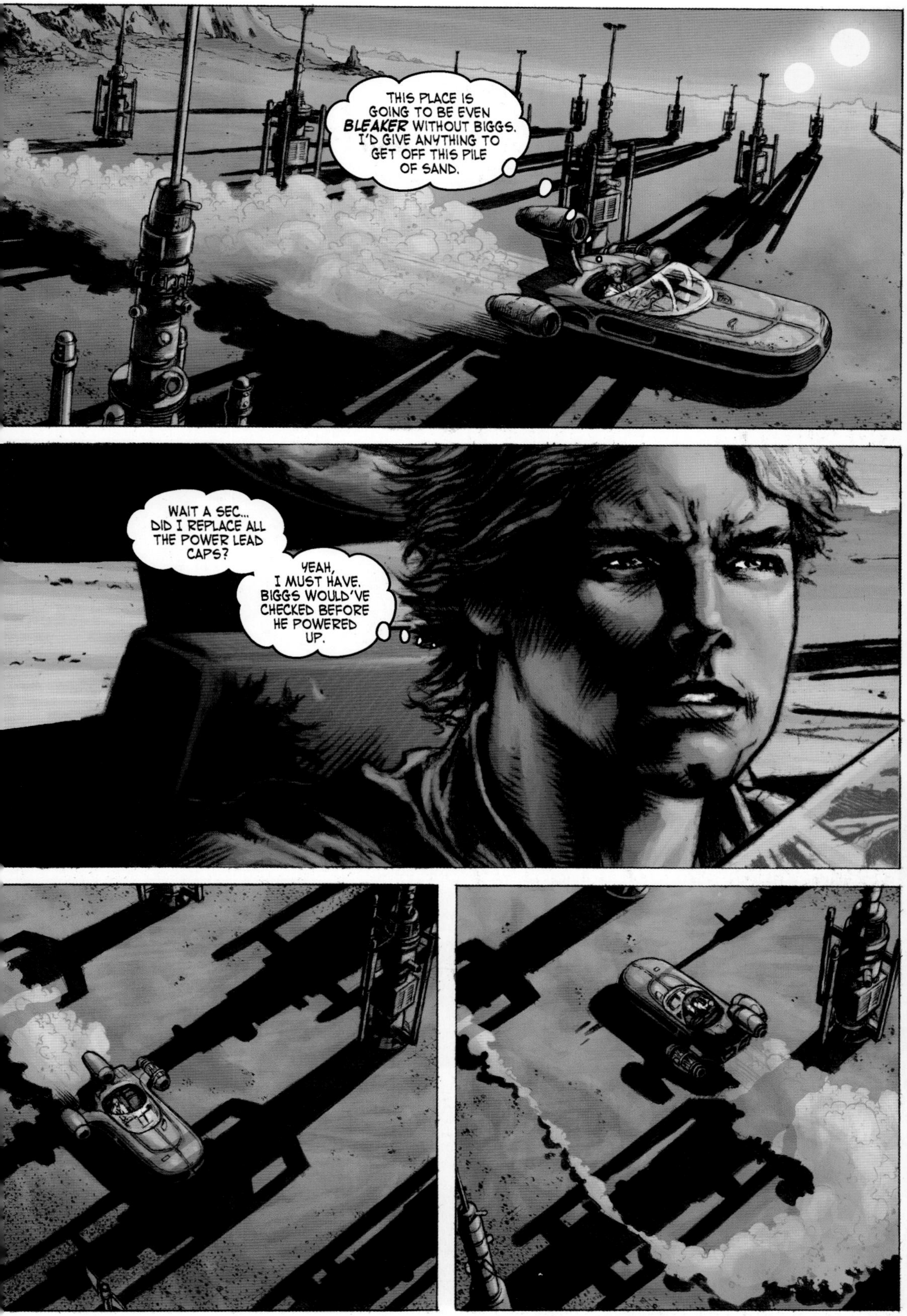
THIS PLACE IS GOING TO BE EVEN BLEAKER WITHOUT BIGGS. I'D GIVE ANYTHING TO GET OFF THIS PILE OF SAND.
WAIT A SEC... DID I REPLACE ALL THE POWER LEAD CAPS?
YEAH, I MUST HAVE. BIGGS WOULD'VE CHECKED BEFORE HE POWERED UP.

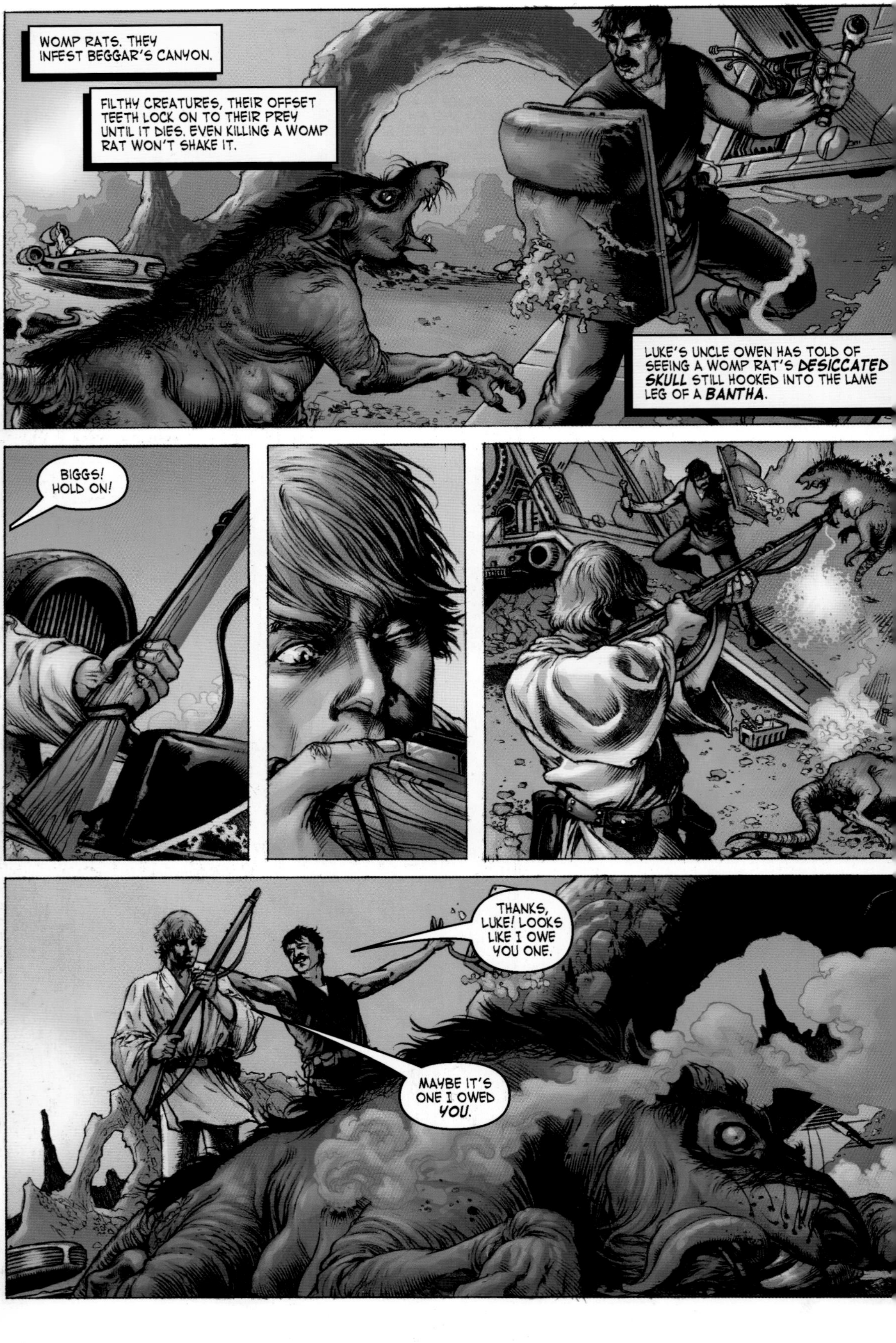
WOMP RATS. THEY INFEST BEGGAR'S CANYON.
FILTHY CREATURES, THEIR OFFSET TEETH LOCK ON TO THEIR PREY UNTIL IT DIES. EVEN KILLING A WOMP RAT WON'T SHAKE IT.
LUKE'S UNCLE OWEN HAS TOLD OF SEEING A WOMP RAT'S DESICCATED SKULL STILL HOOKED INTO THE LAME LEG OF A BANTHA.
BIGGS! HOLD ON!
THANKS, LUKE! LOOKS LIKE I OWE YOU ONE.
MAYBE IT'S ONE I OWED YOU.

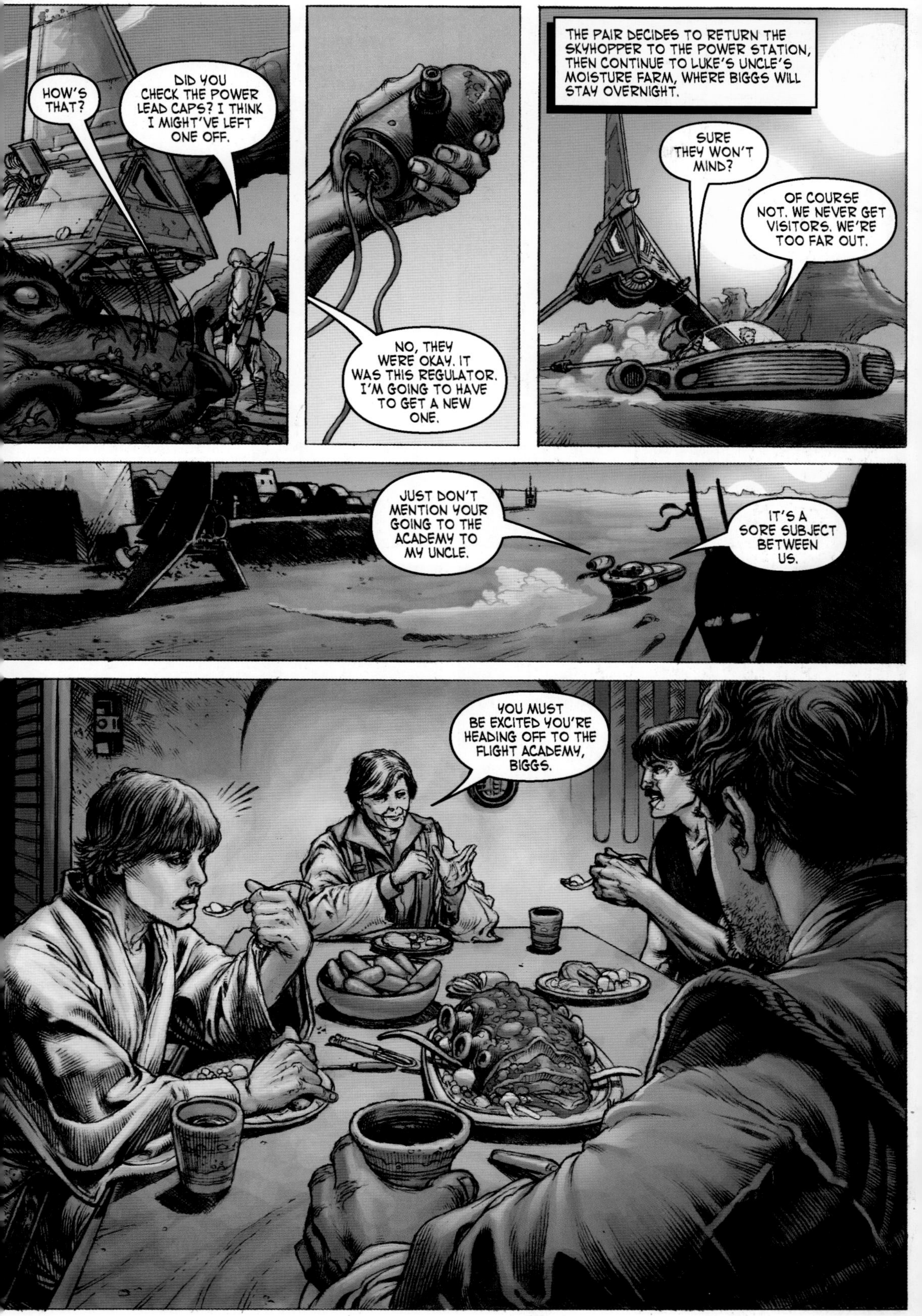
HOW'S THAT?
DID YOU CHECK THE POWER LEAD CAPS? I THINK I MIGHT'VE LEFT ONE OFF.
NO, THEY WERE OKAY. IT WAS THIS REGULATOR. I'M GOING TO HAVE TO GET A NEW ONE.
THE PAIR DECIDES TO RETURN THE SKYHOPPER TO THE POWER STATION, THEN CONTINUE TO LUKE'S UNCLE'S MOISTURE FARM, WHERE BIGGS WILL STAY OVERNIGHT.
SURE THEY WON'T MIND?
OF COURSE NOT. WE NEVER GET VISITORS. WE'RE TOO FAR OUT.
JUST DON'T MENTION YOUR GOING TO THE ACADEMY TO MY UNCLE.
IT'S A SORE SUBJECT BETWEEN US.
YOU MUST BE EXCITED YOU'RE HEADING OFF TO THE FLIGHT ACADEMY, BIGGS.

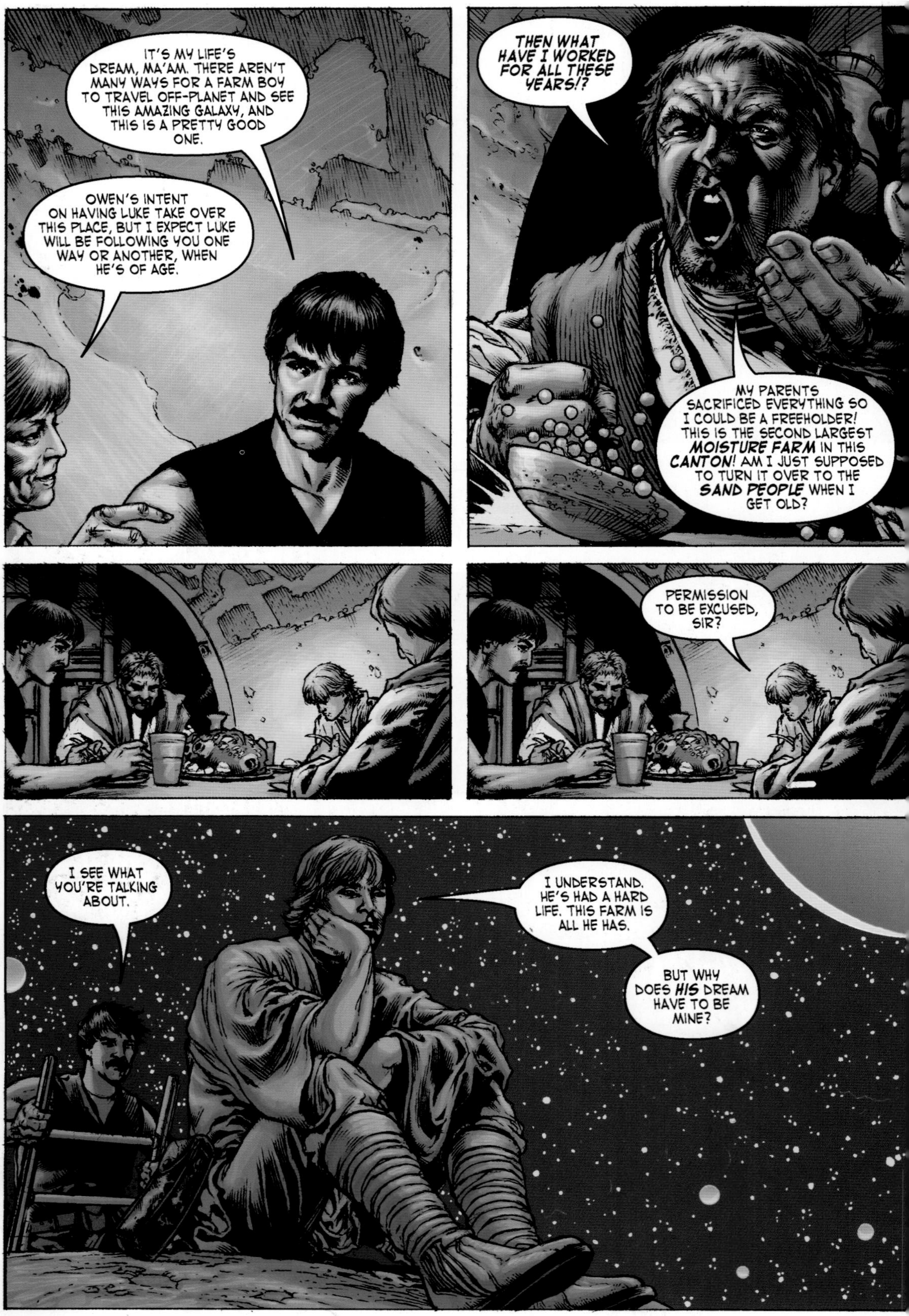
IT'S MY LIFE'S DREAM, MA'AM. THERE AREN'T MANY WAYS FOR A FARM BOY TO TRAVEL OFF-PLANET AND SEE THIS AMAZING GALAXY, AND THIS IS A PRETTY GOOD ONE.
OWEN'S INTENT ON HAVING LUKE TAKE OVER THIS PLACE, BUT I EXPECT LUKE WILL BE FOLLOWING YOU ONE WAY OR ANOTHER, WHEN HE'S OF AGE.
THEN WHAT HAVE I WORKED FOR ALL THESE YEARS!?
MY PARENTS SACRIFICED EVERYTHING SO I COULD BE A FREEHOLDER! THIS IS THE SECOND LARGEST MOISTURE FARM IN THIS CANTON! AM I JUST SUPPOSED TO TURN IT OVER TO THE SAND PEOPLE WHEN I GET OLD?
PERMISSION TO BE EXCUSED, SIR?
I SEE WHAT YOU'RE TALKING ABOUT.
I UNDERSTAND. HE'S HAD A HARD LIFE. THIS FARM IS ALL HE HAS.
BUT WHY DOES HIS DREAM HAVE TO BE MINE?

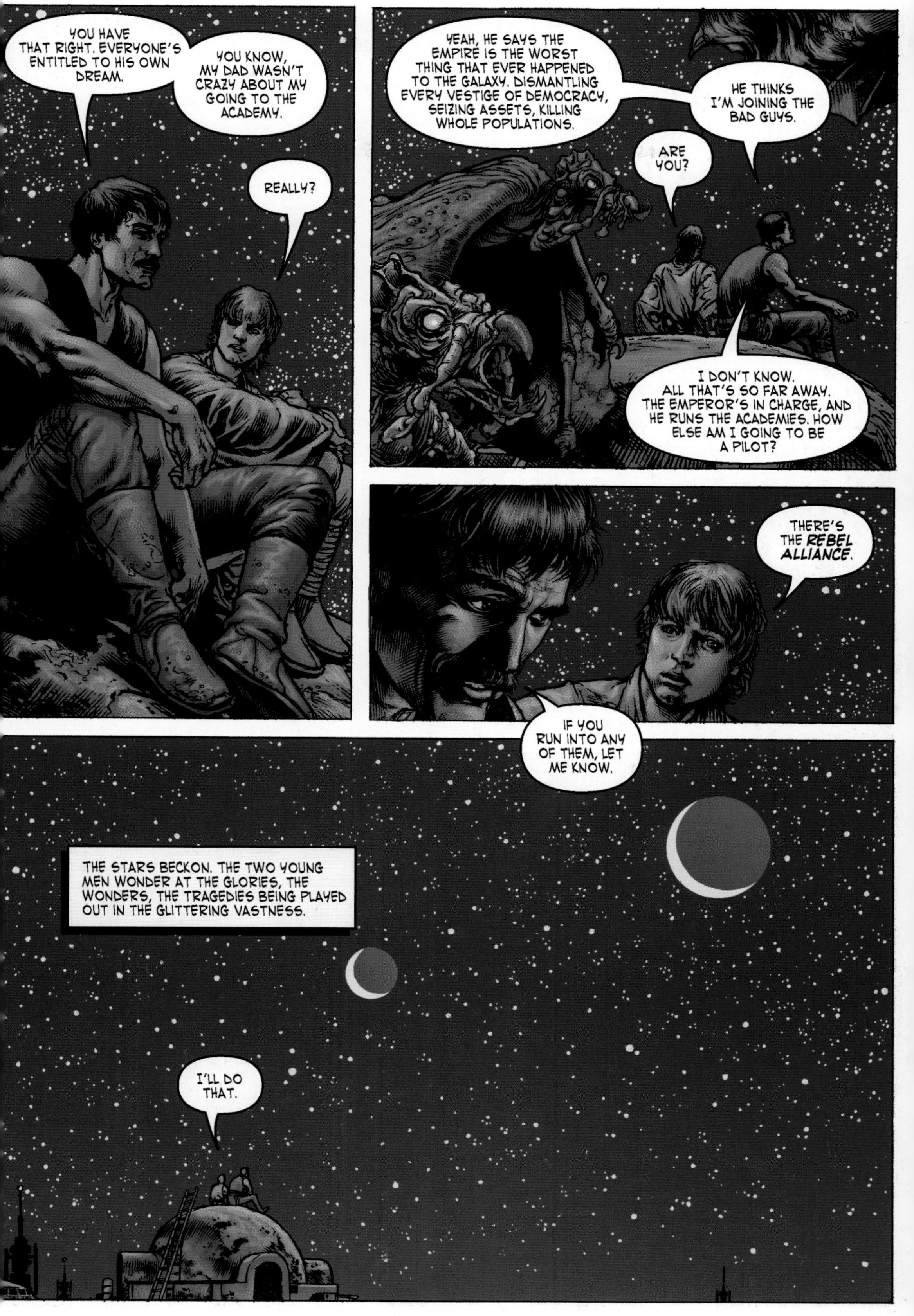
YOU HAVE THAT RIGHT. EVERYONE'S ENTITLED TO HIS OWN DREAM.
YOU KNOW, MY DAD WASN'T CRAZY ABOUT MY GOING TO THE ACADEMY.
REALLY?
YEAH, HE SAYS THE EMPIRE IS THE WORST THING THAT EVER HAPPENED TO THE GALAXY. DISMANTLING EVERY VESTIGE OF DEMOCRACY, SEIZING ASSETS, KILLING WHOLE POPULATIONS.
HE THINKS I'M JOINING THE BAD GUYS.
ARE YOU?
I DON'T KNOW. ALL THAT'S SO FAR AWAY. THE EMPEROR'S IN CHARGE, AND HE RUNS THE ACADEMIES. HOW ELSE AM I GOING TO BE A PILOT?
THERE'S THE *REBEL ALLIANCE*.
IF YOU RUN INTO ANY OF THEM, LET ME KNOW.
THE STARS BECKON. THE TWO YOUNG MEN WONDER AT THE GLORIES, THE WONDERS, THE TRAGEDIES BEING PLAYED OUT IN THE GLITTERING VASTNESS.
I'LL DO THAT.

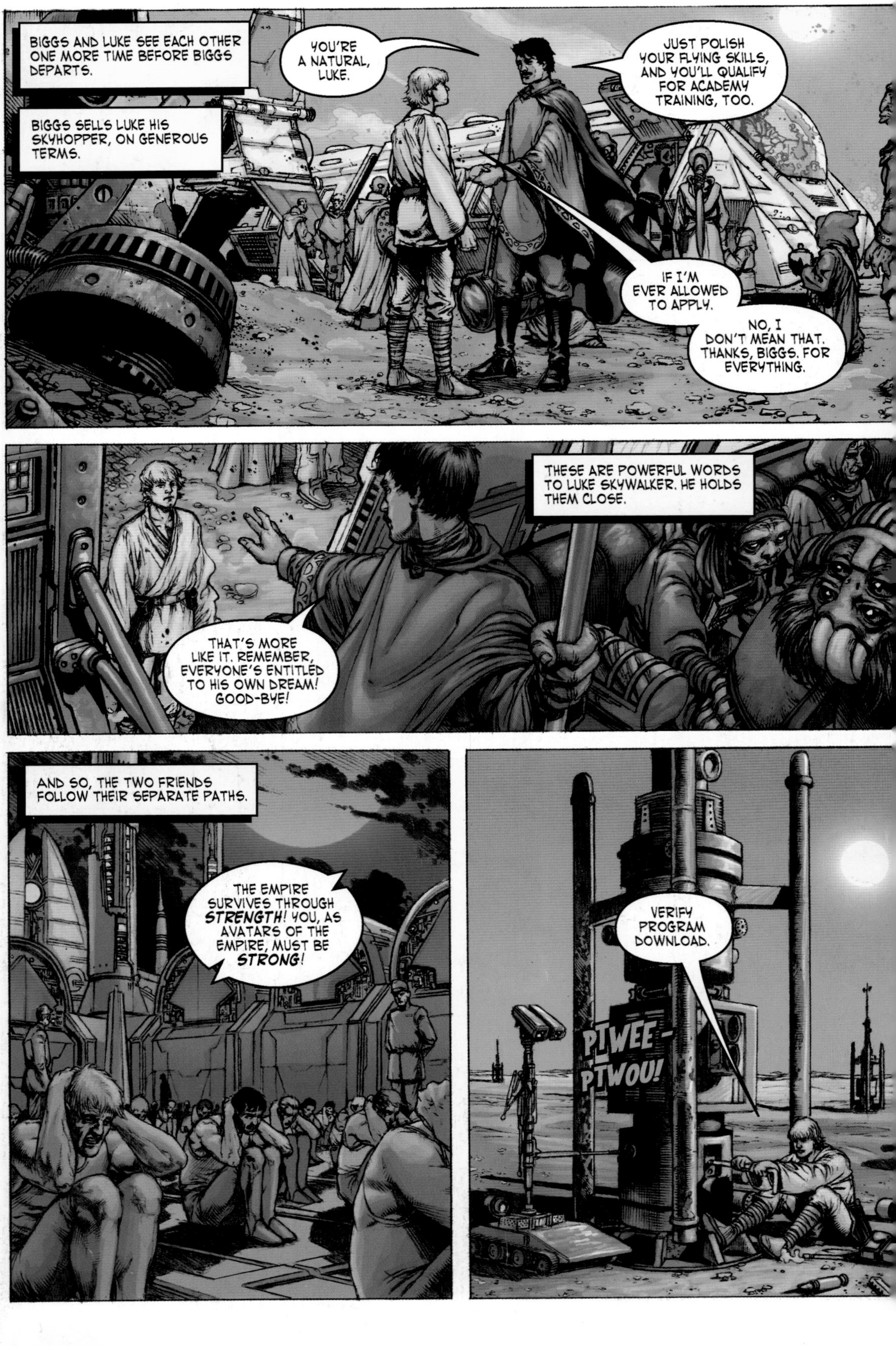
BIGGS AND LUKE SEE EACH OTHER ONE MORE TIME BEFORE BIGGS DEPARTS.
BIGGS SELLS LUKE HIS SKYHOPPER, ON GENEROUS TERMS.
YOU'RE A NATURAL, LUKE.
JUST POLISH YOUR FLYING SKILLS, AND YOU'LL QUALIFY FOR ACADEMY TRAINING, TOO.
IF I'M EVER ALLOWED TO APPLY.
NO, I DON'T MEAN THAT. THANKS, BIGGS. FOR EVERYTHING.
THESE ARE POWERFUL WORDS TO LUKE SKYWALKER. HE HOLDS THEM CLOSE.
THAT'S MORE LIKE IT. REMEMBER, EVERYONE'S ENTITLED TO HIS OWN DREAM! GOOD-BYE!
AND SO, THE TWO FRIENDS FOLLOW THEIR SEPARATE PATHS.
THE EMPIRE SURVIVES THROUGH STRENGTH! YOU, AS AVATARS OF THE EMPIRE, MUST BE STRONG!
VERIFY PROGRAM DOWNLOAD.
PTWEE-PTWOU!

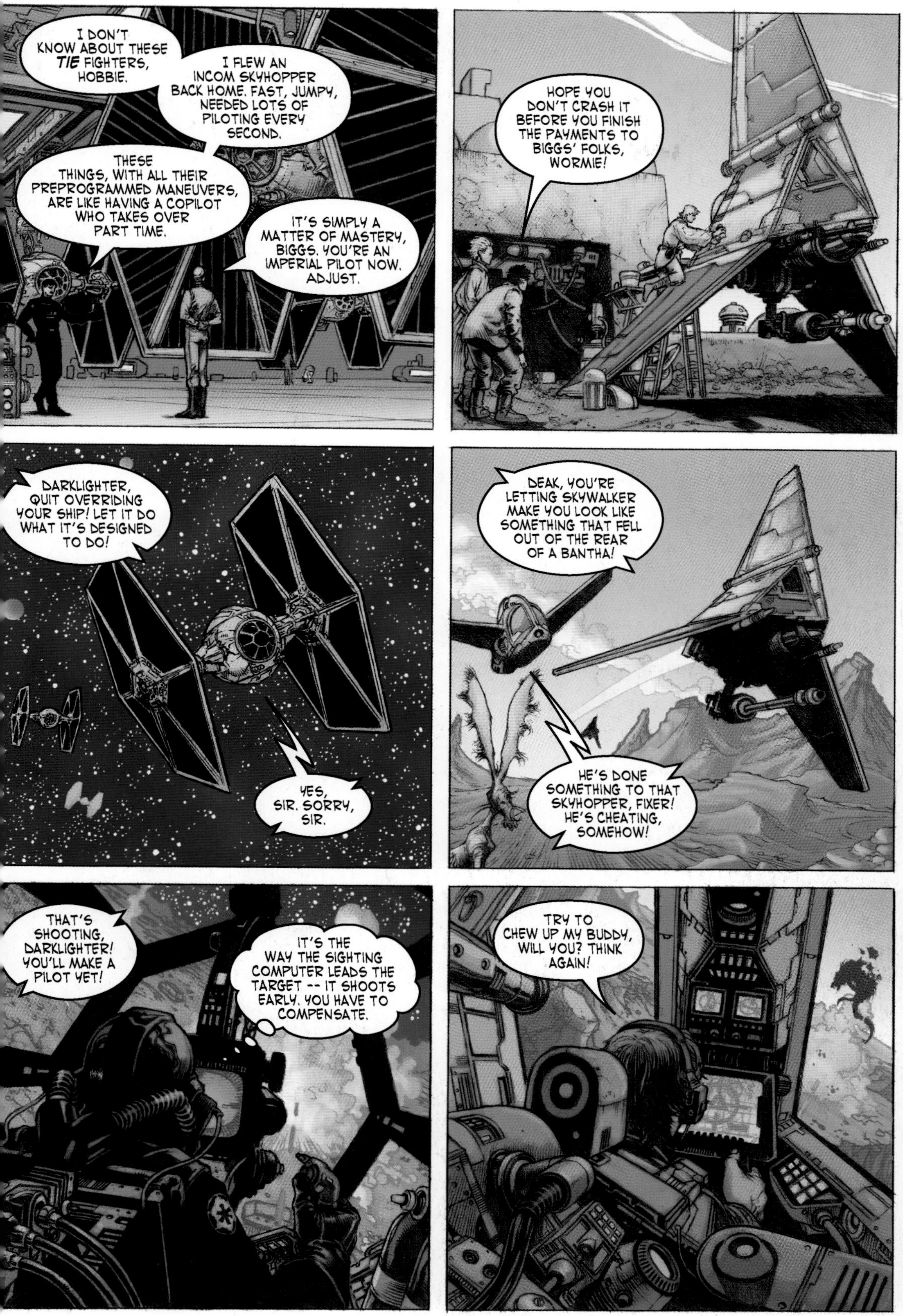
I DON'T KNOW ABOUT THESE *TIE* FIGHTERS, HOBBIE.
I FLEW AN INCOM SKYHOPPER BACK HOME. FAST, JUMPY, NEEDED LOTS OF PILOTING EVERY SECOND.
THESE THINGS, WITH ALL THEIR PREPROGRAMMED MANEUVERS, ARE LIKE HAVING A COPILOT WHO TAKES OVER PART TIME.
IT'S SIMPLY A MATTER OF MASTERY, BIGGS. YOU'RE AN IMPERIAL PILOT NOW. ADJUST.
HOPE YOU DON'T CRASH IT BEFORE YOU FINISH THE PAYMENTS TO BIGGS' FOLKS, WORMIE!
DARKLIGHTER, QUIT OVERRIDING YOUR SHIP! LET IT DO WHAT IT'S DESIGNED TO DO!
YES, SIR. SORRY, SIR.
DEAK, YOU'RE LETTING SKYWALKER MAKE YOU LOOK LIKE SOMETHING THAT FELL OUT OF THE REAR OF A BANTHA!
HE'S DONE SOMETHING TO THAT SKYHOPPER, FIXER! HE'S CHEATING, SOMEHOW!
THAT'S SHOOTING, DARKLIGHTER! YOU'LL MAKE A PILOT YET!
IT'S THE WAY THE SIGHTING COMPUTER LEADS THE TARGET -- IT SHOOTS EARLY. YOU HAVE TO COMPENSATE.
TRY TO CHEW UP MY BUDDY, WILL YOU? THINK AGAIN!

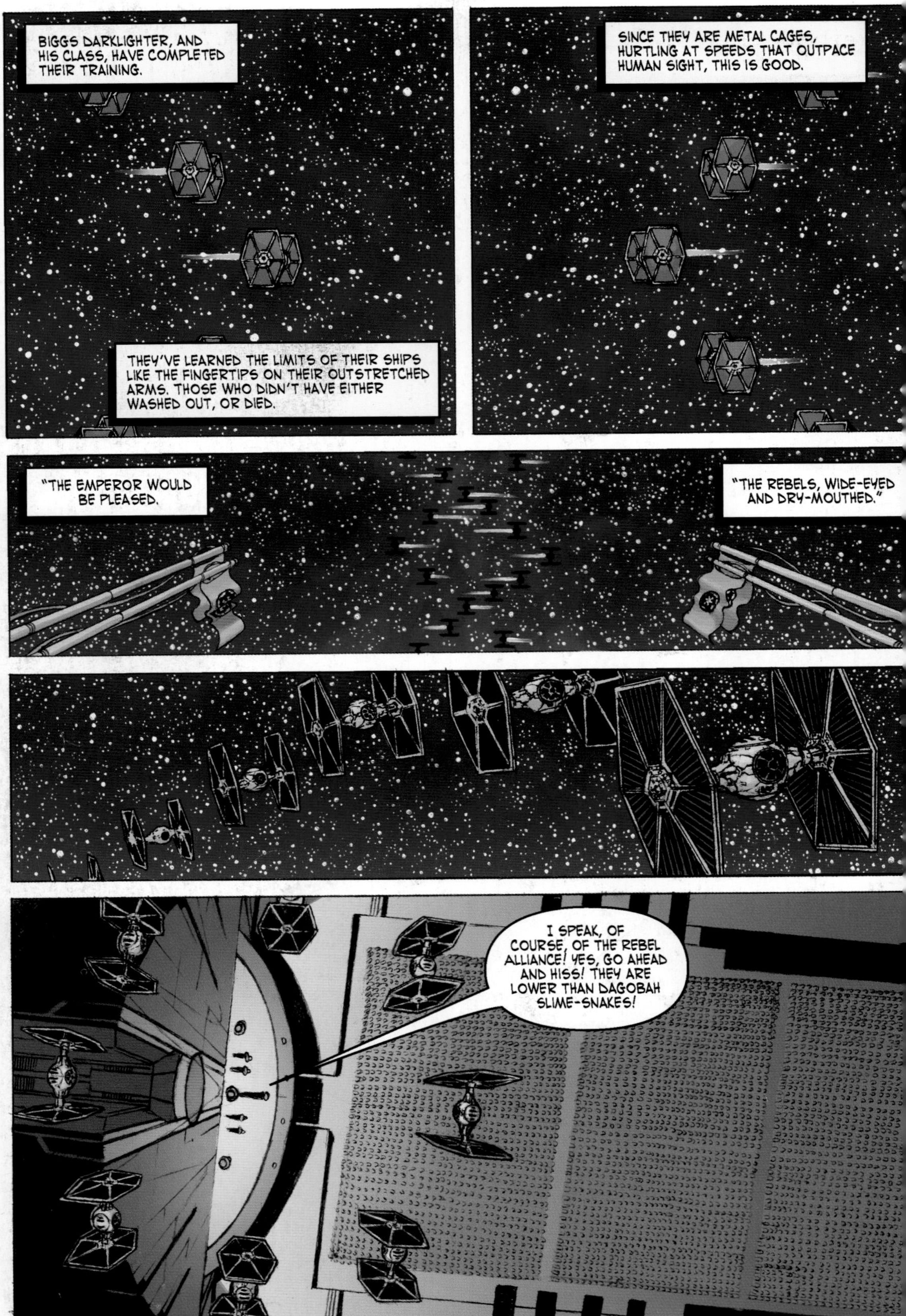
BIGGS DARKLIGHTER, AND HIS CLASS, HAVE COMPLETED THEIR TRAINING.
THEY'VE LEARNED THE LIMITS OF THEIR SHIPS LIKE THE FINGERTIPS ON THEIR OUTSTRETCHED ARMS. THOSE WHO DIDN'T HAVE EITHER WASHED OUT, OR DIED.
SINCE THEY ARE METAL CAGES, HURTLING AT SPEEDS THAT OUTPACE HUMAN SIGHT, THIS IS GOOD.
"THE EMPEROR WOULD BE PLEASED.
"THE REBELS, WIDE-EYED AND DRY-MOUTHED."
I SPEAK, OF COURSE, OF THE REBEL ALLIANCE! YES, GO AHEAD AND HISS! THEY ARE LOWER THAN DAGOBAH SLIME-SNAKES!

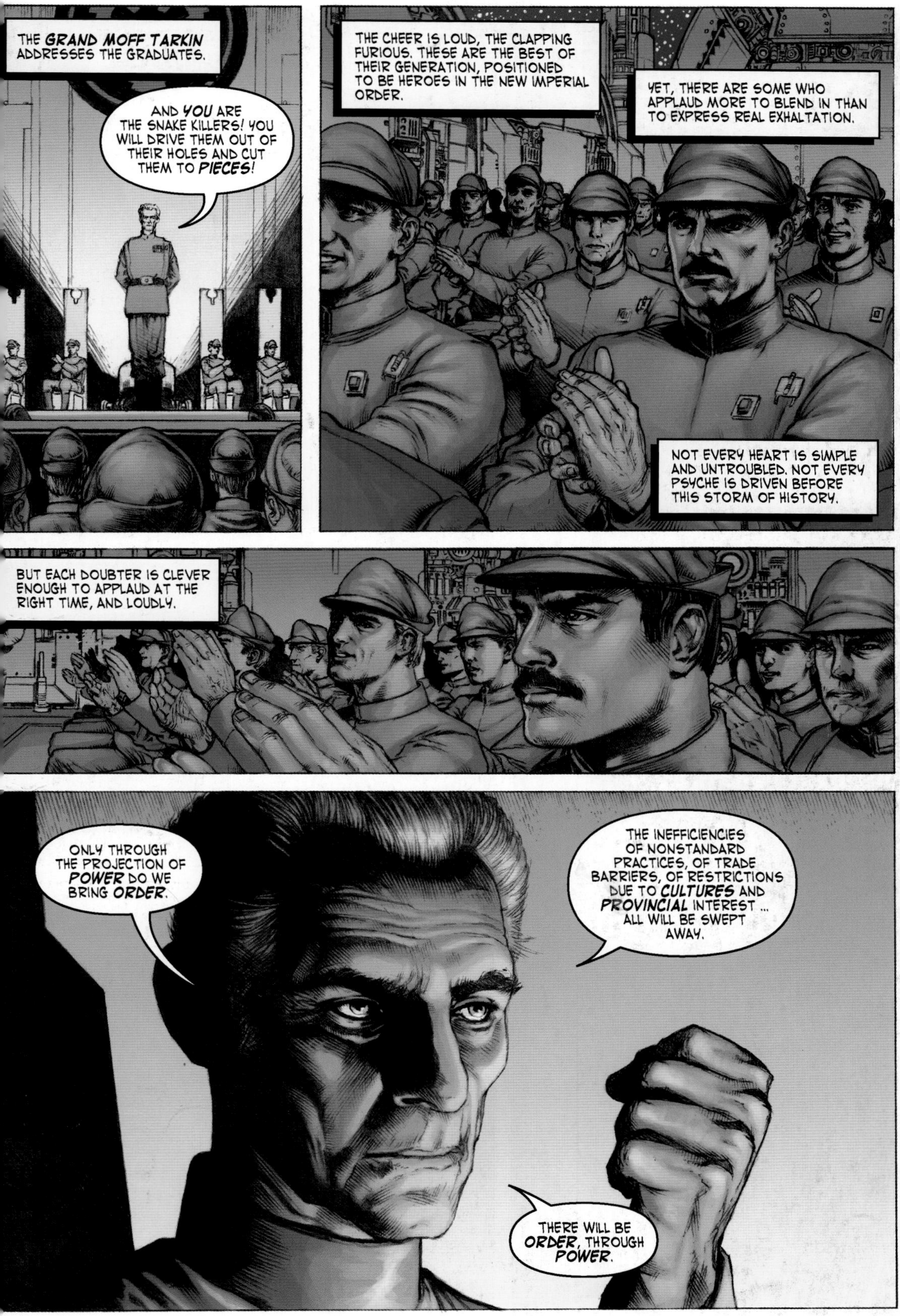
THE GRAND MOFF TARKIN ADDRESSES THE GRADUATES.
AND YOU ARE THE SNAKE KILLERS! YOU WILL DRIVE THEM OUT OF THEIR HOLES AND CUT THEM TO PIECES!
THE CHEER IS LOUD, THE CLAPPING FURIOUS. THESE ARE THE BEST OF THEIR GENERATION, POSITIONED TO BE HEROES IN THE NEW IMPERIAL ORDER.
YET, THERE ARE SOME WHO APPLAUD MORE TO BLEND IN THAN TO EXPRESS REAL EXHALTATION.
NOT EVERY HEART IS SIMPLE AND UNTROUBLED. NOT EVERY PSYCHE IS DRIVEN BEFORE THIS STORM OF HISTORY.
BUT EACH DOUBTER IS CLEVER ENOUGH TO APPLAUD AT THE RIGHT TIME, AND LOUDLY.
ONLY THROUGH THE PROJECTION OF POWER DO WE BRING ORDER.
THE INEFFICIENCIES OF NONSTANDARD PRACTICES, OF TRADE BARRIERS, OF RESTRICTIONS DUE TO CULTURES AND PROVINCIAL INTEREST ... ALL WILL BE SWEPT AWAY.
THERE WILL BE ORDER, THROUGH POWER.

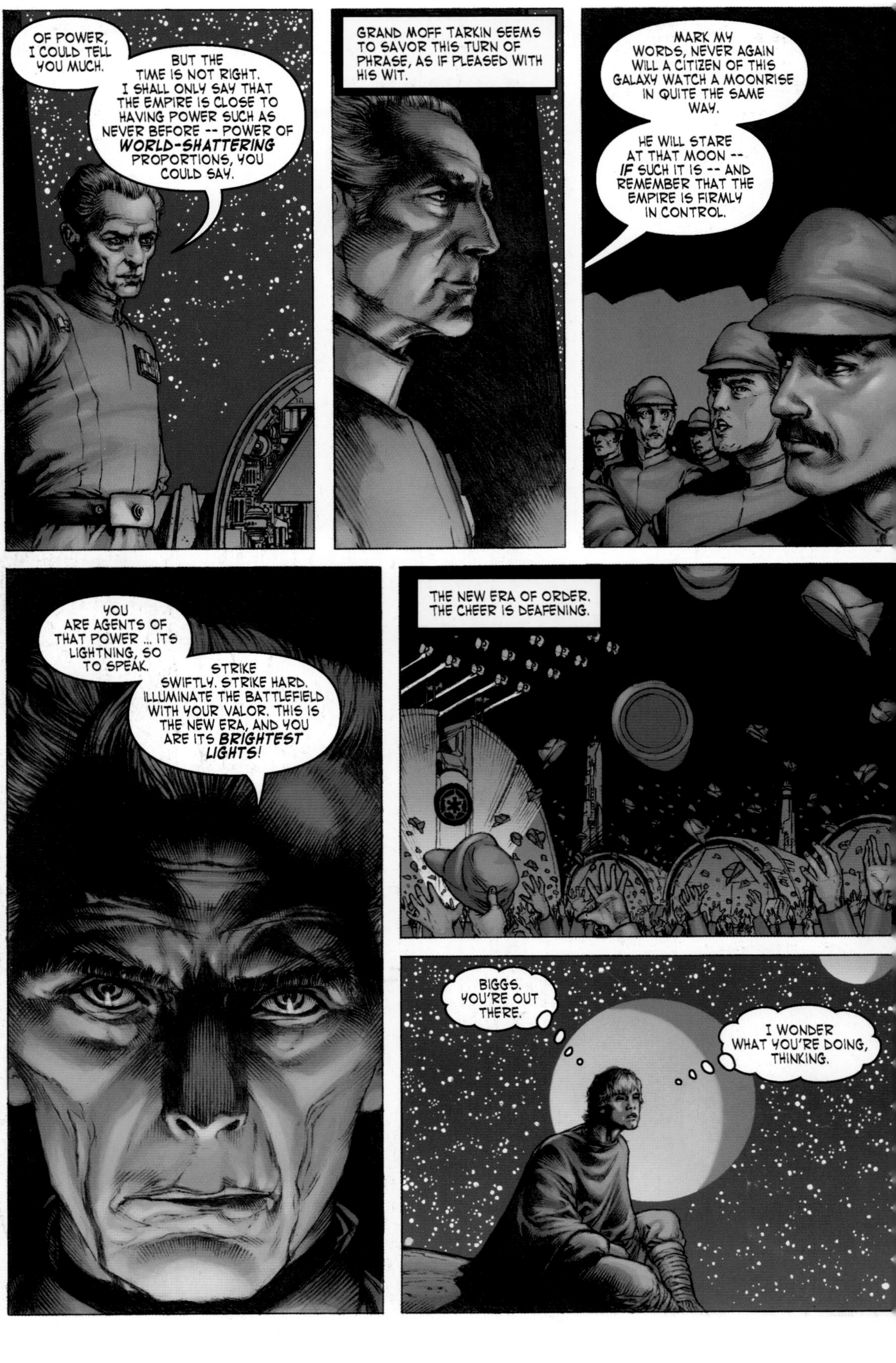
OF POWER, I COULD TELL YOU MUCH.
BUT THE TIME IS NOT RIGHT. I SHALL ONLY SAY THAT THE EMPIRE IS CLOSE TO HAVING POWER SUCH AS NEVER BEFORE -- POWER OF **WORLD-SHATTERING** PROPORTIONS, YOU COULD SAY.
GRAND MOFF TARKIN SEEMS TO SAVOR THIS TURN OF PHRASE, AS IF PLEASED WITH HIS WIT.
MARK MY WORDS, NEVER AGAIN WILL A CITIZEN OF THIS GALAXY WATCH A MOONRISE IN QUITE THE SAME WAY.
HE WILL STARE AT THAT MOON -- ***IF*** SUCH IT IS -- AND REMEMBER THAT THE EMPIRE IS FIRMLY IN CONTROL.
YOU ARE AGENTS OF THAT POWER ... ITS LIGHTNING, SO TO SPEAK.
STRIKE SWIFTLY. STRIKE HARD. ILLUMINATE THE BATTLEFIELD WITH YOUR VALOR. THIS IS THE NEW ERA, AND YOU ARE ITS ***BRIGHTEST LIGHTS!***
THE NEW ERA OF ORDER. THE CHEER IS DEAFENING.
BIGGS. YOU'RE OUT THERE.
I WONDER WHAT YOU'RE DOING, THINKING.

BIGGS, IF YOU WANT SOME OF THIS HAPPY JUICE, YOU'D BETTER GET IT NOW.

WHAT'RE YOU MOONIN' ABOUT, ANYWAY? WITH YOUR CLASS RANK, YOU'RE BOUND TO GET A PLUM ASSIGNMENT TOMORROW.

I'M JUST WONDERING WHAT GRAND MOFF TARKIN WAS TALKING ABOUT.

FEED ME TO THE FISHES OF NABOO IF I KNOW!

I BET IT'S THE BLAYLOCK EFFECT. THAT THING THAT PROJECTS IMAGES IN AN ATMOSPHERE. SCARE THE FIGHT RIGHT OUT OF A REBELLIOUS PLANET.

IMAGINE TEN THOUSAND BATTLE CRUISERS, CRISSCROSSING THE SKY!

CAN IT PROJECT ON A MOON?

I DON'T KNOW IF IT EVEN *WORKS*. THEY WERE HAVING TROUBLE WITH IT, LAST I HEARD.

IN THE HALL OUTSIDE, SOMEONE APPROACHES, TOO QUIETLY TO BE HEARD.

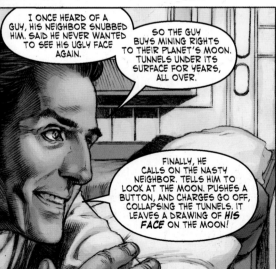

I ONCE HEARD OF A GUY, HIS NEIGHBOR SNUBBED HIM. SAID HE NEVER WANTED TO SEE HIS UGLY FACE AGAIN.

SO THE GUY BUYS MINING RIGHTS TO THEIR PLANET'S MOON. TUNNELS UNDER ITS SURFACE FOR YEARS, ALL OVER.

FINALLY, HE CALLS ON THE NASTY NEIGHBOR. TELLS HIM TO LOOK AT THE MOON. PUSHES A BUTTON, AND CHARGES GO OFF, COLLAPSING THE TUNNELS. IT LEAVES A DRAWING OF *HIS FACE* ON THE MOON!

MAYBE THEY'VE GOT A WAY TO BLOW UP MOONS.

OR SOMETHING ELSE.

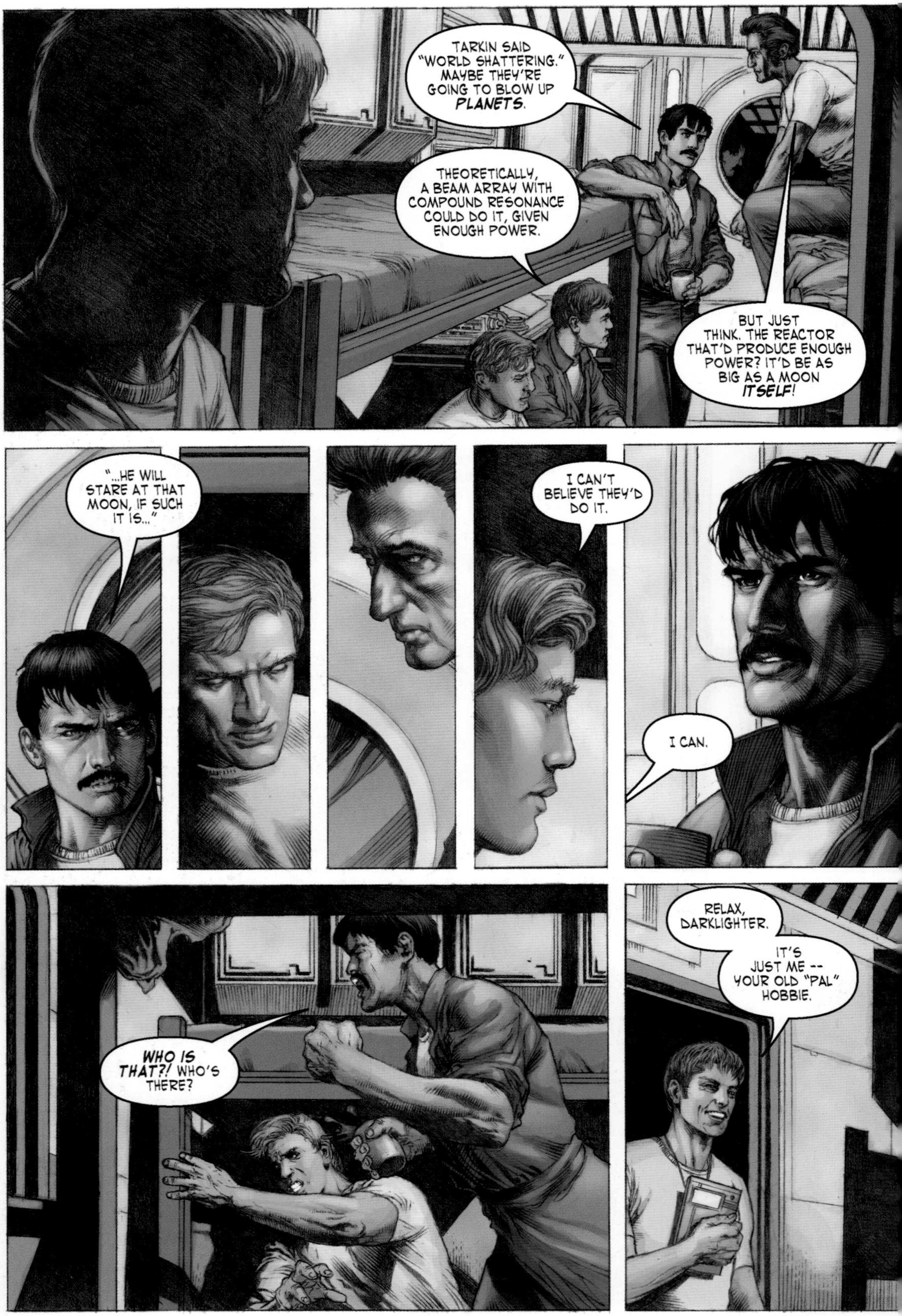
TARKIN SAID "WORLD SHATTERING." MAYBE THEY'RE GOING TO BLOW UP *PLANETS*.
THEORETICALLY, A BEAM ARRAY WITH COMPOUND RESONANCE COULD DO IT, GIVEN ENOUGH POWER.
BUT JUST THINK. THE REACTOR THAT'D PRODUCE ENOUGH POWER? IT'D BE AS BIG AS A MOON *ITSELF*!
"...HE WILL STARE AT THAT MOON, IF SUCH IT IS..."
I CAN'T BELIEVE THEY'D DO IT.
I CAN.
WHO IS THAT?! WHO'S THERE?
RELAX, DARKLIGHTER.
IT'S JUST ME -- YOUR OLD "PAL" HOBBIE.

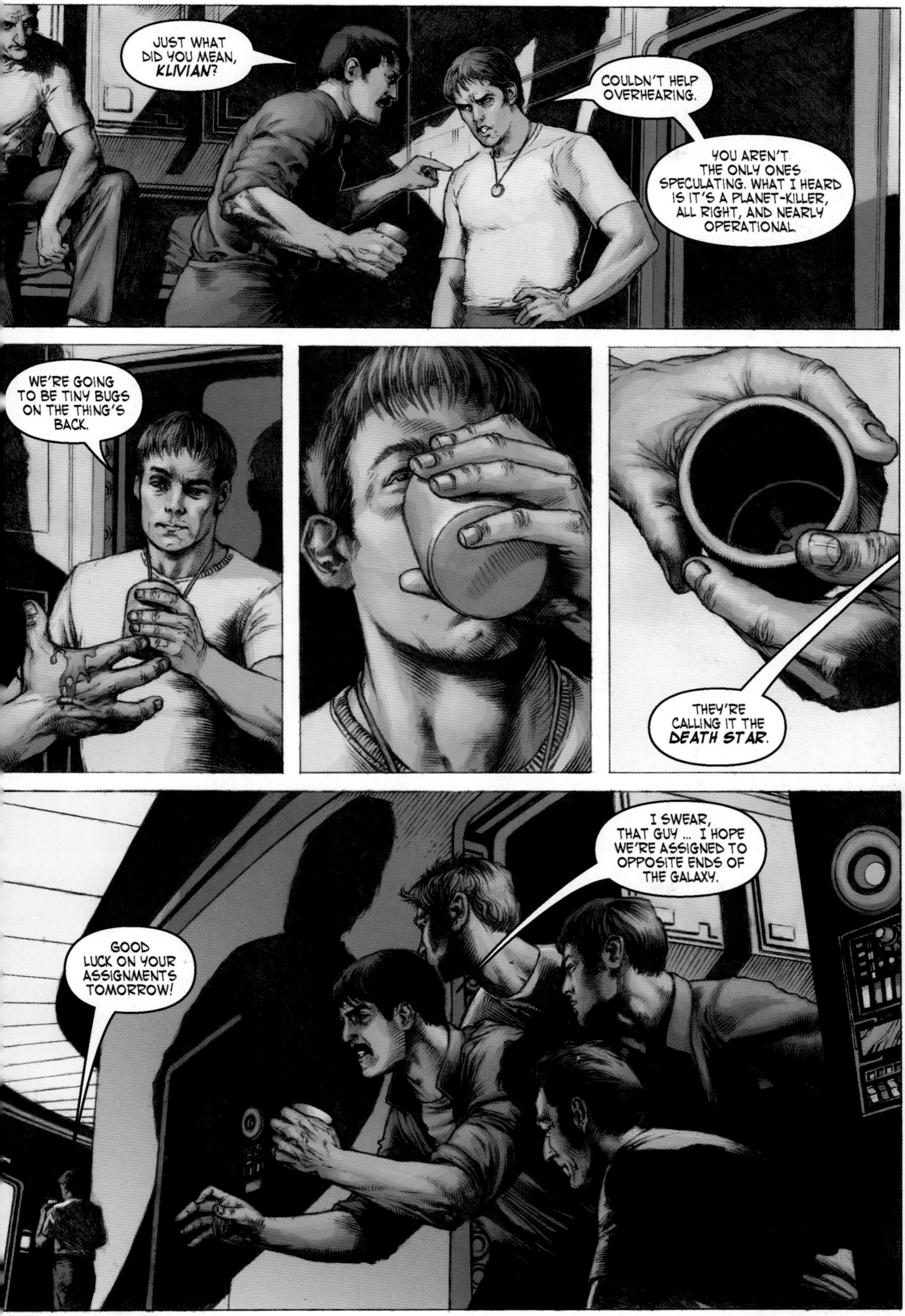
JUST WHAT DID YOU MEAN, KLIVIAN?
COULDN'T HELP OVERHEARING.
YOU AREN'T THE ONLY ONES SPECULATING. WHAT I HEARD IS IT'S A PLANET-KILLER, ALL RIGHT, AND NEARLY OPERATIONAL.
WE'RE GOING TO BE TINY BUGS ON THE THING'S BACK.
THEY'RE CALLING IT THE DEATH STAR.
I SWEAR, THAT GUY ... I HOPE WE'RE ASSIGNED TO OPPOSITE ENDS OF THE GALAXY.
GOOD LUCK ON YOUR ASSIGNMENTS TOMORROW!

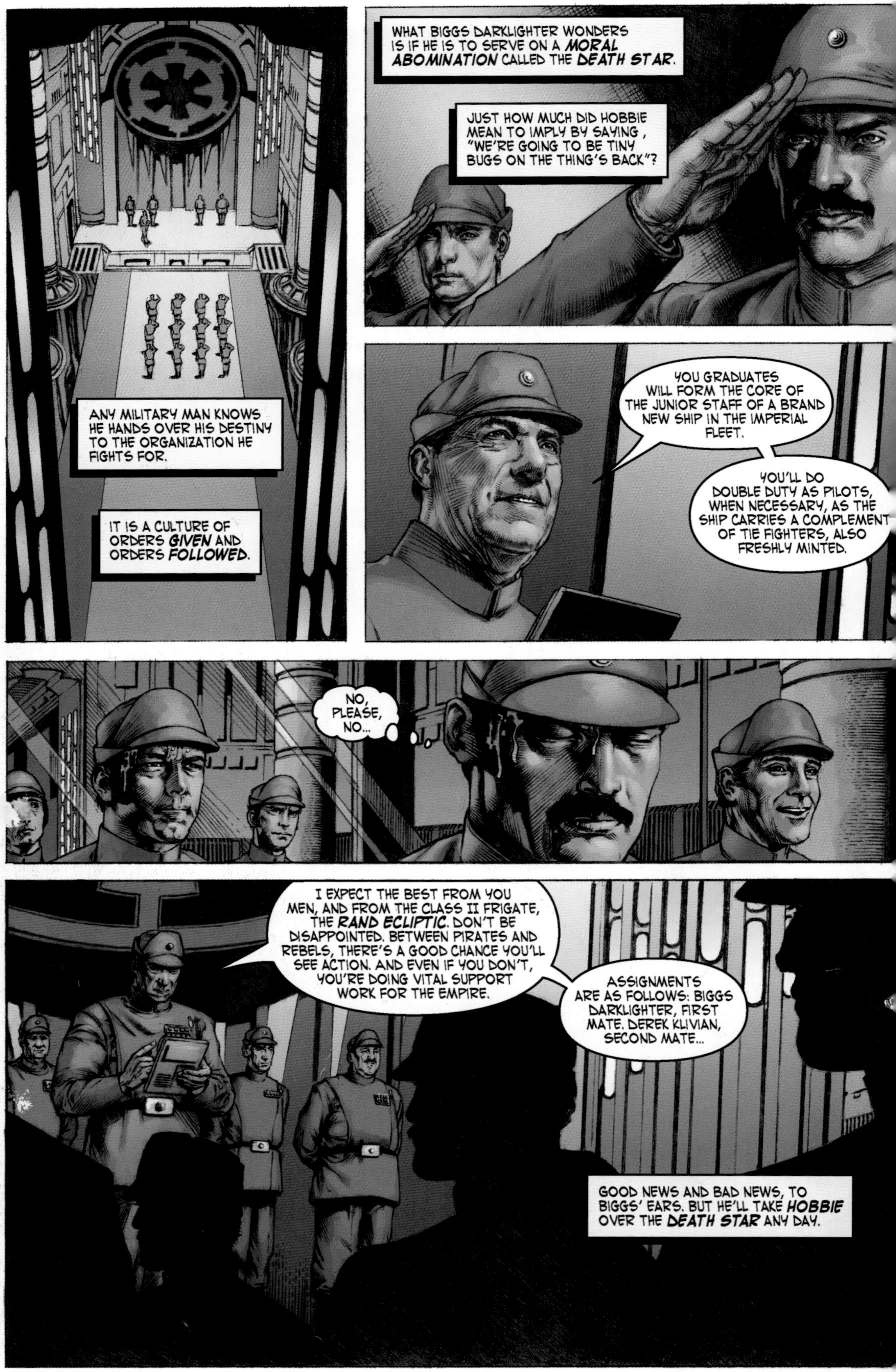
ANY MILITARY MAN KNOWS HE HANDS OVER HIS DESTINY TO THE ORGANIZATION HE FIGHTS FOR.
IT IS A CULTURE OF ORDERS GIVEN AND ORDERS FOLLOWED.
WHAT BIGGS DARKLIGHTER WONDERS IS IF HE IS TO SERVE ON A MORAL ABOMINATION CALLED THE DEATH STAR.
JUST HOW MUCH DID HOBBIE MEAN TO IMPLY BY SAYING, "WE'RE GOING TO BE TINY BUGS ON THE THING'S BACK"?
YOU GRADUATES WILL FORM THE CORE OF THE JUNIOR STAFF OF A BRAND NEW SHIP IN THE IMPERIAL FLEET.
YOU'LL DO DOUBLE DUTY AS PILOTS, WHEN NECESSARY, AS THE SHIP CARRIES A COMPLEMENT OF TIE FIGHTERS, ALSO FRESHLY MINTED.
NO, PLEASE, NO...
I EXPECT THE BEST FROM YOU MEN, AND FROM THE CLASS II FRIGATE, THE RAND ECLIPTIC. DON'T BE DISAPPOINTED. BETWEEN PIRATES AND REBELS, THERE'S A GOOD CHANCE YOU'LL SEE ACTION. AND EVEN IF YOU DON'T, YOU'RE DOING VITAL SUPPORT WORK FOR THE EMPIRE.
ASSIGNMENTS ARE AS FOLLOWS: BIGGS DARKLIGHTER, FIRST MATE. DEREK KLIVIAN, SECOND MATE...
GOOD NEWS AND BAD NEWS, TO BIGGS' EARS. BUT HE'LL TAKE HOBBIE OVER THE DEATH STAR ANY DAY.

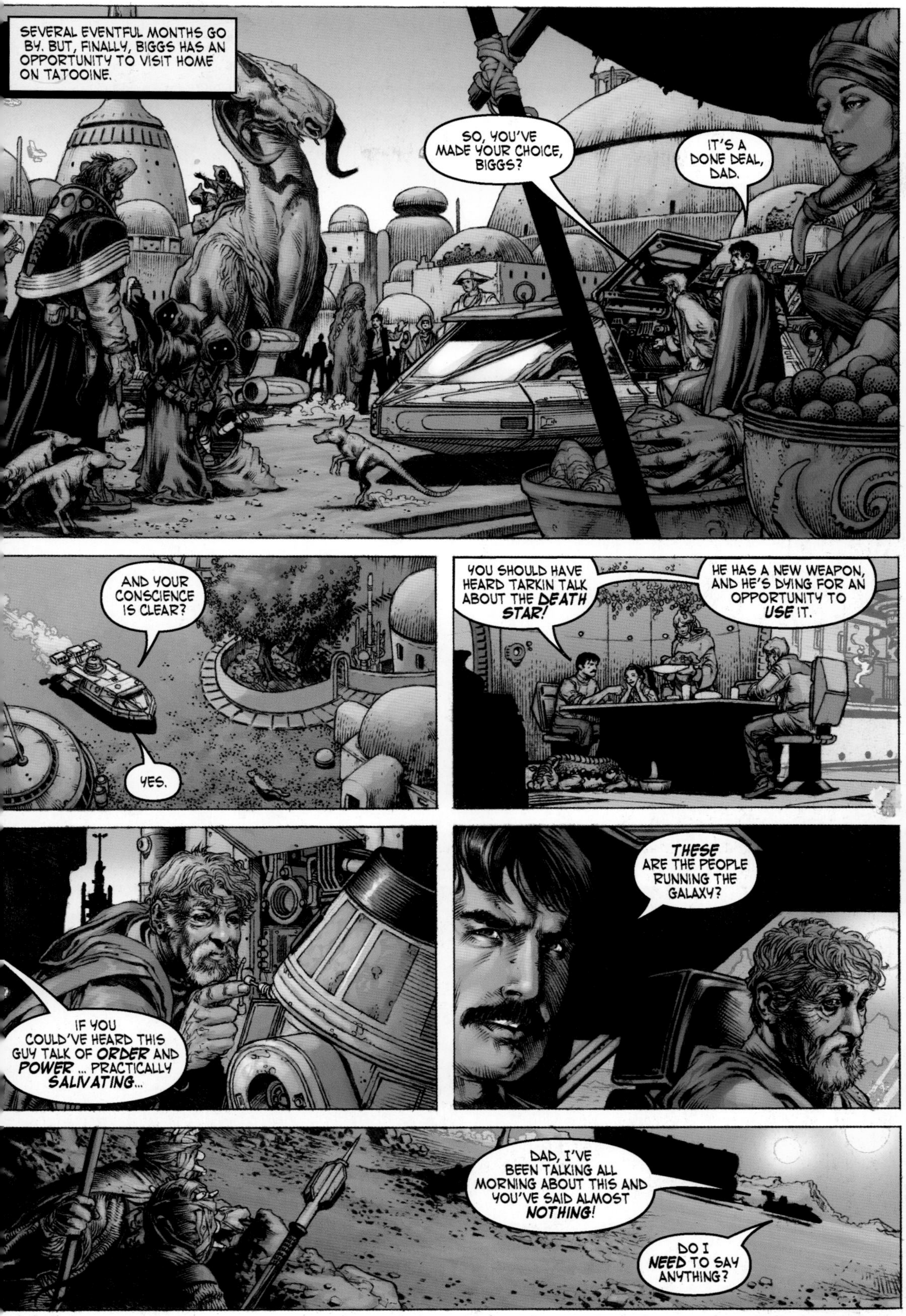
SEVERAL EVENTFUL MONTHS GO BY. BUT, FINALLY, BIGGS HAS AN OPPORTUNITY TO VISIT HOME ON TATOOINE.
SO, YOU'VE MADE YOUR CHOICE, BIGGS?
IT'S A DONE DEAL, DAD.
AND YOUR CONSCIENCE IS CLEAR?
YES.
YOU SHOULD HAVE HEARD TARKIN TALK ABOUT THE DEATH STAR!
HE HAS A NEW WEAPON, AND HE'S DYING FOR AN OPPORTUNITY TO USE IT.
IF YOU COULD'VE HEARD THIS GUY TALK OF ORDER AND POWER ... PRACTICALLY SALIVATING...
THESE ARE THE PEOPLE RUNNING THE GALAXY?
DAD, I'VE BEEN TALKING ALL MORNING ABOUT THIS AND YOU'VE SAID ALMOST NOTHING!
DO I NEED TO SAY ANYTHING?

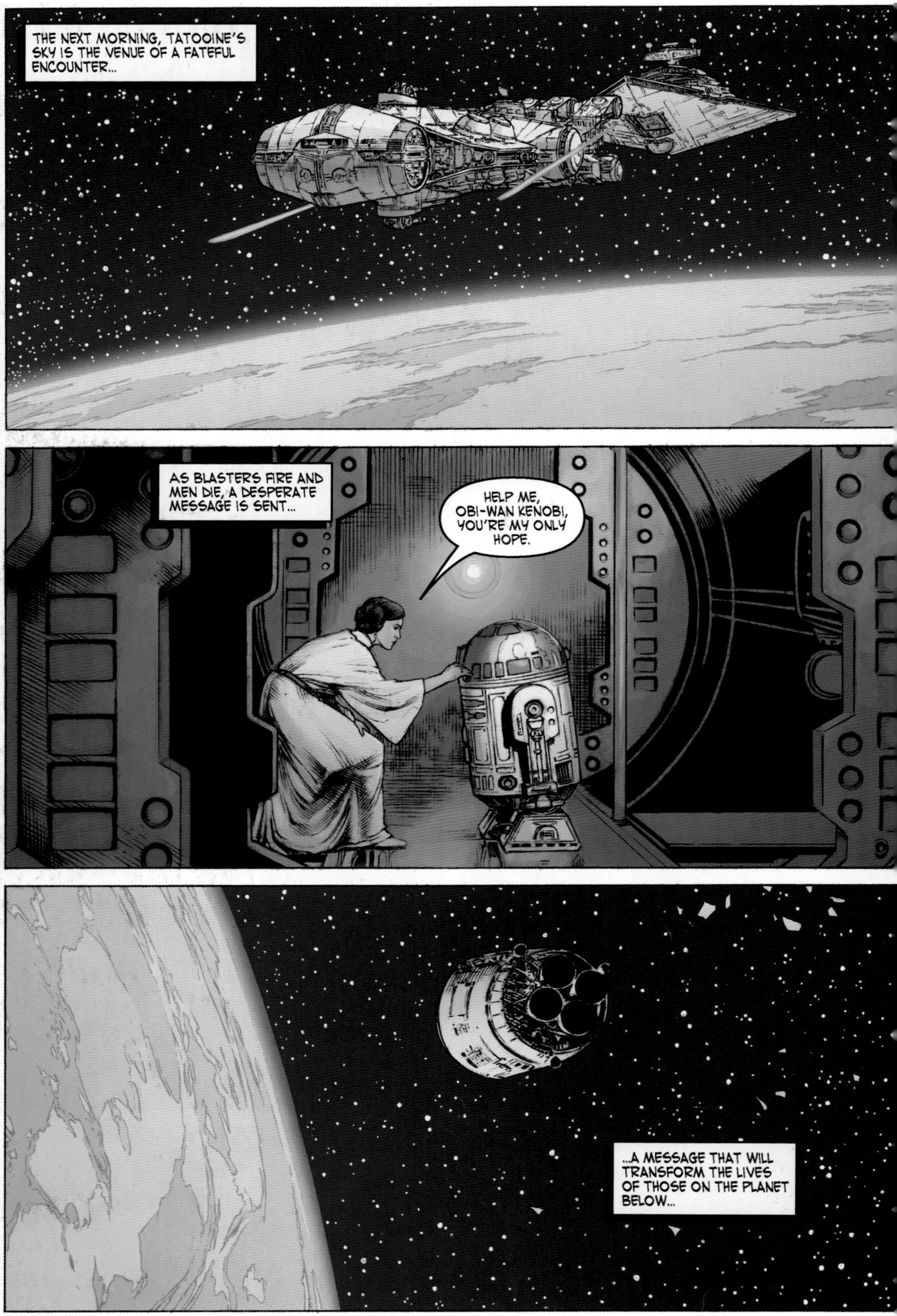
THE NEXT MORNING, TATOOINE'S SKY IS THE VENUE OF A FATEFUL ENCOUNTER...
AS BLASTERS FIRE AND MEN DIE, A DESPERATE MESSAGE IS SENT...
HELP ME, OBI-WAN KENOBI, YOU'RE MY ONLY HOPE.
...A MESSAGE THAT WILL TRANSFORM THE LIVES OF THOSE ON THE PLANET BELOW...

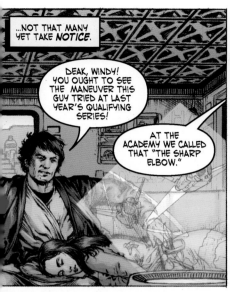

...NOT THAT MANY YET TAKE *NOTICE*.

DEAK, WINDY! YOU OUGHT TO SEE THE MANEUVER THIS GUY TRIED AT LAST YEAR'S QUALIFYING SERIES!

AT THE ACADEMY WE CALLED THAT "THE SHARP ELBOW."

BIGGS! WHERE'D YOU COME FROM?

WHERE DO YOU THINK?

OOH, YOU LOOK LIKE A SPACE HERO!

ALL RIGHT, CAMIE, DON'T PUSH IT.

I MEAN IT, CAMIE, LET GO.

COME ON, FIXER. BIGGS HAS BEEN AWAY FOR -- HOW LONG?

I SAID *LET GO!*

YOU LET GO, FIXER-BOY!

HEY!!

EVERYBODY, *OUT HERE!* YOU HAVE TO *SEE* THIS!

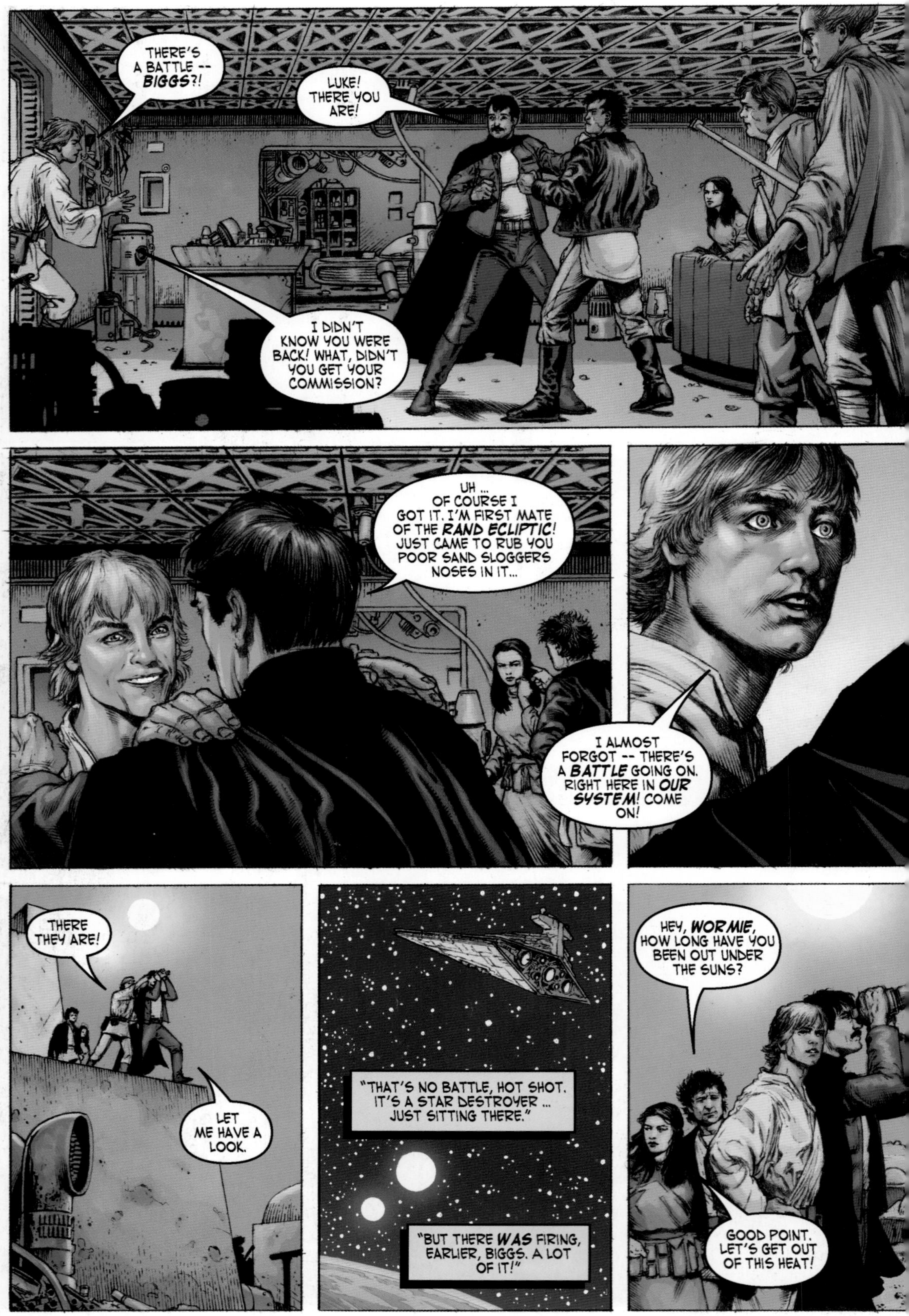
THERE'S A BATTLE -- BIGGS?!
LUKE! THERE YOU ARE!
I DIDN'T KNOW YOU WERE BACK! WHAT, DIDN'T YOU GET YOUR COMMISSION?
UH ... OF COURSE I GOT IT. I'M FIRST MATE OF THE RAND ECLIPTIC! JUST CAME TO RUB YOU POOR SAND SLOGGERS NOSES IN IT...
I ALMOST FORGOT -- THERE'S A BATTLE GOING ON. RIGHT HERE IN OUR SYSTEM! COME ON!
THERE THEY ARE!
LET ME HAVE A LOOK.
"THAT'S NO BATTLE, HOT SHOT. IT'S A STAR DESTROYER ... JUST SITTING THERE."
"BUT THERE WAS FIRING, EARLIER, BIGGS. A LOT OF IT!"
HEY, WORMIE, HOW LONG HAVE YOU BEEN OUT UNDER THE SUNS?
GOOD POINT. LET'S GET OUT OF THIS HEAT!

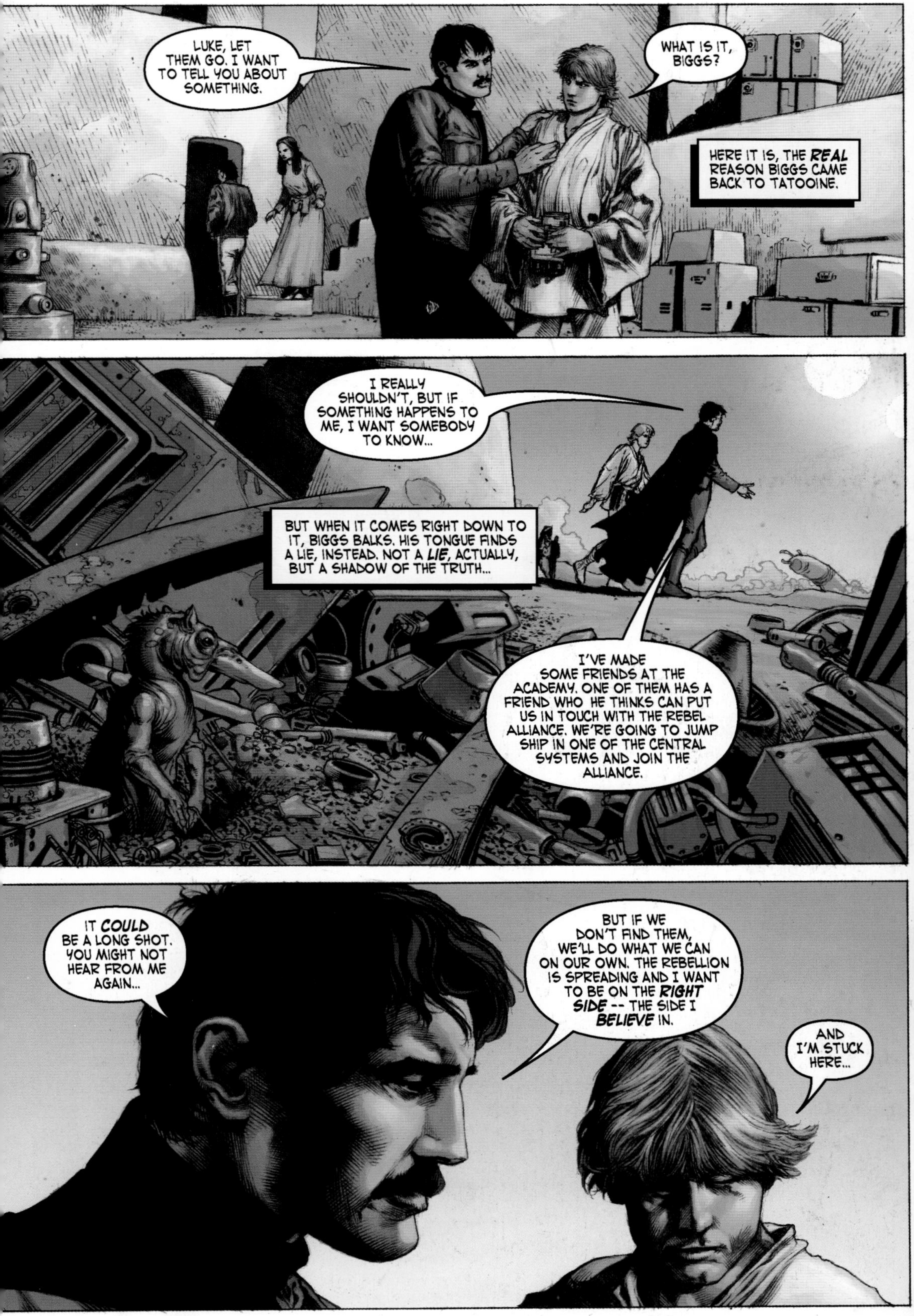
LUKE, LET THEM GO. I WANT TO TELL YOU ABOUT SOMETHING.
WHAT IS IT, BIGGS?
HERE IT IS, THE *REAL* REASON BIGGS CAME BACK TO TATOOINE.
I REALLY SHOULDN'T, BUT IF SOMETHING HAPPENS TO ME, I WANT SOMEBODY TO KNOW...
BUT WHEN IT COMES RIGHT DOWN TO IT, BIGGS BALKS. HIS TONGUE FINDS A LIE, INSTEAD. NOT A *LIE*, ACTUALLY, BUT A SHADOW OF THE TRUTH...
I'VE MADE SOME FRIENDS AT THE ACADEMY. ONE OF THEM HAS A FRIEND WHO HE THINKS CAN PUT US IN TOUCH WITH THE REBEL ALLIANCE. WE'RE GOING TO JUMP SHIP IN ONE OF THE CENTRAL SYSTEMS AND JOIN THE ALLIANCE.
IT *COULD* BE A LONG SHOT. YOU MIGHT NOT HEAR FROM ME AGAIN...
BUT IF WE DON'T FIND THEM, WE'LL DO WHAT WE CAN ON OUR OWN. THE REBELLION IS SPREADING AND I WANT TO BE ON THE *RIGHT SIDE* -- THE SIDE I *BELIEVE* IN.
AND I'M STUCK HERE...

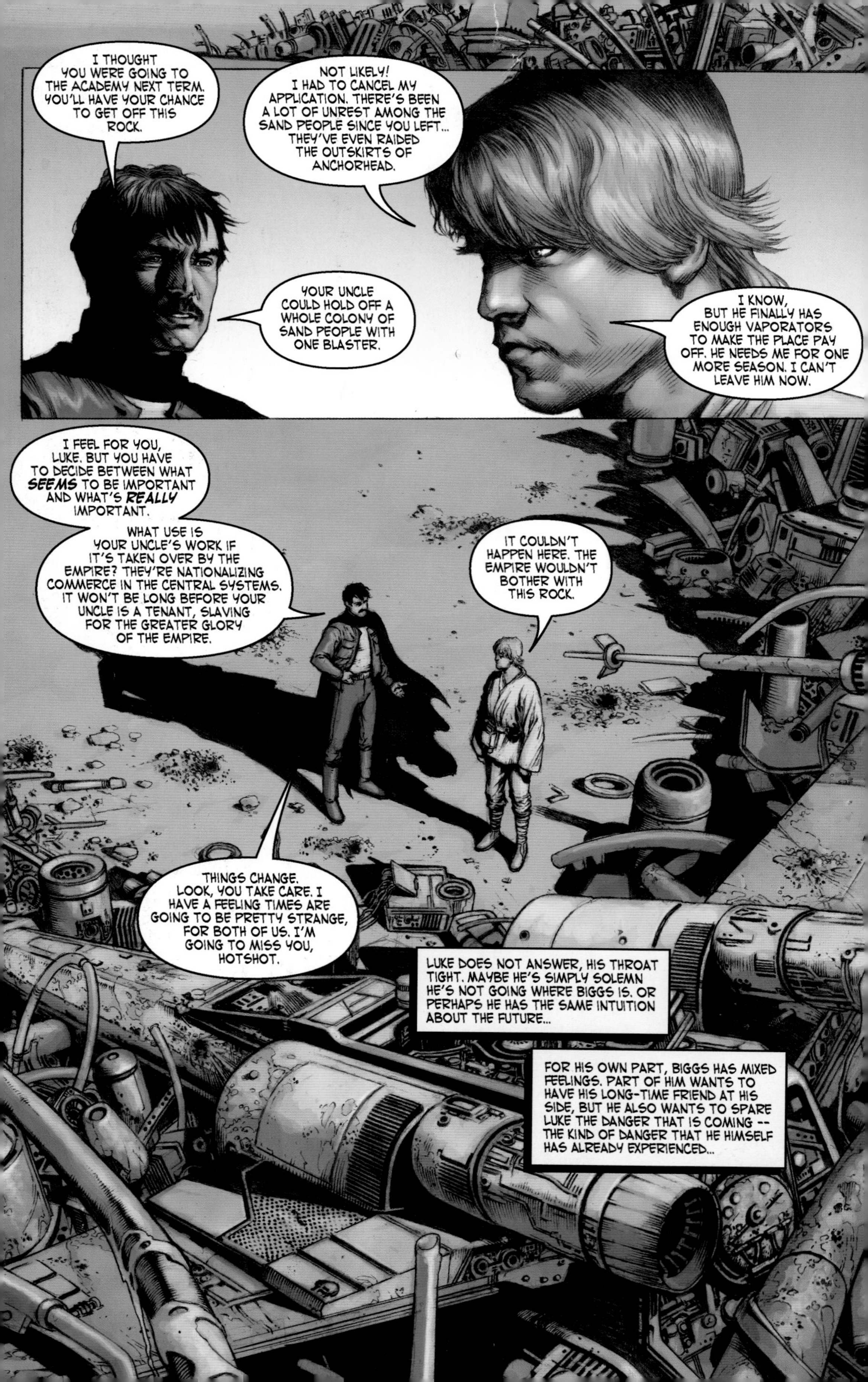
I THOUGHT YOU WERE GOING TO THE ACADEMY NEXT TERM. YOU'LL HAVE YOUR CHANCE TO GET OFF THIS ROCK.
NOT LIKELY! I HAD TO CANCEL MY APPLICATION. THERE'S BEEN A LOT OF UNREST AMONG THE SAND PEOPLE SINCE YOU LEFT... THEY'VE EVEN RAIDED THE OUTSKIRTS OF ANCHORHEAD.
YOUR UNCLE COULD HOLD OFF A WHOLE COLONY OF SAND PEOPLE WITH ONE BLASTER.
I KNOW, BUT HE FINALLY HAS ENOUGH VAPORATORS TO MAKE THE PLACE PAY OFF. HE NEEDS ME FOR ONE MORE SEASON. I CAN'T LEAVE HIM NOW.
I FEEL FOR YOU, LUKE. BUT YOU HAVE TO DECIDE BETWEEN WHAT *SEEMS* TO BE IMPORTANT AND WHAT'S *REALLY* IMPORTANT.
WHAT USE IS YOUR UNCLE'S WORK IF IT'S TAKEN OVER BY THE EMPIRE? THEY'RE NATIONALIZING COMMERCE IN THE CENTRAL SYSTEMS. IT WON'T BE LONG BEFORE YOUR UNCLE IS A TENANT, SLAVING FOR THE GREATER GLORY OF THE EMPIRE.
IT COULDN'T HAPPEN HERE. THE EMPIRE WOULDN'T BOTHER WITH THIS ROCK.
THINGS CHANGE. LOOK, YOU TAKE CARE. I HAVE A FEELING TIMES ARE GOING TO BE PRETTY STRANGE, FOR BOTH OF US. I'M GOING TO MISS YOU, HOTSHOT.
LUKE DOES NOT ANSWER, HIS THROAT TIGHT. MAYBE HE'S SIMPLY SOLEMN HE'S NOT GOING WHERE BIGGS IS. OR PERHAPS HE HAS THE SAME INTUITION ABOUT THE FUTURE...
FOR HIS OWN PART, BIGGS HAS MIXED FEELINGS. PART OF HIM WANTS TO HAVE HIS LONG-TIME FRIEND AT HIS SIDE, BUT HE ALSO WANTS TO SPARE LUKE THE DANGER THAT IS COMING -- THE KIND OF DANGER THAT HE HIMSELF HAS ALREADY EXPERIENCED...

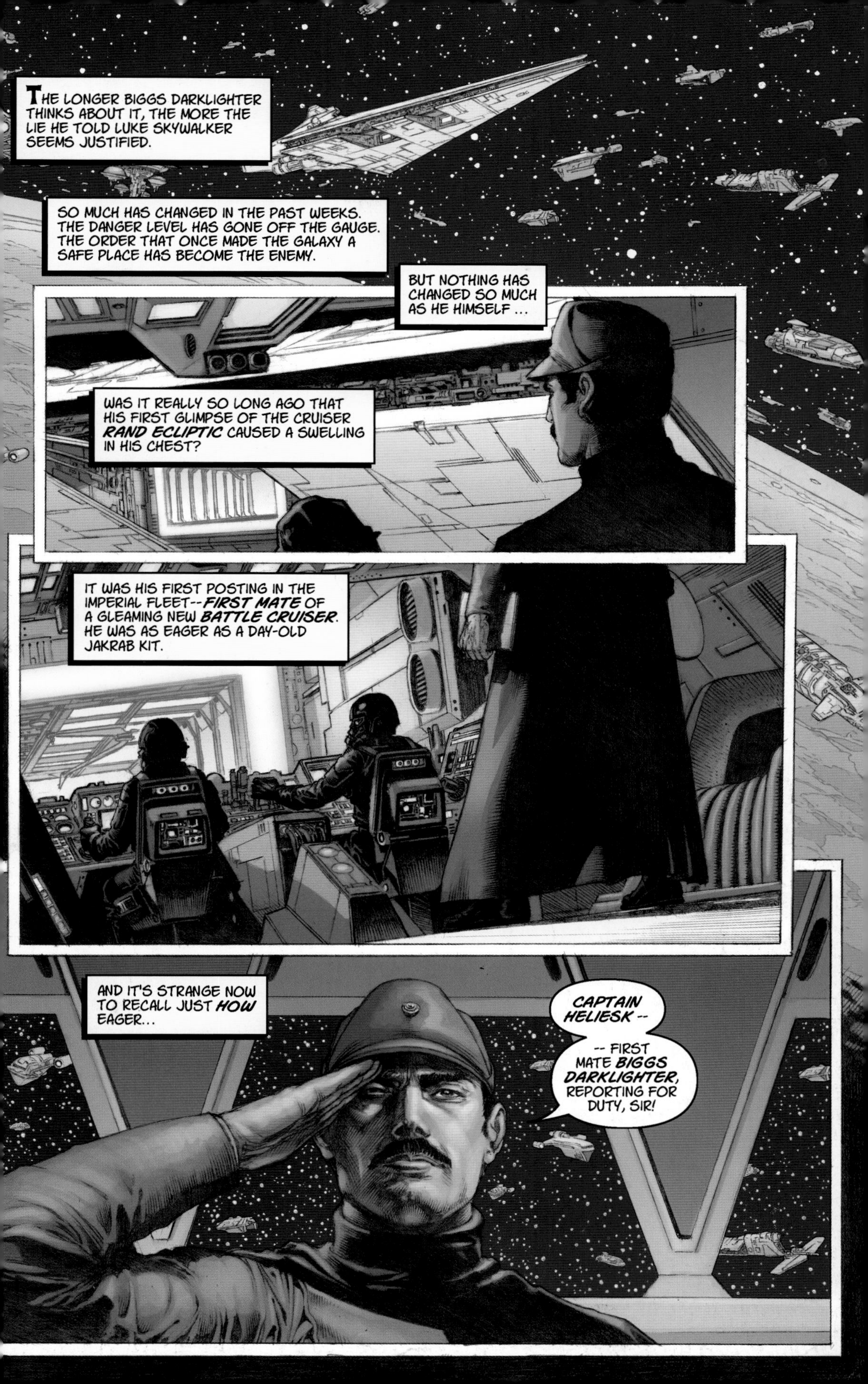
THE LONGER BIGGS DARKLIGHTER THINKS ABOUT IT, THE MORE THE LIE HE TOLD LUKE SKYWALKER SEEMS JUSTIFIED.
SO MUCH HAS CHANGED IN THE PAST WEEKS. THE DANGER LEVEL HAS GONE OFF THE GAUGE. THE ORDER THAT ONCE MADE THE GALAXY A SAFE PLACE HAS BECOME THE ENEMY.
BUT NOTHING HAS CHANGED SO MUCH AS HE HIMSELF ...
WAS IT REALLY SO LONG AGO THAT HIS FIRST GLIMPSE OF THE CRUISER *RAND ECLIPTIC* CAUSED A SWELLING IN HIS CHEST?
IT WAS HIS FIRST POSTING IN THE IMPERIAL FLEET--*FIRST MATE* OF A GLEAMING NEW *BATTLE CRUISER*. HE WAS AS EAGER AS A DAY-OLD JAKRAB KIT.
AND IT'S STRANGE NOW TO RECALL JUST *HOW* EAGER...
CAPTAIN HELIESK --
-- FIRST MATE *BIGGS DARKLIGHTER*, REPORTING FOR DUTY, SIR!

AT EASE, DARKLIGHTER.

YOU KNOW SECOND MATE *KLIVIAN*.

YES, SIR. HELLO, *HOBBIE*.

I'M NOT LATE, AM I, SIR?

NO, OFFICER KLIVIAN ARRIVED EARLY. YOU KNOW THESE STRIVER TYPES.

BIGGS *DOES*, AND HE HAS NEVER TRUSTED HOBBIE, HIS ACADEMY CLASSMATE.

COME WITH ME. I DIDN'T WANT YOU ACADEMY GOLDEN BOYS, BUT THE OFFICERS I'D *REQUESTED* MET WITH SOME *REBELS* AND WERE APPARENTLY *KILLED*.

"APPARENTLY," SIR?

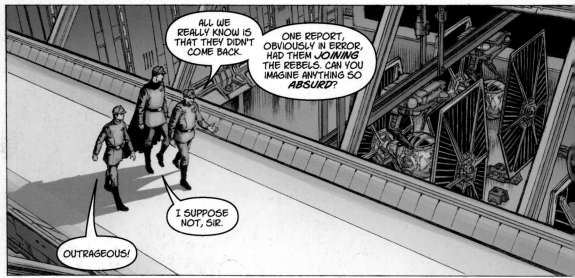

ALL WE REALLY KNOW IS THAT THEY DIDN'T COME BACK.

ONE REPORT, OBVIOUSLY IN ERROR, HAD THEM *JOINING* THE REBELS. CAN YOU IMAGINE ANYTHING SO *ABSURD*?

I SUPPOSE NOT, SIR.

OUTRAGEOUS!

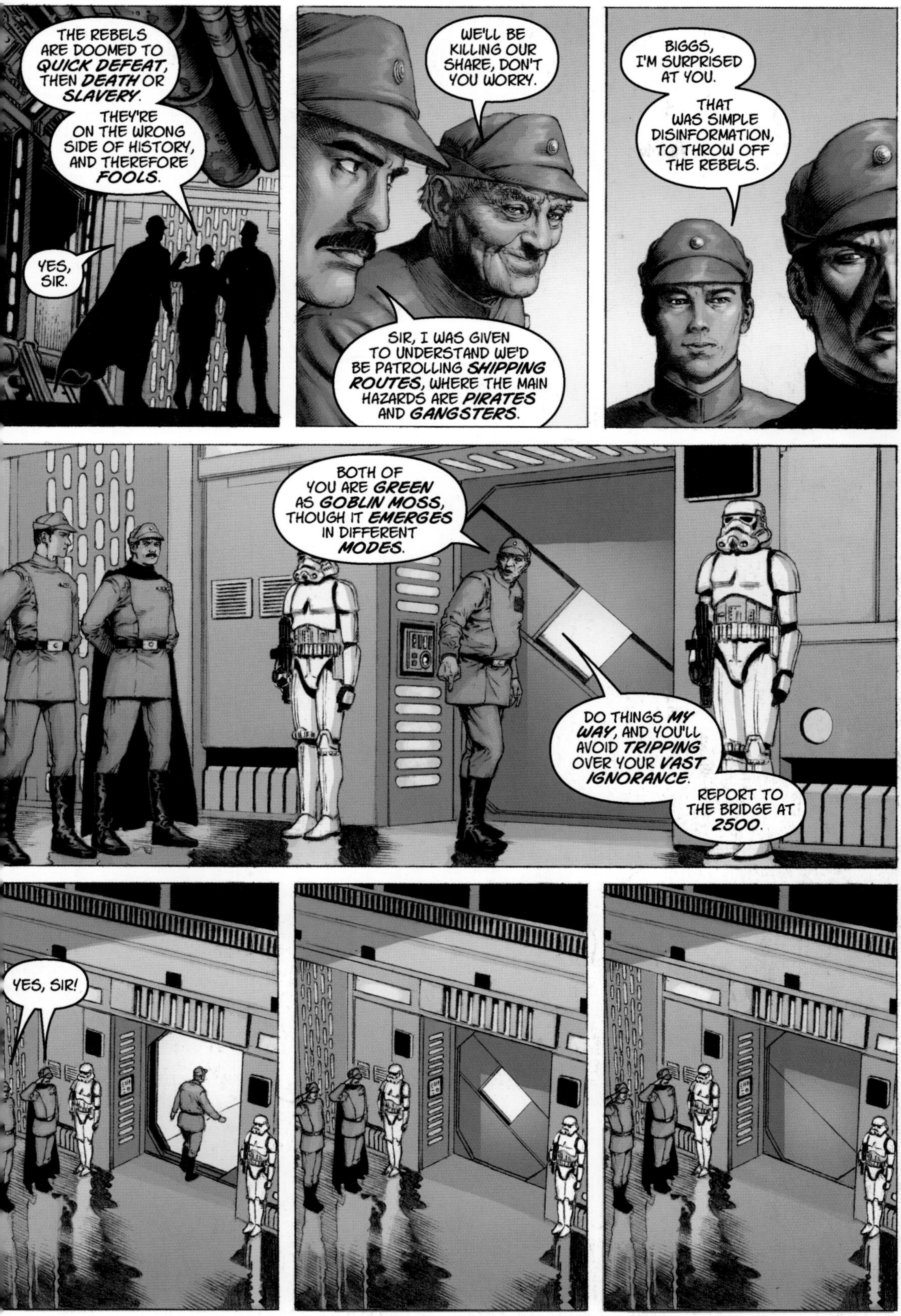
THE REBELS ARE DOOMED TO QUICK DEFEAT, THEN DEATH OR SLAVERY.
THEY'RE ON THE WRONG SIDE OF HISTORY, AND THEREFORE FOOLS.
YES, SIR.
WE'LL BE KILLING OUR SHARE, DON'T YOU WORRY.
SIR, I WAS GIVEN TO UNDERSTAND WE'D BE PATROLLING SHIPPING ROUTES, WHERE THE MAIN HAZARDS ARE PIRATES AND GANGSTERS.
BIGGS, I'M SURPRISED AT YOU.
THAT WAS SIMPLE DISINFORMATION, TO THROW OFF THE REBELS.
BOTH OF YOU ARE GREEN AS GOBLIN MOSS, THOUGH IT EMERGES IN DIFFERENT MODES.
DO THINGS MY WAY, AND YOU'LL AVOID TRIPPING OVER YOUR VAST IGNORANCE.
REPORT TO THE BRIDGE AT 2500.
YES, SIR!

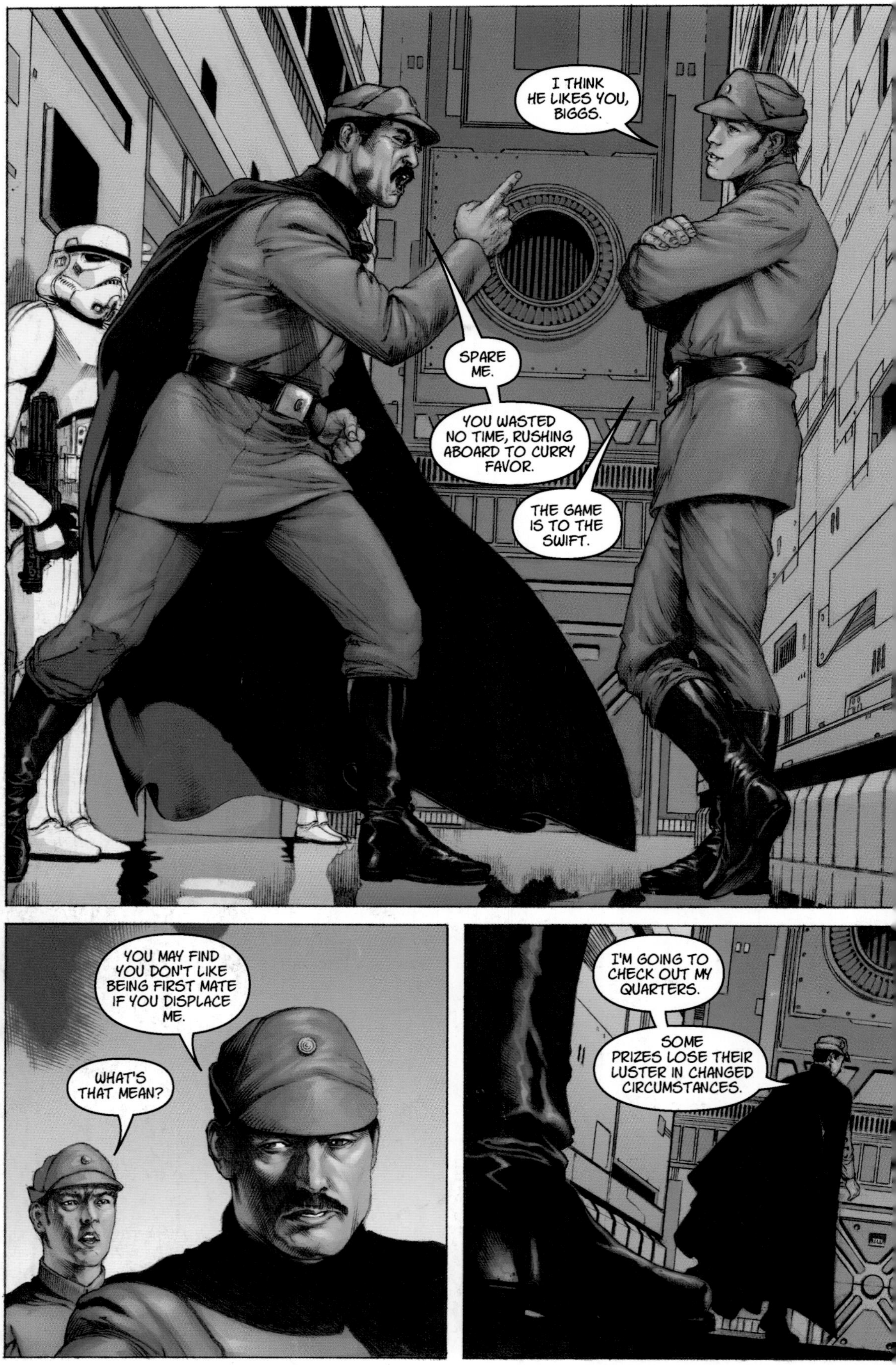

I THINK HE LIKES YOU, BIGGS.
SPARE ME.
YOU WASTED NO TIME, RUSHING ABOARD TO CURRY FAVOR.
THE GAME IS TO THE SWIFT.
YOU MAY FIND YOU DON'T LIKE BEING FIRST MATE IF YOU DISPLACE ME.
WHAT'S THAT MEAN?
I'M GOING TO CHECK OUT MY QUARTERS.
SOME PRIZES LOSE THEIR LUSTER IN CHANGED CIRCUMSTANCES.

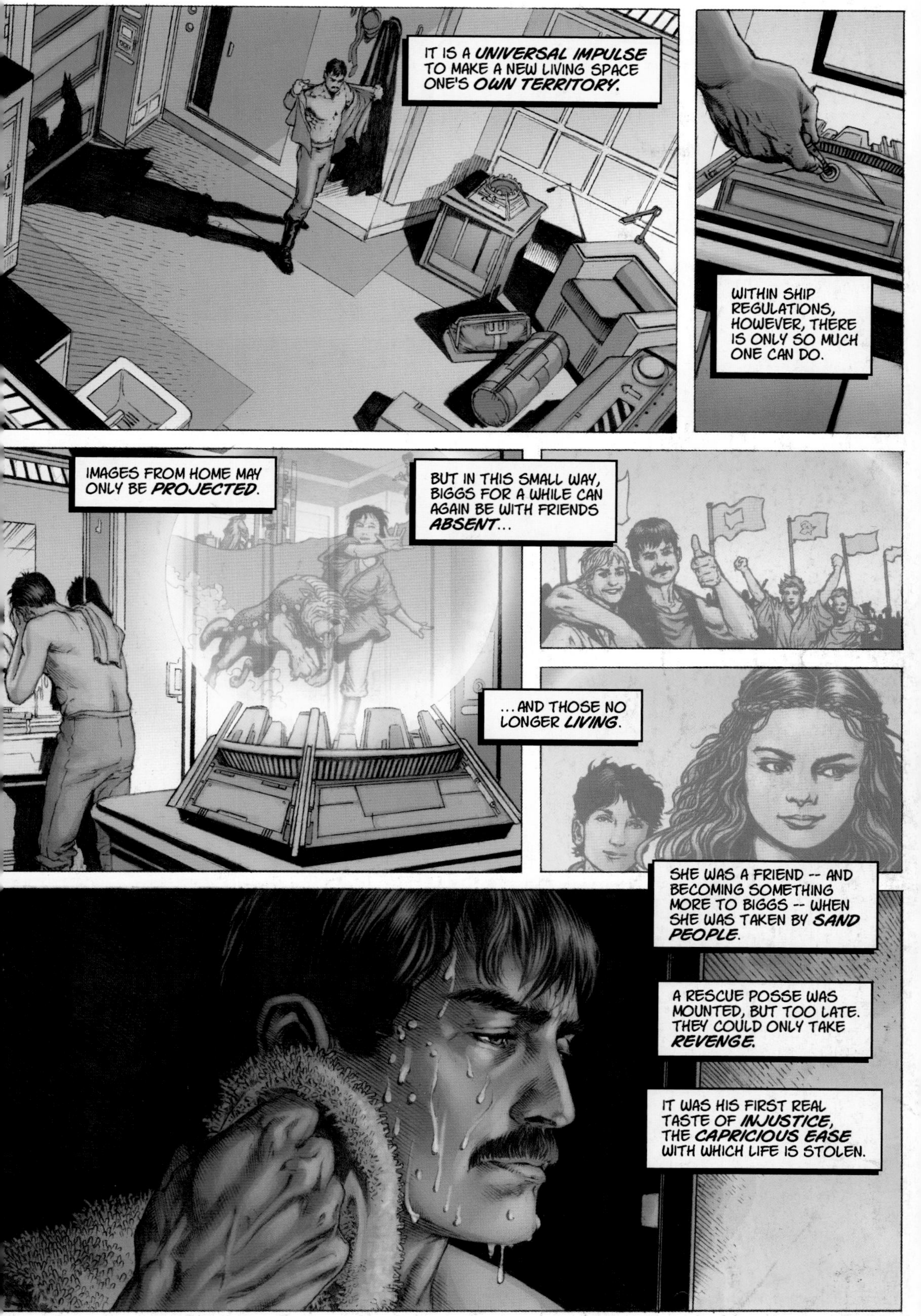
IT IS A UNIVERSAL IMPULSE TO MAKE A NEW LIVING SPACE ONE'S OWN TERRITORY.
WITHIN SHIP REGULATIONS, HOWEVER, THERE IS ONLY SO MUCH ONE CAN DO.
IMAGES FROM HOME MAY ONLY BE PROJECTED.
BUT IN THIS SMALL WAY, BIGGS FOR A WHILE CAN AGAIN BE WITH FRIENDS ABSENT...
...AND THOSE NO LONGER LIVING.
SHE WAS A FRIEND -- AND BECOMING SOMETHING MORE TO BIGGS -- WHEN SHE WAS TAKEN BY SAND PEOPLE.
A RESCUE POSSE WAS MOUNTED, BUT TOO LATE. THEY COULD ONLY TAKE REVENGE.
IT WAS HIS FIRST REAL TASTE OF INJUSTICE, THE CAPRICIOUS EASE WITH WHICH LIFE IS STOLEN.

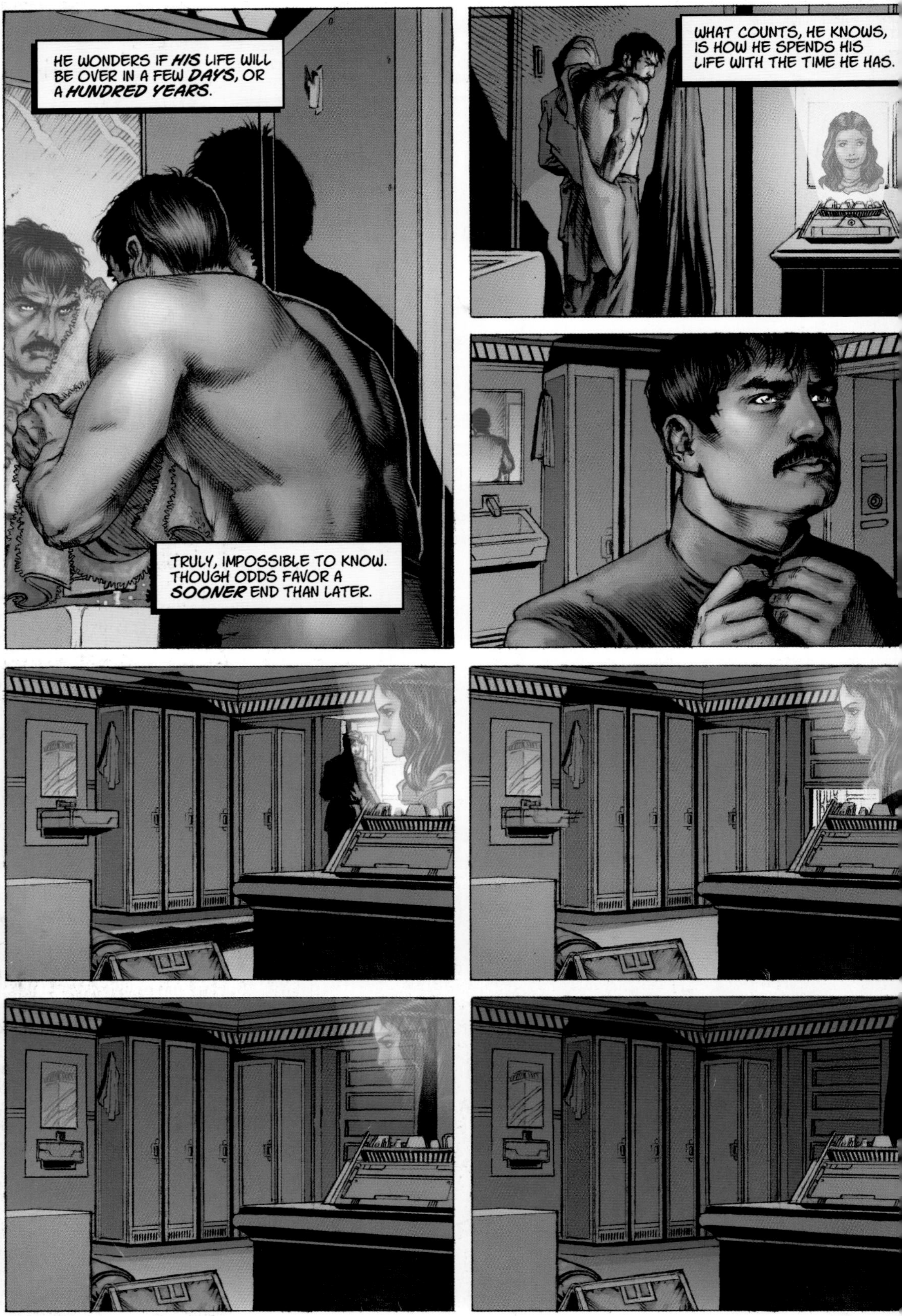
HE WONDERS IF HIS LIFE WILL BE OVER IN A FEW DAYS, OR A HUNDRED YEARS.
TRULY, IMPOSSIBLE TO KNOW. THOUGH ODDS FAVOR A SOONER END THAN LATER.
WHAT COUNTS, HE KNOWS, IS HOW HE SPENDS HIS LIFE WITH THE TIME HE HAS.

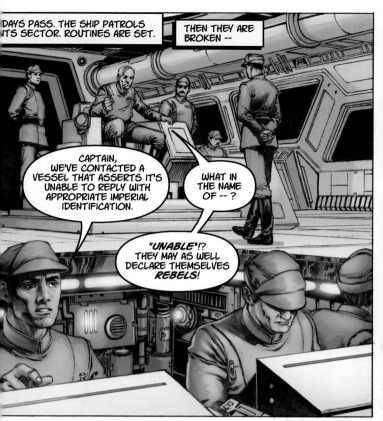

DAYS PASS. THE SHIP PATROLS ITS SECTOR. ROUTINES ARE SET.

THEN THEY ARE BROKEN --

CAPTAIN, WE'VE CONTACTED A VESSEL THAT ASSERTS IT'S UNABLE TO REPLY WITH APPROPRIATE IMPERIAL IDENTIFICATION.

WHAT IN THE NAME OF -- ?

"UNABLE"!? THEY MAY AS WELL DECLARE THEMSELVES REBELS!

DARKLIGHTER, KLIVIAN -- ASSEMBLE YOUR FLYBOYS. I WANT THAT CRAFT ENGAGED, THEN DISABLED -- OR DESTROYED.

SIR, SOME OF THE OUTWORLDS BARELY HAVE IMPERIAL OVERSEERS IN PLACE, MUCH LESS SPACE TRAFFIC PROTOCOLS. MY HOMEWORLD, TATOOINE --

IF THEY DON'T KNOW THE CODES, THEY SHOULDN'T RISK SPACE!

NOW GO!

ALL RIGHT, HERE'S WHERE WE GET TO SHOW WE WERE PAYING ATTENTION!

FOLLOW YOUR CHECKLISTS, AND ASSEMBLE BEHIND ME!

THIS IS TWILIGHT LEADER. LET'S GIVE 'EM THE ATOM. COUNT OFF.

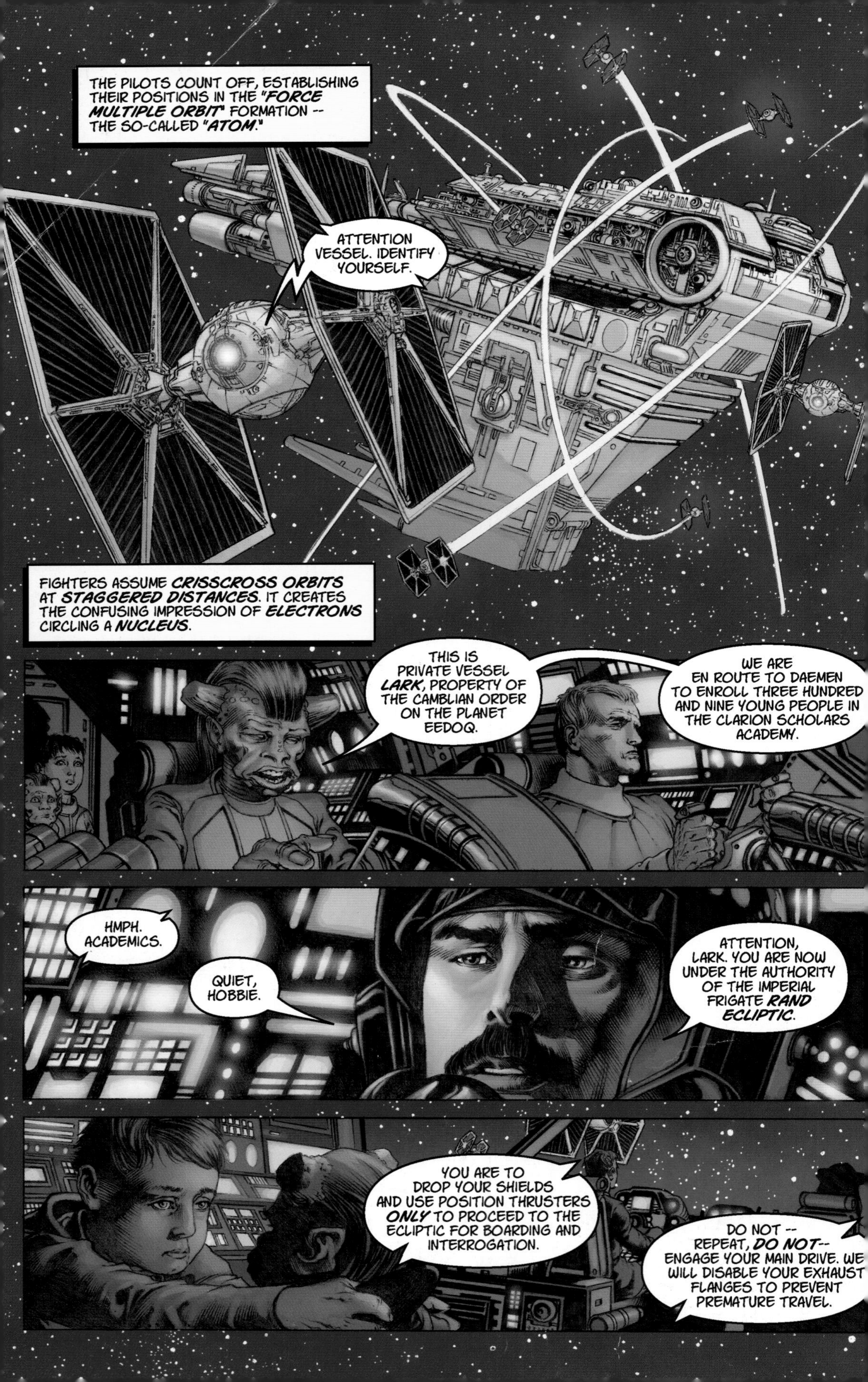
THE PILOTS COUNT OFF, ESTABLISHING THEIR POSITIONS IN THE "FORCE MULTIPLE ORBIT" FORMATION -- THE SO-CALLED "ATOM."
ATTENTION VESSEL. IDENTIFY YOURSELF.
FIGHTERS ASSUME CRISSCROSS ORBITS AT STAGGERED DISTANCES. IT CREATES THE CONFUSING IMPRESSION OF ELECTRONS CIRCLING A NUCLEUS.
THIS IS PRIVATE VESSEL LARK, PROPERTY OF THE CAMBLIAN ORDER ON THE PLANET EEDOQ.
WE ARE EN ROUTE TO DAEMEN TO ENROLL THREE HUNDRED AND NINE YOUNG PEOPLE IN THE CLARION SCHOLARS ACADEMY.
HMPH. ACADEMICS.
QUIET, HOBBIE.
ATTENTION, LARK. YOU ARE NOW UNDER THE AUTHORITY OF THE IMPERIAL FRIGATE RAND ECLIPTIC.
YOU ARE TO DROP YOUR SHIELDS AND USE POSITION THRUSTERS ONLY TO PROCEED TO THE ECLIPTIC FOR BOARDING AND INTERROGATION.
DO NOT -- REPEAT, DO NOT-- ENGAGE YOUR MAIN DRIVE. WE WILL DISABLE YOUR EXHAUST FLANGES TO PREVENT PREMATURE TRAVEL.

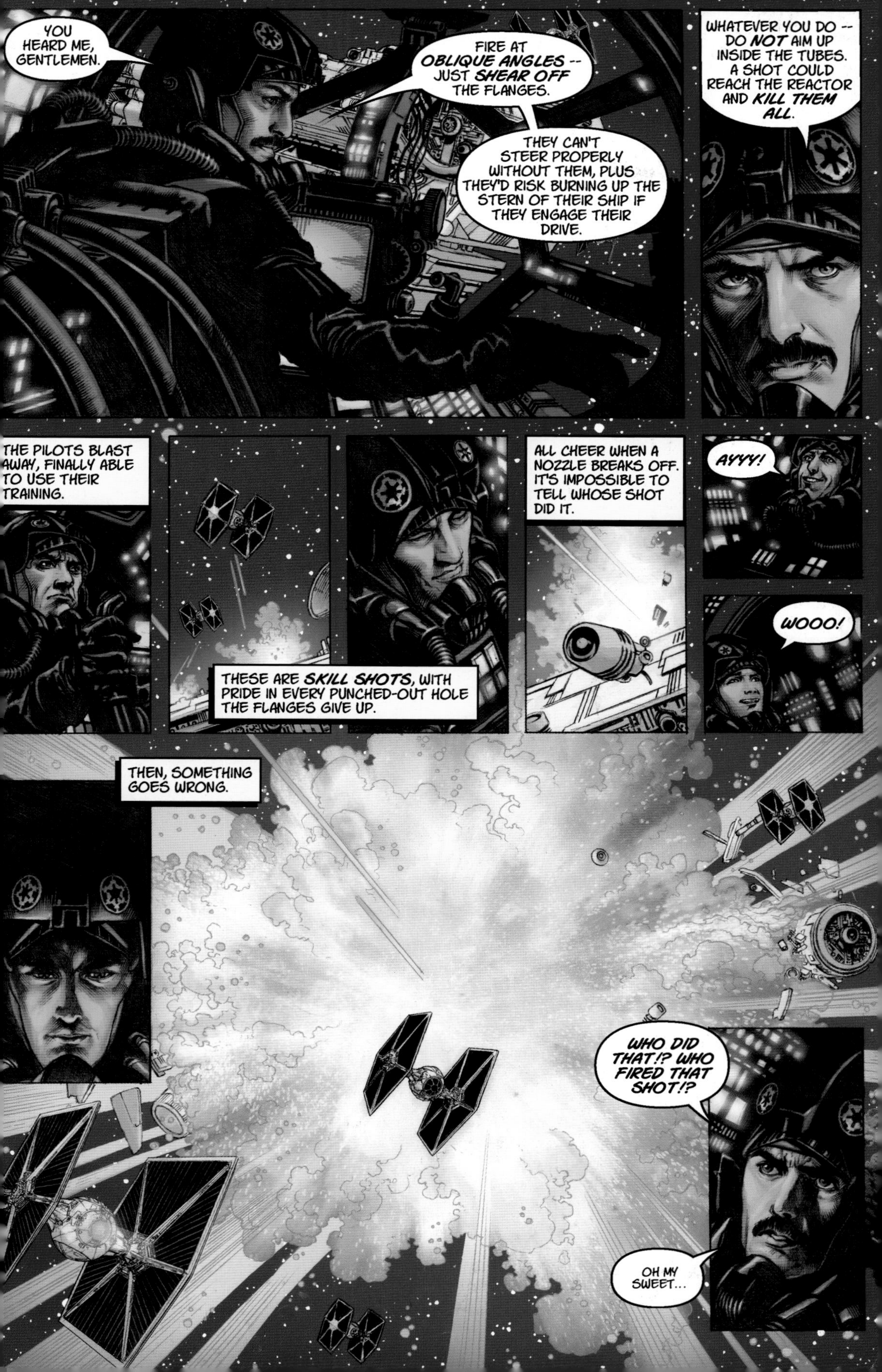
YOU HEARD ME, GENTLEMEN.
FIRE AT OBLIQUE ANGLES -- JUST SHEAR OFF THE FLANGES.
THEY CAN'T STEER PROPERLY WITHOUT THEM, PLUS THEY'D RISK BURNING UP THE STERN OF THEIR SHIP IF THEY ENGAGE THEIR DRIVE.
WHATEVER YOU DO -- DO NOT AIM UP INSIDE THE TUBES. A SHOT COULD REACH THE REACTOR AND KILL THEM ALL.
THE PILOTS BLAST AWAY, FINALLY ABLE TO USE THEIR TRAINING.
THESE ARE SKILL SHOTS, WITH PRIDE IN EVERY PUNCHED-OUT HOLE THE FLANGES GIVE UP.
ALL CHEER WHEN A NOZZLE BREAKS OFF. IT'S IMPOSSIBLE TO TELL WHOSE SHOT DID IT.
AYYY!
WOOO!
THEN, SOMETHING GOES WRONG.
WHO DID THAT!? WHO FIRED THAT SHOT!?
OH MY SWEET...

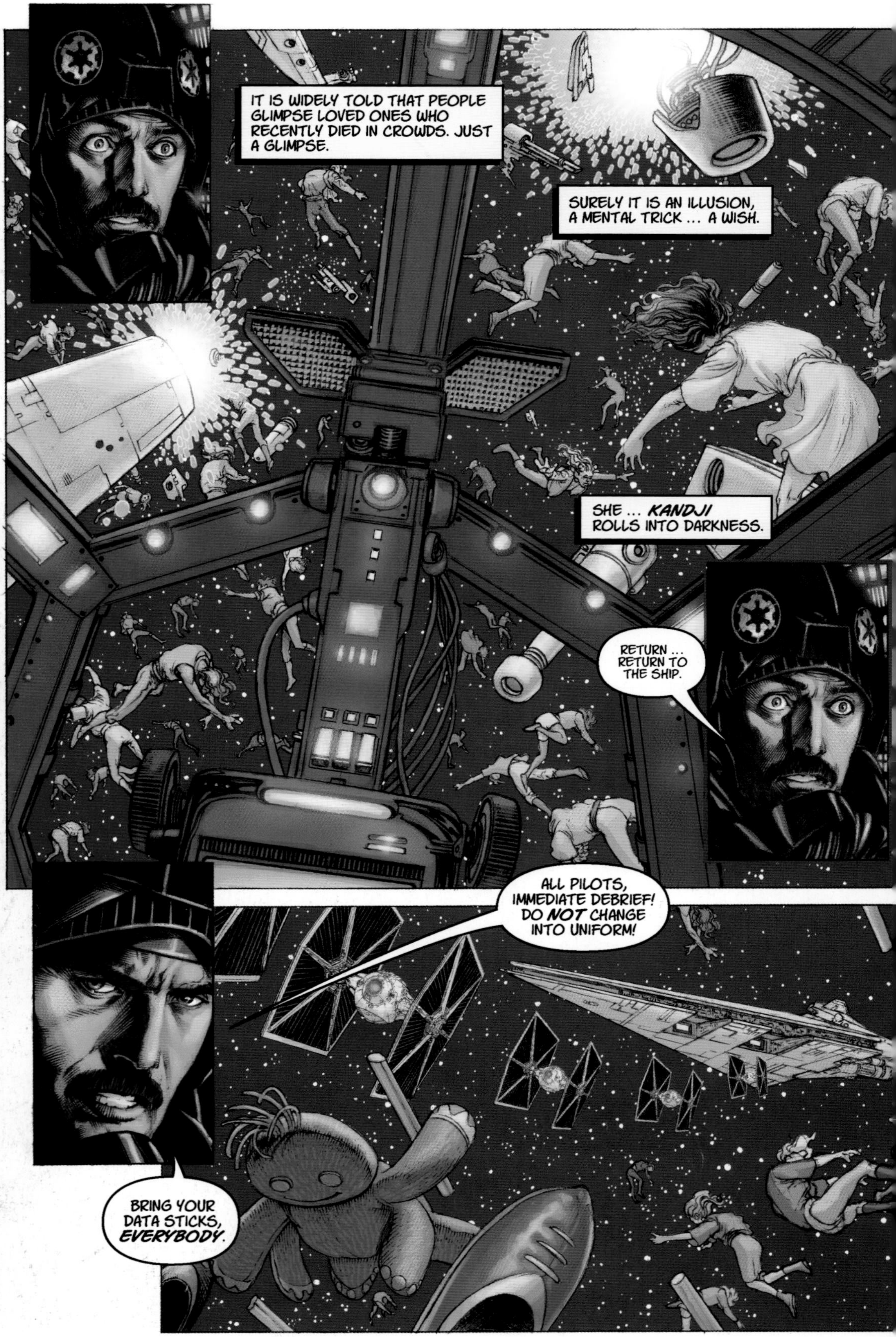
IT IS WIDELY TOLD THAT PEOPLE GLIMPSE LOVED ONES WHO RECENTLY DIED IN CROWDS. JUST A GLIMPSE.
SURELY IT IS AN ILLUSION, A MENTAL TRICK ... A WISH.
SHE ... *KANDJI* ROLLS INTO DARKNESS.
RETURN ... RETURN TO THE SHIP.
ALL PILOTS, IMMEDIATE DEBRIEF! DO *NOT* CHANGE INTO UNIFORM!
BRING YOUR DATA STICKS, *EVERYBODY*.

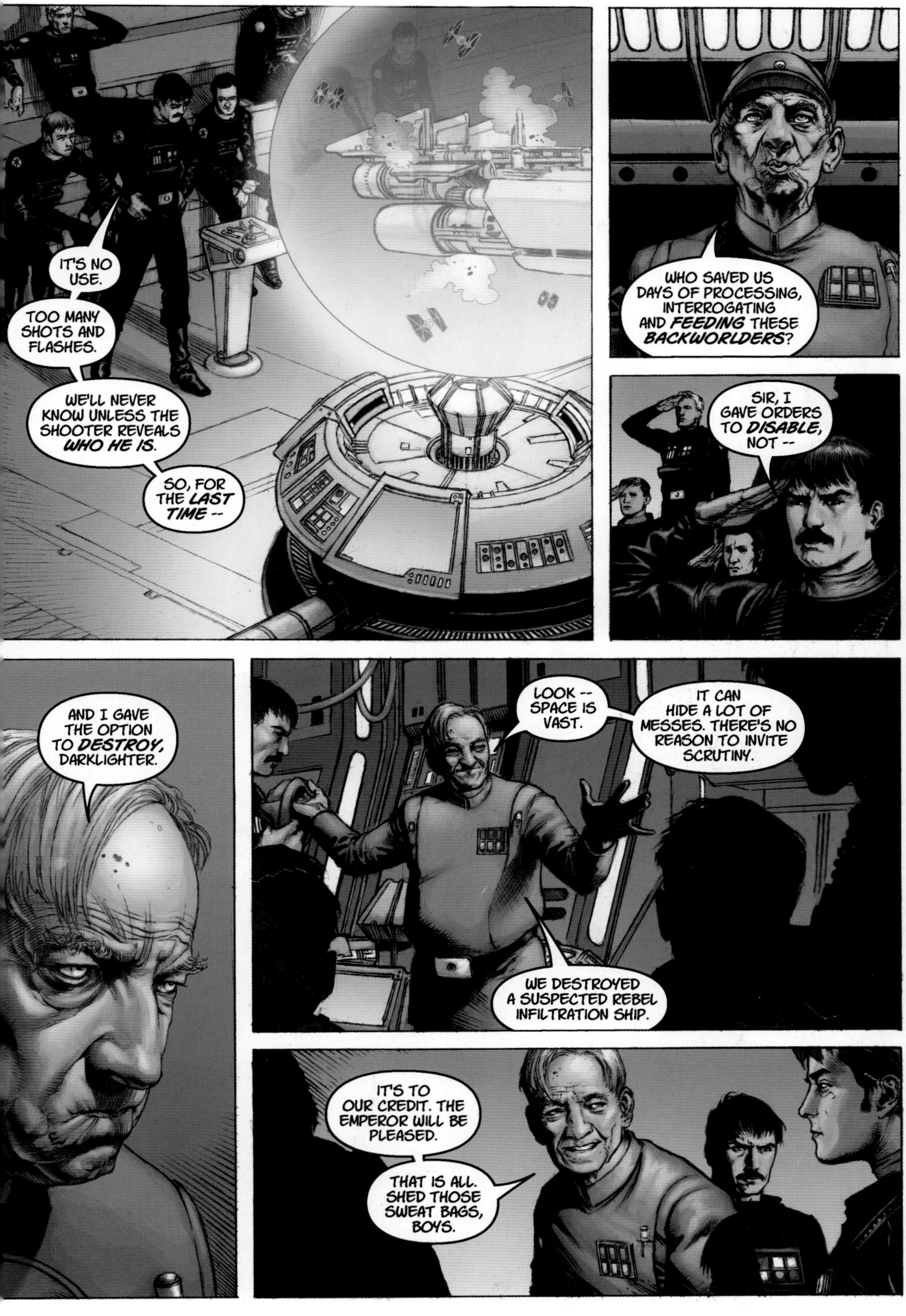
IT'S NO USE.
TOO MANY SHOTS AND FLASHES.
WE'LL NEVER KNOW UNLESS THE SHOOTER REVEALS *WHO HE IS*.
SO, FOR THE *LAST TIME* --
WHO SAVED US DAYS OF PROCESSING, INTERROGATING AND *FEEDING* THESE *BACKWORLDERS*?
SIR, I GAVE ORDERS TO *DISABLE*, NOT --
AND I GAVE THE OPTION TO *DESTROY*, DARKLIGHTER.
LOOK -- SPACE IS VAST.
IT CAN HIDE A LOT OF MESSES. THERE'S NO REASON TO INVITE SCRUTINY.
WE DESTROYED A SUSPECTED REBEL INFILTRATION SHIP.
IT'S TO OUR CREDIT. THE EMPEROR WILL BE PLEASED.
THAT IS ALL. SHED THOSE SWEAT BAGS, BOYS.

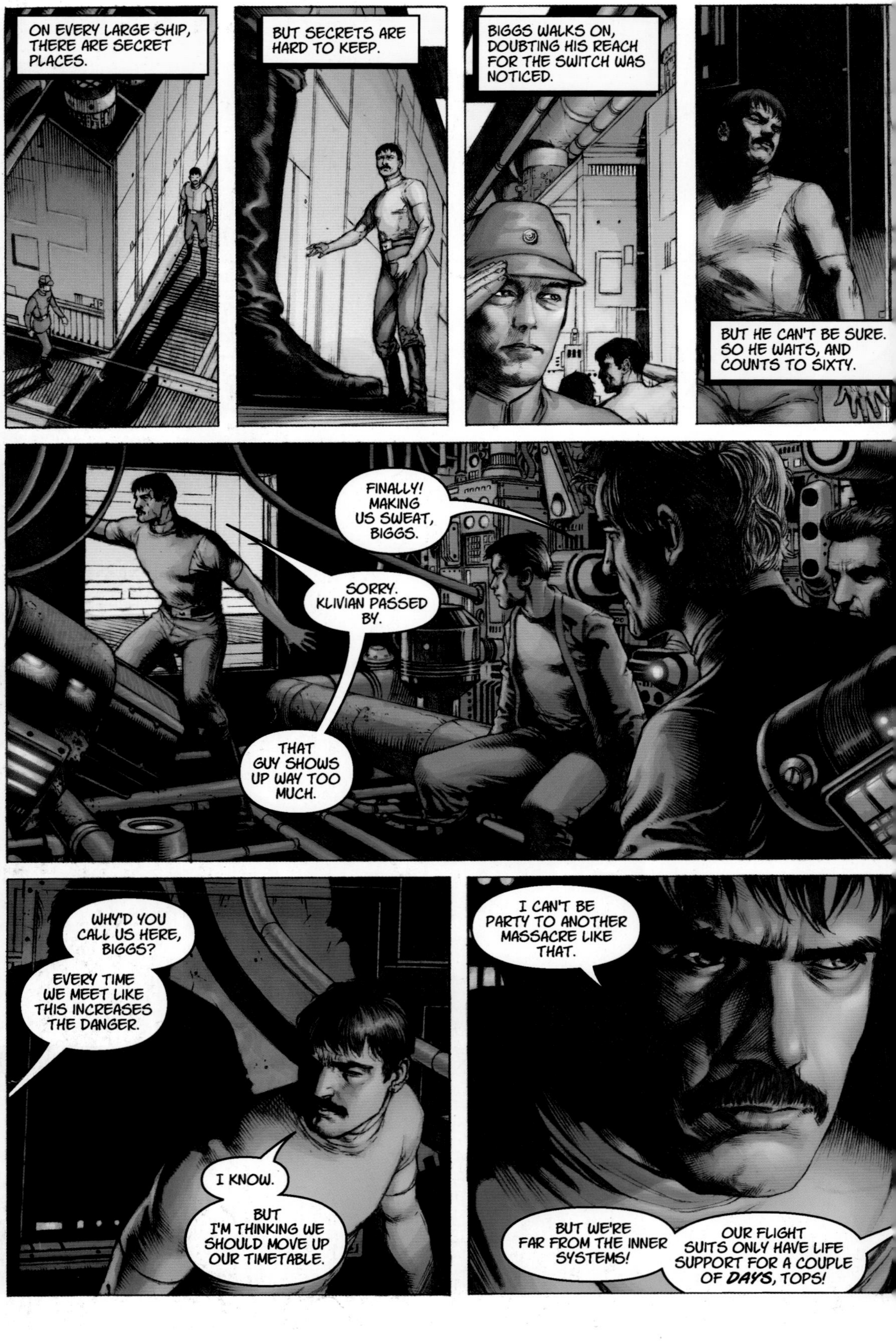
ON EVERY LARGE SHIP, THERE ARE SECRET PLACES.
BUT SECRETS ARE HARD TO KEEP.
BIGGS WALKS ON, DOUBTING HIS REACH FOR THE SWITCH WAS NOTICED.
BUT HE CAN'T BE SURE. SO HE WAITS, AND COUNTS TO SIXTY.
FINALLY! MAKING US SWEAT, BIGGS.
SORRY. KLIVIAN PASSED BY.
THAT GUY SHOWS UP WAY TOO MUCH.
WHY'D YOU CALL US HERE, BIGGS?
EVERY TIME WE MEET LIKE THIS INCREASES THE DANGER.
I KNOW.
BUT I'M THINKING WE SHOULD MOVE UP OUR TIMETABLE.
I CAN'T BE PARTY TO ANOTHER MASSACRE LIKE THAT.
BUT WE'RE FAR FROM THE INNER SYSTEMS!
OUR FLIGHT SUITS ONLY HAVE LIFE SUPPORT FOR A COUPLE OF *DAYS*, TOPS!

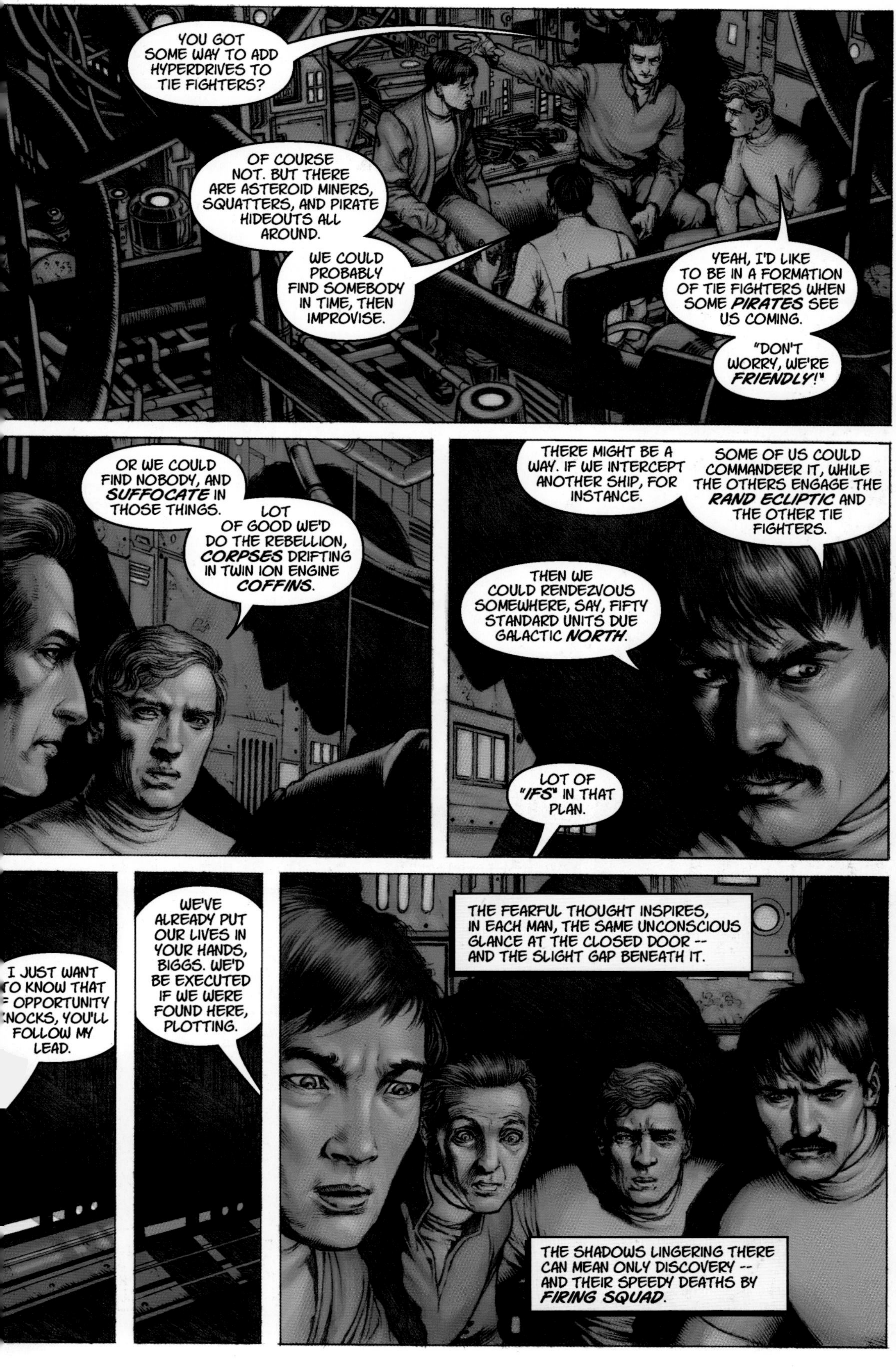
YOU GOT SOME WAY TO ADD HYPERDRIVES TO TIE FIGHTERS?
OF COURSE NOT. BUT THERE ARE ASTEROID MINERS, SQUATTERS, AND PIRATE HIDEOUTS ALL AROUND.
WE COULD PROBABLY FIND SOMEBODY IN TIME, THEN IMPROVISE.
YEAH, I'D LIKE TO BE IN A FORMATION OF TIE FIGHTERS WHEN SOME PIRATES SEE US COMING.
"DON'T WORRY, WE'RE FRIENDLY!"
OR WE COULD FIND NOBODY, AND SUFFOCATE IN THOSE THINGS.
LOT OF GOOD WE'D DO THE REBELLION, CORPSES DRIFTING IN TWIN ION ENGINE COFFINS.
THERE MIGHT BE A WAY. IF WE INTERCEPT ANOTHER SHIP, FOR INSTANCE.
SOME OF US COULD COMMANDEER IT, WHILE THE OTHERS ENGAGE THE RAND ECLIPTIC AND THE OTHER TIE FIGHTERS.
THEN WE COULD RENDEZVOUS SOMEWHERE, SAY, FIFTY STANDARD UNITS DUE GALACTIC NORTH.
LOT OF "IFS" IN THAT PLAN.
I JUST WANT TO KNOW THAT IF OPPORTUNITY KNOCKS, YOU'LL FOLLOW MY LEAD.
WE'VE ALREADY PUT OUR LIVES IN YOUR HANDS, BIGGS. WE'D BE EXECUTED IF WE WERE FOUND HERE, PLOTTING.
THE FEARFUL THOUGHT INSPIRES, IN EACH MAN, THE SAME UNCONSCIOUS GLANCE AT THE CLOSED DOOR -- AND THE SLIGHT GAP BENEATH IT.
THE SHADOWS LINGERING THERE CAN MEAN ONLY DISCOVERY -- AND THEIR SPEEDY DEATHS BY FIRING SQUAD.

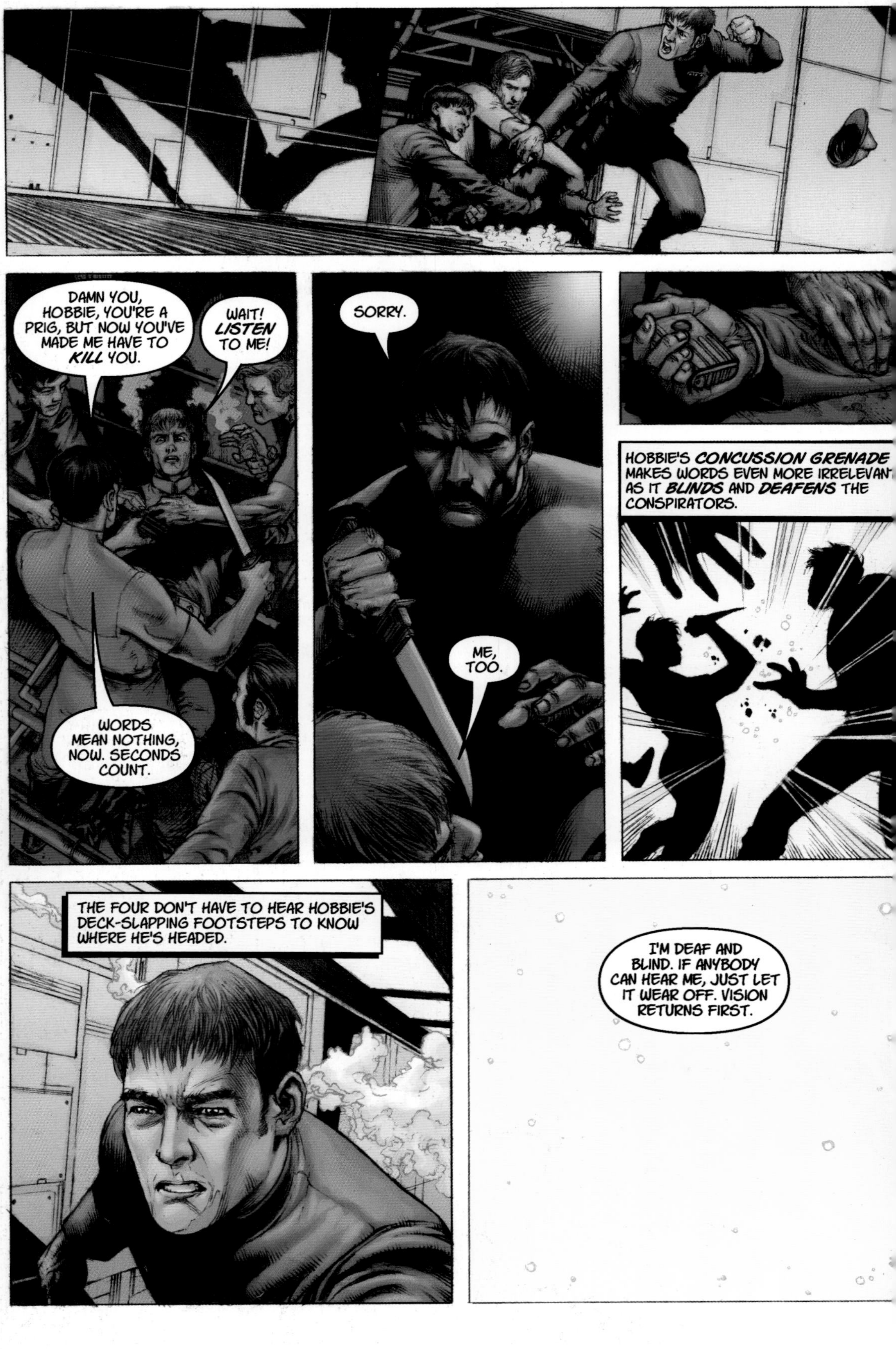
DAMN YOU, HOBBIE, YOU'RE A PRIG, BUT NOW YOU'VE MADE ME HAVE TO KILL YOU.
WAIT! LISTEN TO ME!
WORDS MEAN NOTHING, NOW. SECONDS COUNT.
SORRY.
ME, TOO.
HOBBIE'S CONCUSSION GRENADE MAKES WORDS EVEN MORE IRRELEVAN AS IT BLINDS AND DEAFENS THE CONSPIRATORS.
THE FOUR DON'T HAVE TO HEAR HOBBIE'S DECK-SLAPPING FOOTSTEPS TO KNOW WHERE HE'S HEADED.
I'M DEAF AND BLIND. IF ANYBODY CAN HEAR ME, JUST LET IT WEAR OFF. VISION RETURNS FIRST.

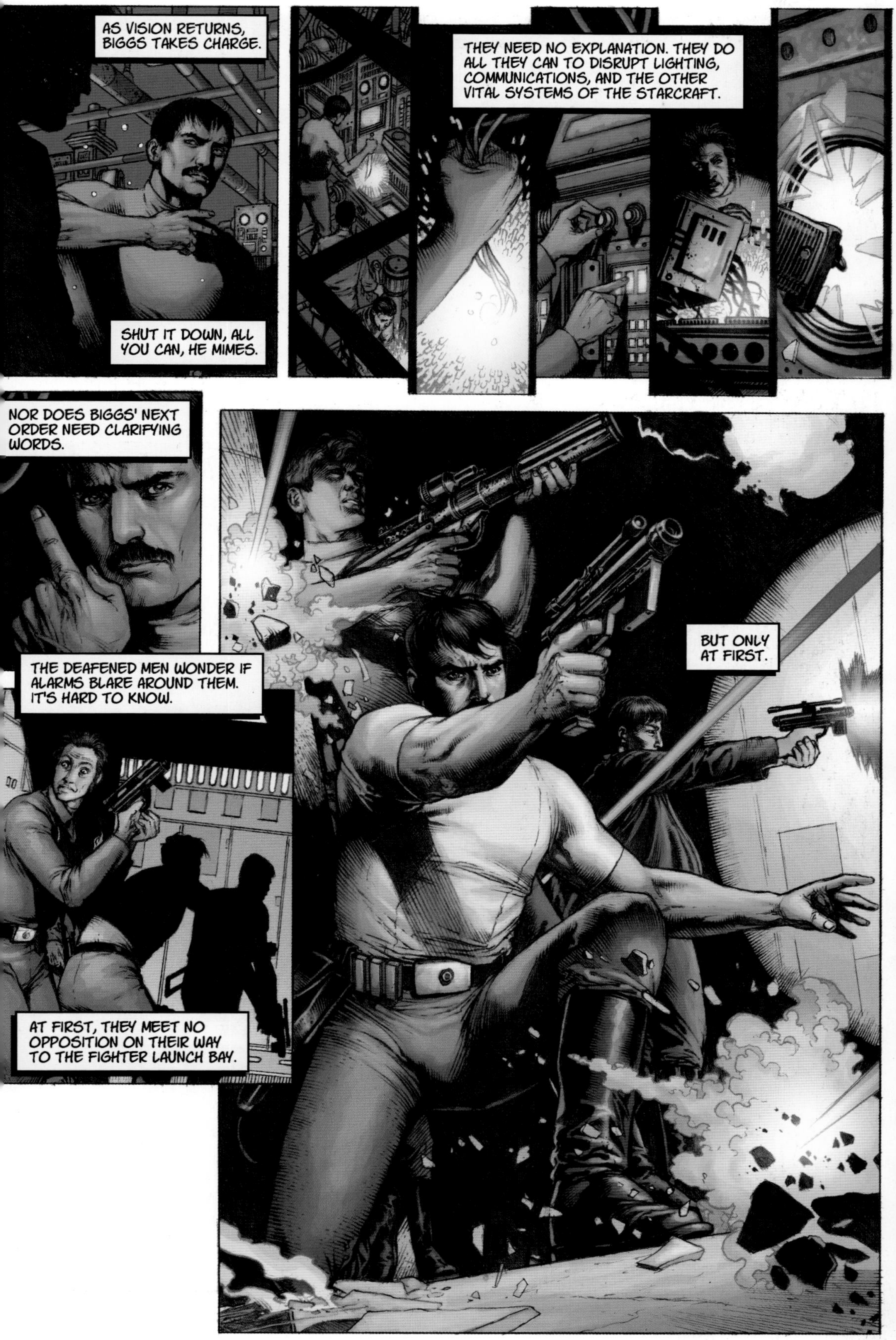
AS VISION RETURNS, BIGGS TAKES CHARGE.
SHUT IT DOWN, ALL YOU CAN, HE MIMES.
THEY NEED NO EXPLANATION. THEY DO ALL THEY CAN TO DISRUPT LIGHTING, COMMUNICATIONS, AND THE OTHER VITAL SYSTEMS OF THE STARCRAFT.
NOR DOES BIGGS' NEXT ORDER NEED CLARIFYING WORDS.
THE DEAFENED MEN WONDER IF ALARMS BLARE AROUND THEM. IT'S HARD TO KNOW.
AT FIRST, THEY MEET NO OPPOSITION ON THEIR WAY TO THE FIGHTER LAUNCH BAY.
BUT ONLY AT FIRST.

WITHOUT WORDS, IT'S UNDERSTOOD THAT BIGGS WILL COVER THE ESCAPE OF THE OTHERS.

THE MOST DANGEROUS MOMENT WILL BE THE TIME IT TAKES THEM TO SUIT UP.

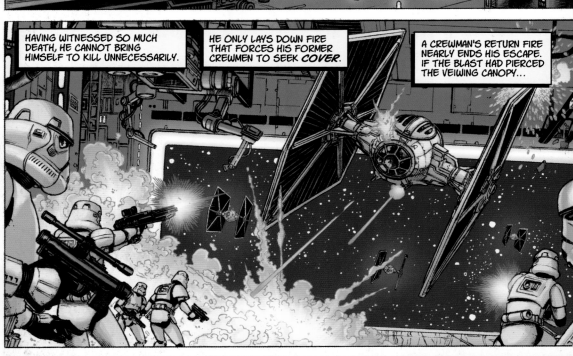

HAVING WITNESSED SO MUCH DEATH, HE CANNOT BRING HIMSELF TO KILL UNNECESSARILY.

HE ONLY LAYS DOWN FIRE THAT FORCES HIS FORMER CREWMEN TO SEEK *COVER*.

A CREWMAN'S RETURN FIRE NEARLY ENDS HIS ESCAPE. IF THE BLAST HAD PIERCED THE VEIWING CANOPY...

FIGHTER SPEEDS BEING WHAT THEY ARE, THE OTHERS ARE OUT OF SIGHT AND SENSOR RANGE ALREADY. BIGGS IS ALONE TO WONDER HOW THEY ESCAPED SO EASILY.

PERHAPS THEY CRIPPLED THE SHIP BETTER THAN HE HAD DARED HOPE, IN THE SERVICE COMPARTMENT.

THEN HE HAS A THOUGHT.

PERHAPS THE OTHERS WILL REMEMBER HIS WORDS, JUST BEFORE DISCOVERY.

HE HEADS *GALACTIC NORTH*.

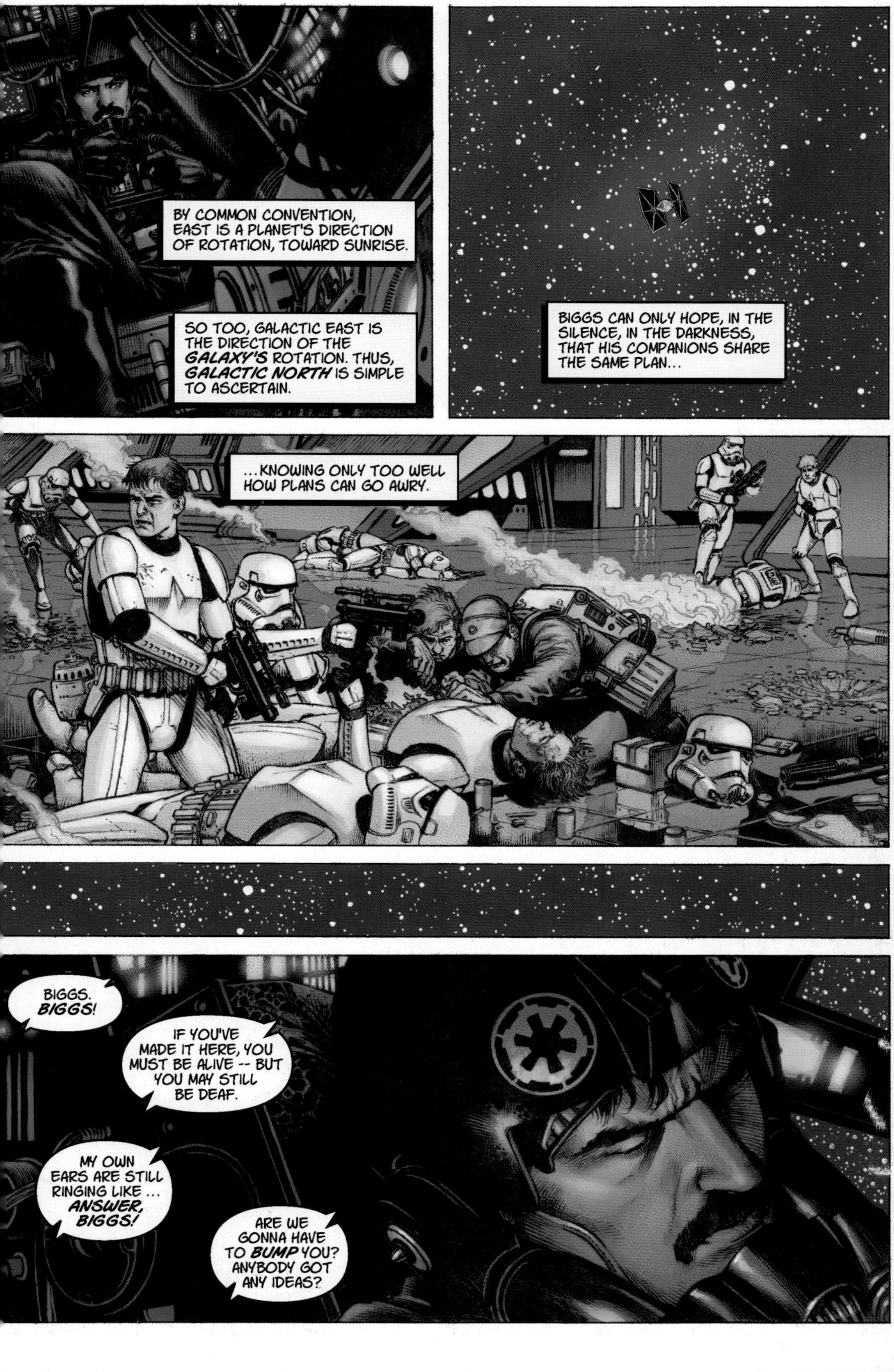
BY COMMON CONVENTION, EAST IS A PLANET'S DIRECTION OF ROTATION, TOWARD SUNRISE.
SO TOO, GALACTIC EAST IS THE DIRECTION OF THE *GALAXY'S* ROTATION. THUS, *GALACTIC NORTH* IS SIMPLE TO ASCERTAIN.
BIGGS CAN ONLY HOPE, IN THE SILENCE, IN THE DARKNESS, THAT HIS COMPANIONS SHARE THE SAME PLAN...
...KNOWING ONLY TOO WELL HOW PLANS CAN GO AWRY.
BIGGS. *BIGGS!*
IF YOU'VE MADE IT HERE, YOU MUST BE ALIVE -- BUT YOU MAY STILL BE DEAF.
MY OWN EARS ARE STILL RINGING LIKE ... *ANSWER, BIGGS!*
ARE WE GONNA HAVE TO *BUMP* YOU? ANYBODY GOT ANY IDEAS?

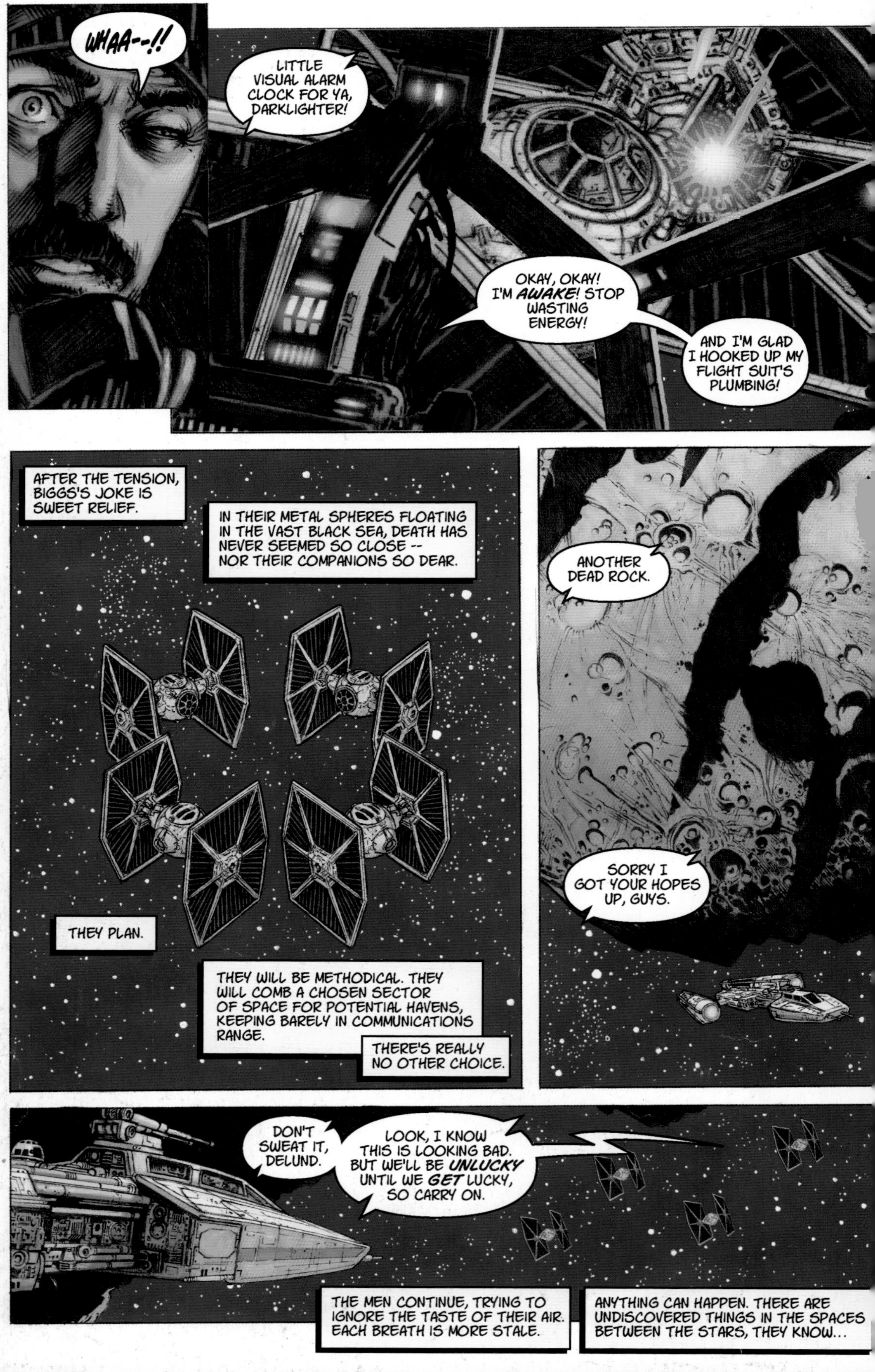
WHAA--!!
LITTLE VISUAL ALARM CLOCK FOR YA, DARKLIGHTER!
OKAY, OKAY! I'M AWAKE! STOP WASTING ENERGY!
AND I'M GLAD I HOOKED UP MY FLIGHT SUIT'S PLUMBING!
AFTER THE TENSION, BIGGS'S JOKE IS SWEET RELIEF.
IN THEIR METAL SPHERES FLOATING IN THE VAST BLACK SEA, DEATH HAS NEVER SEEMED SO CLOSE -- NOR THEIR COMPANIONS SO DEAR.
THEY PLAN.
THEY WILL BE METHODICAL. THEY WILL COMB A CHOSEN SECTOR OF SPACE FOR POTENTIAL HAVENS, KEEPING BARELY IN COMMUNICATIONS RANGE.
THERE'S REALLY NO OTHER CHOICE.
ANOTHER DEAD ROCK.
SORRY I GOT YOUR HOPES UP, GUYS.
DON'T SWEAT IT, DELUND.
LOOK, I KNOW THIS IS LOOKING BAD. BUT WE'LL BE UNLUCKY UNTIL WE GET LUCKY, SO CARRY ON.
THE MEN CONTINUE, TRYING TO IGNORE THE TASTE OF THEIR AIR. EACH BREATH IS MORE STALE.
ANYTHING CAN HAPPEN. THERE ARE UNDISCOVERED THINGS IN THE SPACES BETWEEN THE STARS, THEY KNOW...

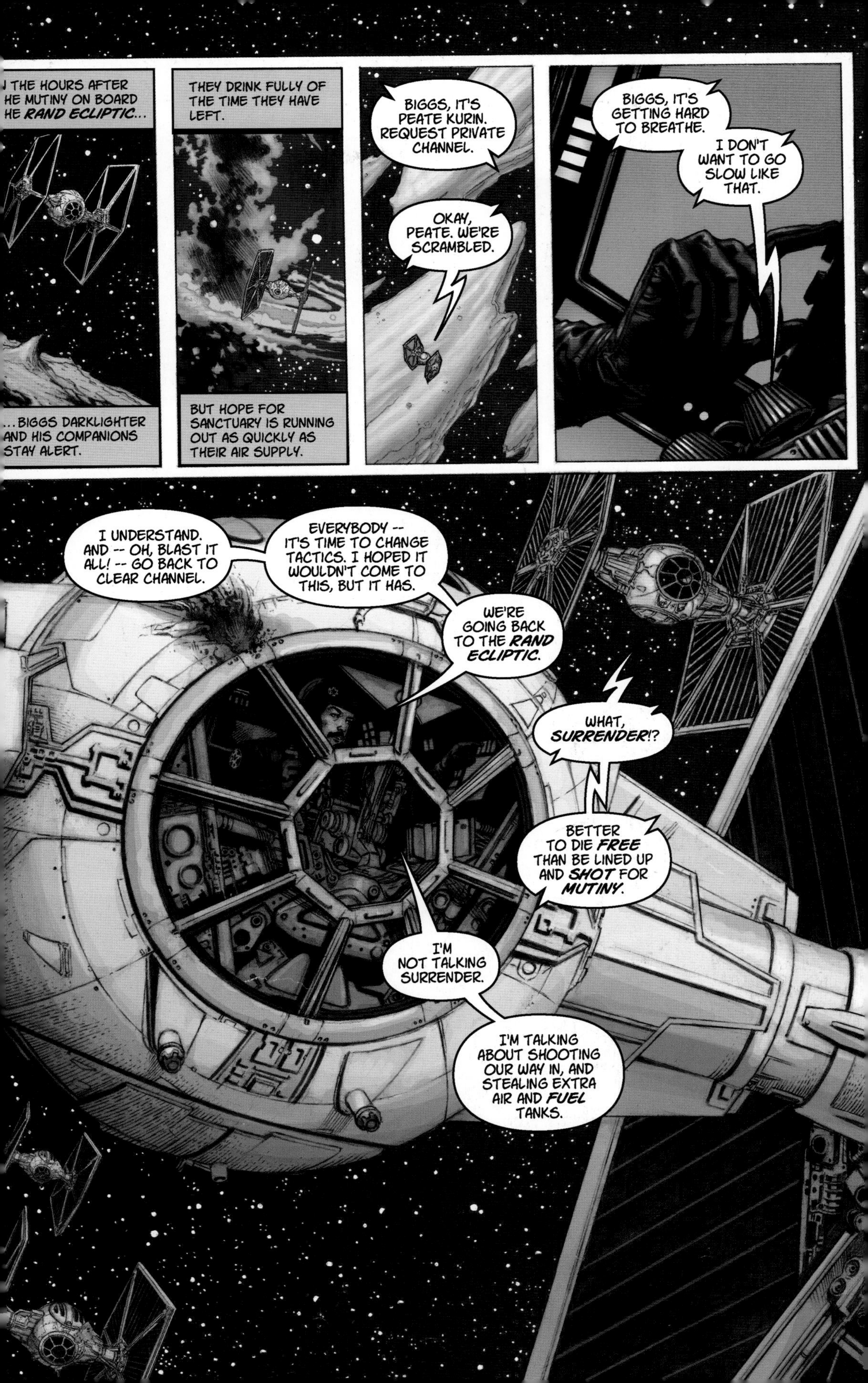

N THE HOURS AFTER HE MUTINY ON BOARD HE *RAND ECLIPTIC*...
...BIGGS DARKLIGHTER AND HIS COMPANIONS STAY ALERT.
THEY DRINK FULLY OF THE TIME THEY HAVE LEFT.
BUT HOPE FOR SANCTUARY IS RUNNING OUT AS QUICKLY AS THEIR AIR SUPPLY.
BIGGS, IT'S PEATE KURIN. REQUEST PRIVATE CHANNEL.
OKAY, PEATE. WE'RE SCRAMBLED.
BIGGS, IT'S GETTING HARD TO BREATHE.
I DON'T WANT TO GO SLOW LIKE THAT.
I UNDERSTAND. AND -- OH, BLAST IT ALL! -- GO BACK TO CLEAR CHANNEL.
EVERYBODY -- IT'S TIME TO CHANGE TACTICS. I HOPED IT WOULDN'T COME TO THIS, BUT IT HAS.
WE'RE GOING BACK TO THE *RAND ECLIPTIC*.
WHAT, *SURRENDER*!?
BETTER TO DIE *FREE* THAN BE LINED UP AND *SHOT* FOR *MUTINY*.
I'M NOT TALKING SURRENDER.
I'M TALKING ABOUT SHOOTING OUR WAY IN, AND STEALING EXTRA AIR AND *FUEL* TANKS.

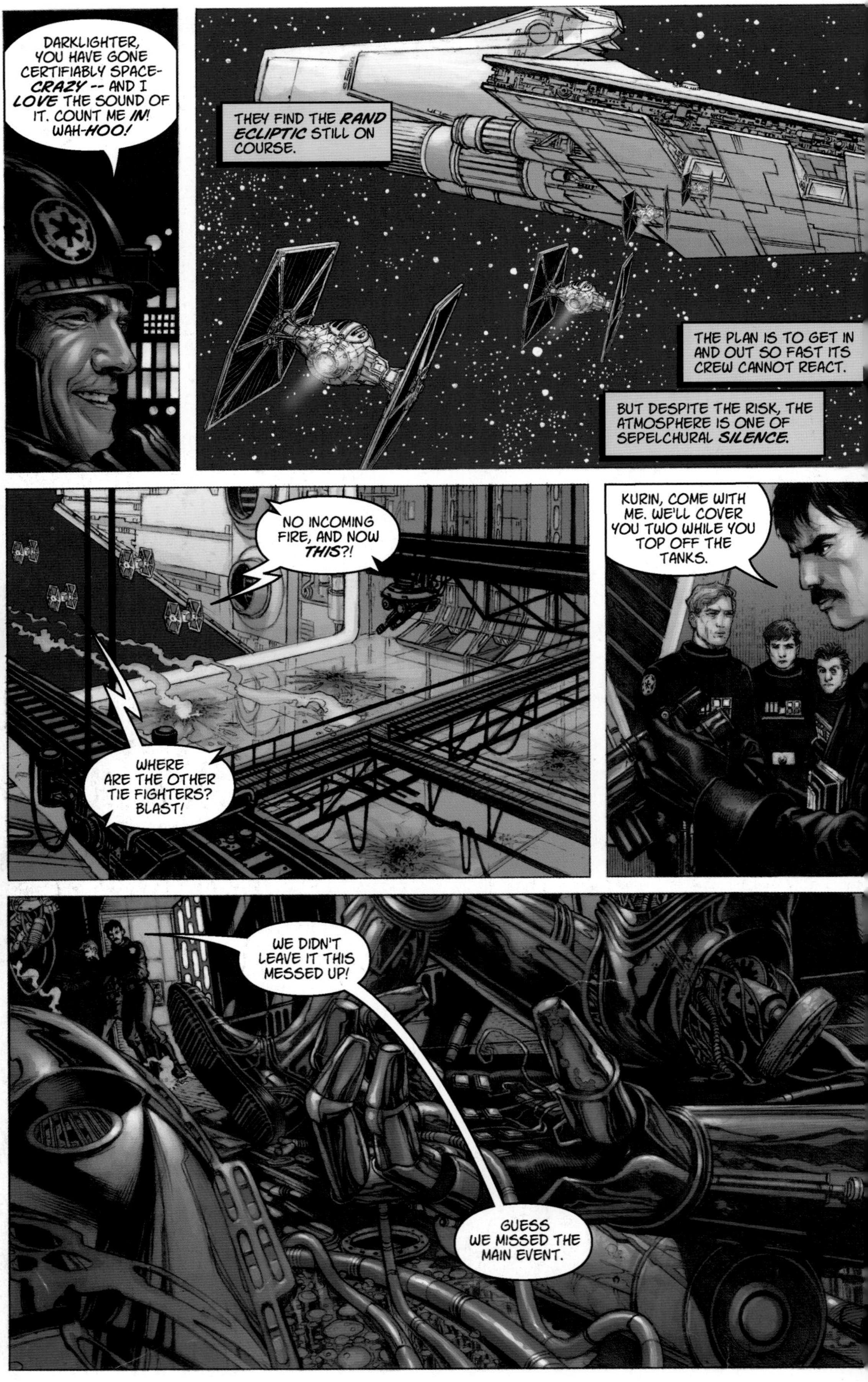
DARKLIGHTER, YOU HAVE GONE CERTIFIABLY SPACE-CRAZY -- AND I LOVE THE SOUND OF IT. COUNT ME IN! WAH-HOO!
THEY FIND THE RAND ECLIPTIC STILL ON COURSE.
THE PLAN IS TO GET IN AND OUT SO FAST ITS CREW CANNOT REACT.
BUT DESPITE THE RISK, THE ATMOSPHERE IS ONE OF SEPELCHURAL SILENCE.
NO INCOMING FIRE, AND NOW THIS?!
WHERE ARE THE OTHER TIE FIGHTERS? BLAST!
KURIN, COME WITH ME. WE'LL COVER YOU TWO WHILE YOU TOP OFF THE TANKS.
WE DIDN'T LEAVE IT THIS MESSED UP!
GUESS WE MISSED THE MAIN EVENT.

SHHH.

KONK
SHUUNK
KONK
SHUUNK

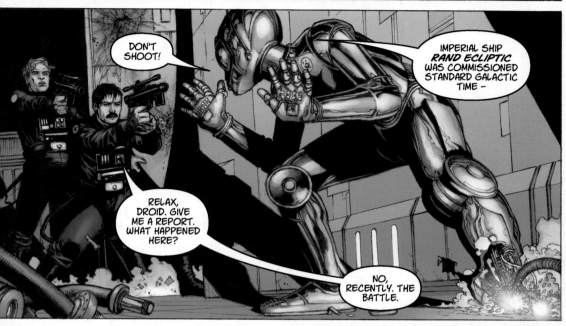

DON'T SHOOT!

IMPERIAL SHIP *RAND ECLIPTIC* WAS COMMISSIONED STANDARD GALACTIC TIME —

RELAX, DROID. GIVE ME A REPORT. WHAT HAPPENED HERE?

NO, RECENTLY. THE BATTLE.

I BELIEVE IT WAS A *MUTINY*, SIR. QUITE A BRAWL, IF I MAY DARE TO OFFER AN OPINION.

WHO WON? WHO'S IN CHARGE?

I BELIEVE THAT WOULD BE SECOND MATE *KLIVIAN*, SIR. HE LED THE MUTINY.

OR WOULD THAT BE *CAPTAIN* KLIVIAN, NOW?

YOU REALLY FORCED MY HAND, *DARKLIGHTER*. IF YOU'D JUST LET ME GET A WORD OUT BEFORE TRYING TO SLIT MY THROAT, YOU WOULD'VE LEARNED YOURS WASN'T THE *ONLY* REBEL CELL ON THE *RAND ECLIPTIC*.

IN FACT, TWO *MORE* CELLS TURNED UP, ONCE THE FIGHTING STARTED. IT TOOK A WHILE TO SORT OUT *WHO* WAS *WHOM*.

CLEVER OF YOU TO DISRUPT ALL THOSE *SHIP SYSTEMS*. THAT REALLY HELPED OUR SIDE.

AND THE TIE FIGHTERS?

A GROUP WITH IMPERIAL SYMPATHIES CHOSE TO ABSENT THEMSELVES, ONCE THEY SAW HOW THE BATTLE WENT. WE LET THEM GO, ALL BUT **ONE**.

WHY THE ONE?

OUR ACADEMY CLASSMATE **TARS NANDY**. IT WAS HE WHO DESTROYED THE **LARK**, KILLING ALL THOSE PEOPLE.

I SAW HIM DO IT, BUT THOUGHT IT WISE TO HOLD MY TONGUE AT THE DEBRIEFING.

BOY, I'M SORRY I WASN'T AROUND FOR ALL THE ACTION.

ME, TOO.

OLD "WRONG-SIDE-OF-HISTORY" HERE LOCKED HIMSELF IN HIS QUARTERS.

WE WOULD HAVE LEFT HIM THERE, IF NOT FOR SOME TECHNICAL QUESTIONS ABOUT IMPERIAL COMMUNICATIONS CODES.

HUUFF!!

SO, BIGGS ... GOING TO PULL RANK ON ME, AND TAKE OVER?

WELL, HOBBIE...

...I DON'T KNOW HOW THE REBEL ALLIANCE COMMAND STRUCTURE WORKS...

...BUT IT'S PLAIN TO SEE YOU'VE **EARNED** COMMAND OF THIS VESSEL, AND UNTIL THE **ALLIANCE** SAYS DIFFERENTLY, WELL...

...FIRST MATE BIGGS DARKLIGHTER REPORTING FOR DUTY, **SIR**!

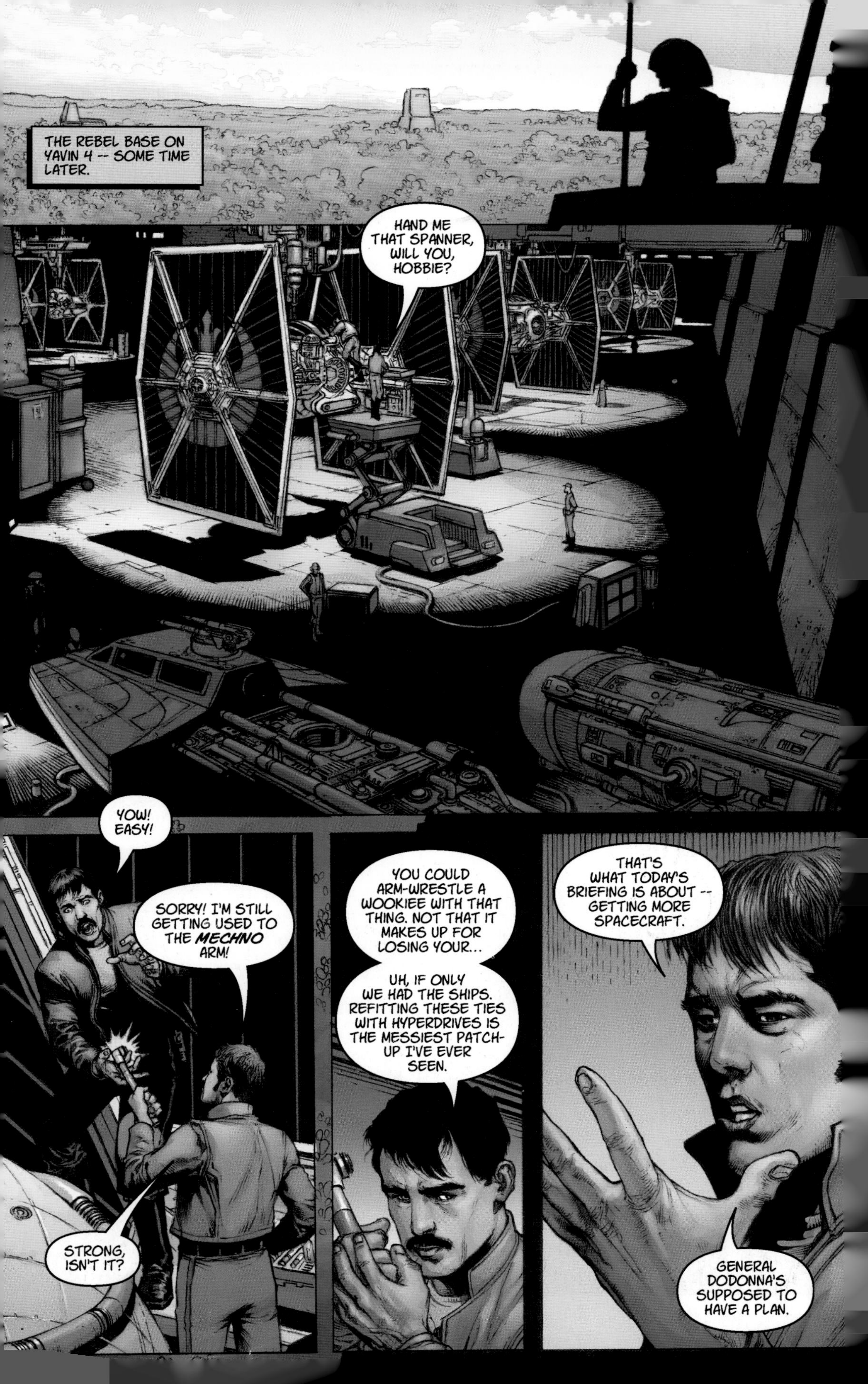
THE REBEL BASE ON YAVIN 4 -- SOME TIME LATER.
HAND ME THAT SPANNER, WILL YOU, HOBBIE?
YOW! EASY!
SORRY! I'M STILL GETTING USED TO THE *MECHNO* ARM!
STRONG, ISN'T IT?
YOU COULD ARM-WRESTLE A WOOKIEE WITH THAT THING. NOT THAT IT MAKES UP FOR LOSING YOUR...
UH, IF ONLY WE HAD THE SHIPS. REFITTING THESE TIES WITH HYPERDRIVES IS THE MESSIEST PATCH-UP I'VE EVER SEEN.
THAT'S WHAT TODAY'S BRIEFING IS ABOUT -- GETTING MORE SPACECRAFT.
GENERAL DODONNA'S SUPPOSED TO HAVE A PLAN.

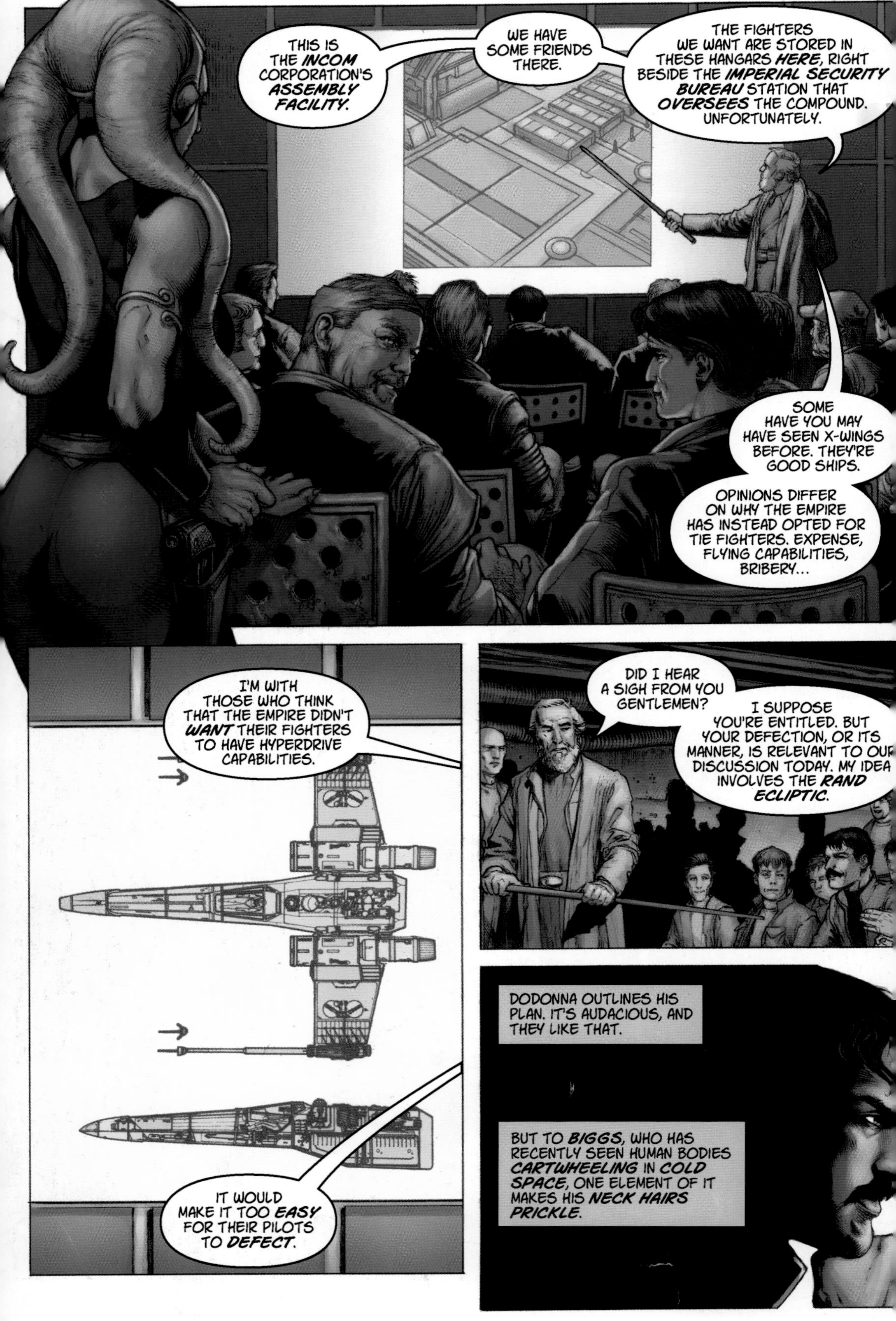
THIS IS THE INCOM CORPORATION'S ASSEMBLY FACILITY.
WE HAVE SOME FRIENDS THERE.
THE FIGHTERS WE WANT ARE STORED IN THESE HANGARS HERE, RIGHT BESIDE THE IMPERIAL SECURITY BUREAU STATION THAT OVERSEES THE COMPOUND. UNFORTUNATELY.
SOME HAVE YOU MAY HAVE SEEN X-WINGS BEFORE. THEY'RE GOOD SHIPS.
OPINIONS DIFFER ON WHY THE EMPIRE HAS INSTEAD OPTED FOR TIE FIGHTERS. EXPENSE, FLYING CAPABILITIES, BRIBERY...
I'M WITH THOSE WHO THINK THAT THE EMPIRE DIDN'T WANT THEIR FIGHTERS TO HAVE HYPERDRIVE CAPABILITIES.
IT WOULD MAKE IT TOO EASY FOR THEIR PILOTS TO DEFECT.
DID I HEAR A SIGH FROM YOU GENTLEMEN?
I SUPPOSE YOU'RE ENTITLED. BUT YOUR DEFECTION, OR ITS MANNER, IS RELEVANT TO OUR DISCUSSION TODAY. MY IDEA INVOLVES THE RAND ECLIPTIC.
DODONNA OUTLINES HIS PLAN. IT'S AUDACIOUS, AND THEY LIKE THAT.
BUT TO BIGGS, WHO HAS RECENTLY SEEN HUMAN BODIES CARTWHEELING IN COLD SPACE, ONE ELEMENT OF IT MAKES HIS NECK HAIRS PRICKLE.

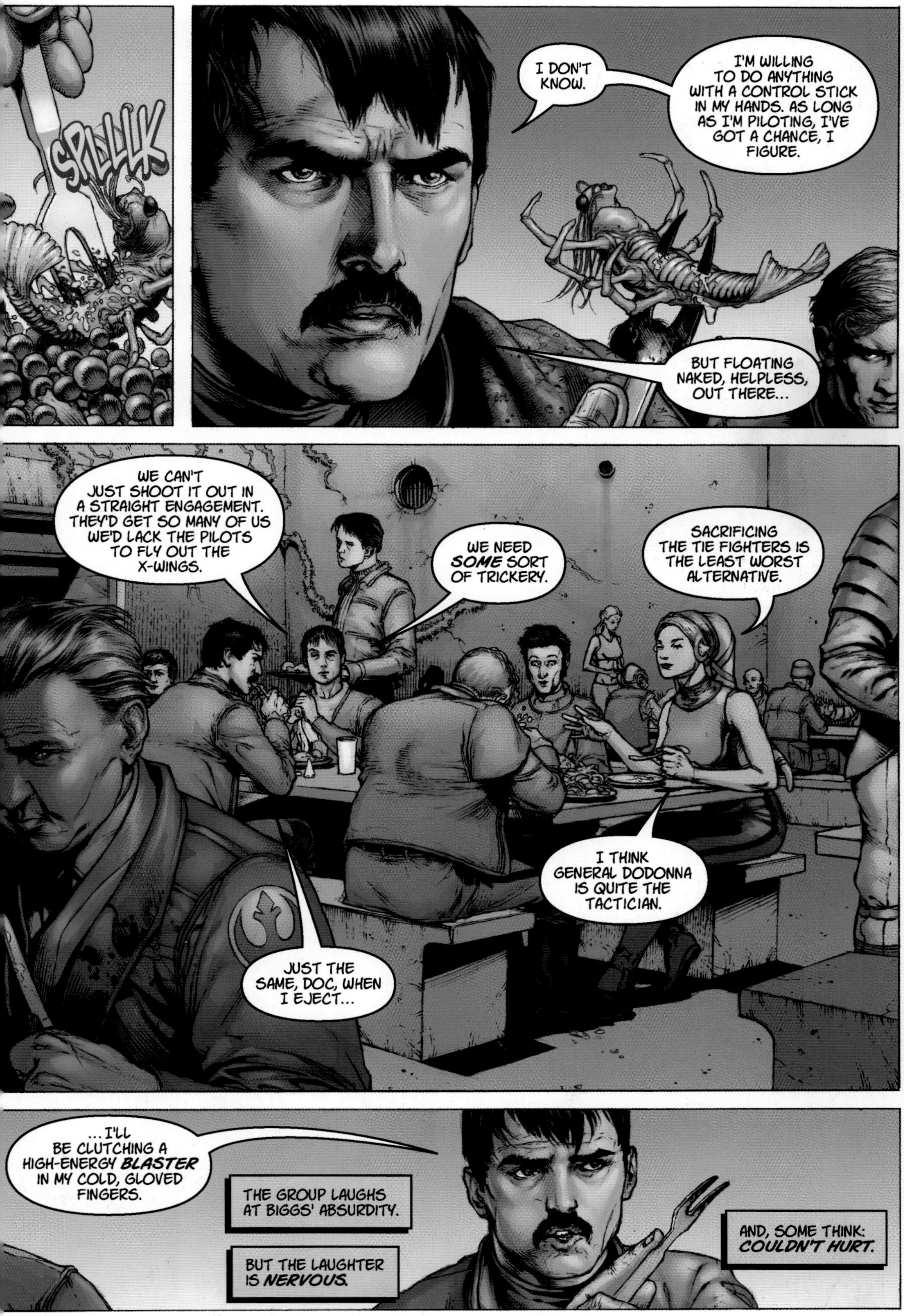
SPLLLK
I DON'T KNOW.
I'M WILLING TO DO ANYTHING WITH A CONTROL STICK IN MY HANDS. AS LONG AS I'M PILOTING, I'VE GOT A CHANCE, I FIGURE.
BUT FLOATING NAKED, HELPLESS, OUT THERE...
WE CAN'T JUST SHOOT IT OUT IN A STRAIGHT ENGAGEMENT. THEY'D GET SO MANY OF US WE'D LACK THE PILOTS TO FLY OUT THE X-WINGS.
WE NEED SOME SORT OF TRICKERY.
SACRIFICING THE TIE FIGHTERS IS THE LEAST WORST ALTERNATIVE.
I THINK GENERAL DODONNA IS QUITE THE TACTICIAN.
JUST THE SAME, DOC, WHEN I EJECT...
...I'LL BE CLUTCHING A HIGH-ENERGY BLASTER IN MY COLD, GLOVED FINGERS.
THE GROUP LAUGHS AT BIGGS' ABSURDITY.
BUT THE LAUGHTER IS NERVOUS.
AND, SOME THINK: COULDN'T HURT.

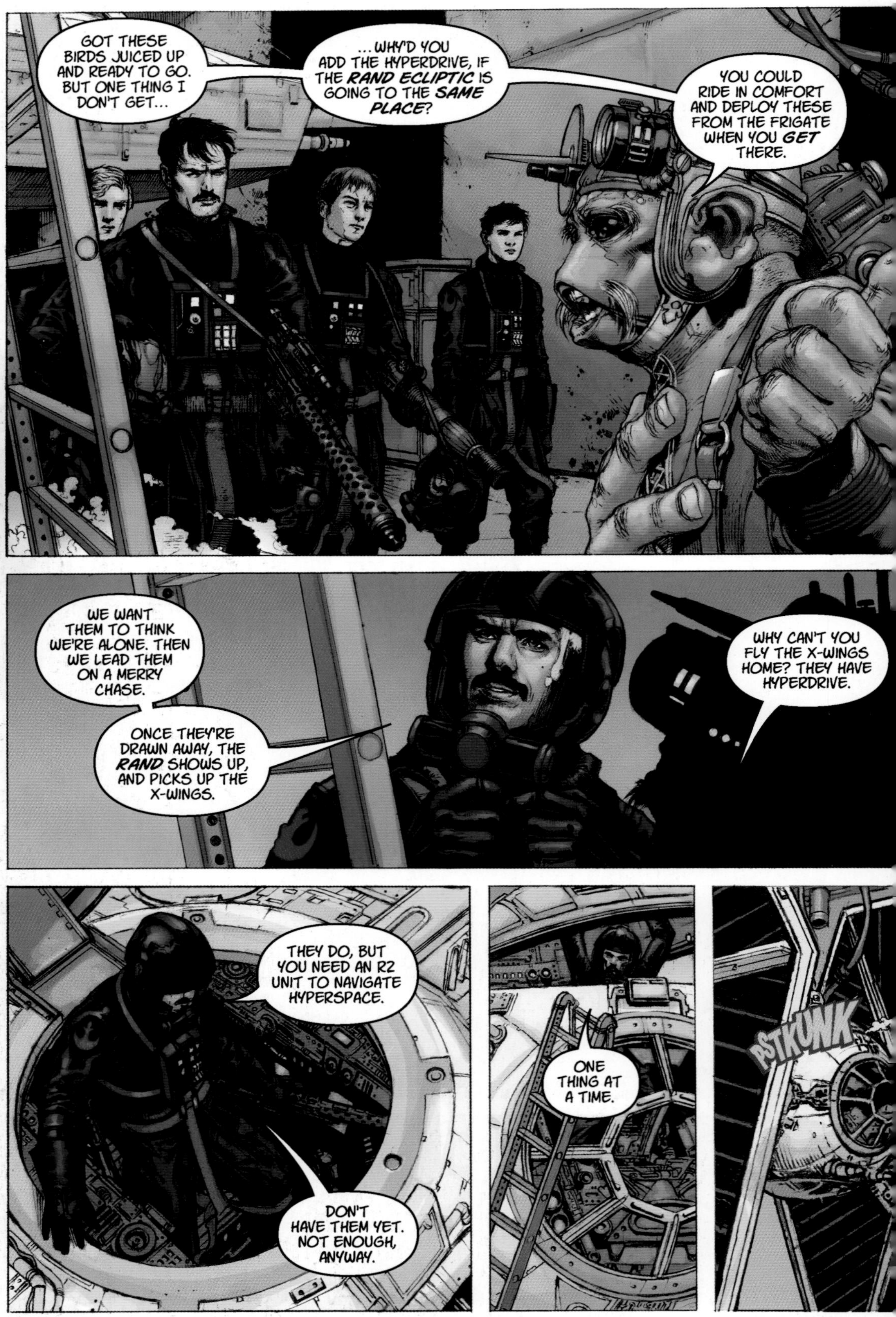
GOT THESE BIRDS JUICED UP AND READY TO GO. BUT ONE THING I DON'T GET...
...WHY'D YOU ADD THE HYPERDRIVE, IF THE RAND ECLIPTIC IS GOING TO THE SAME PLACE?
YOU COULD RIDE IN COMFORT AND DEPLOY THESE FROM THE FRIGATE WHEN YOU GET THERE.
WE WANT THEM TO THINK WE'RE ALONE. THEN WE LEAD THEM ON A MERRY CHASE.
ONCE THEY'RE DRAWN AWAY, THE RAND SHOWS UP, AND PICKS UP THE X-WINGS.
WHY CAN'T YOU FLY THE X-WINGS HOME? THEY HAVE HYPERDRIVE.
THEY DO, BUT YOU NEED AN R2 UNIT TO NAVIGATE HYPERSPACE.
DON'T HAVE THEM YET. NOT ENOUGH, ANYWAY.
ONE THING AT A TIME.
PSTKUNK

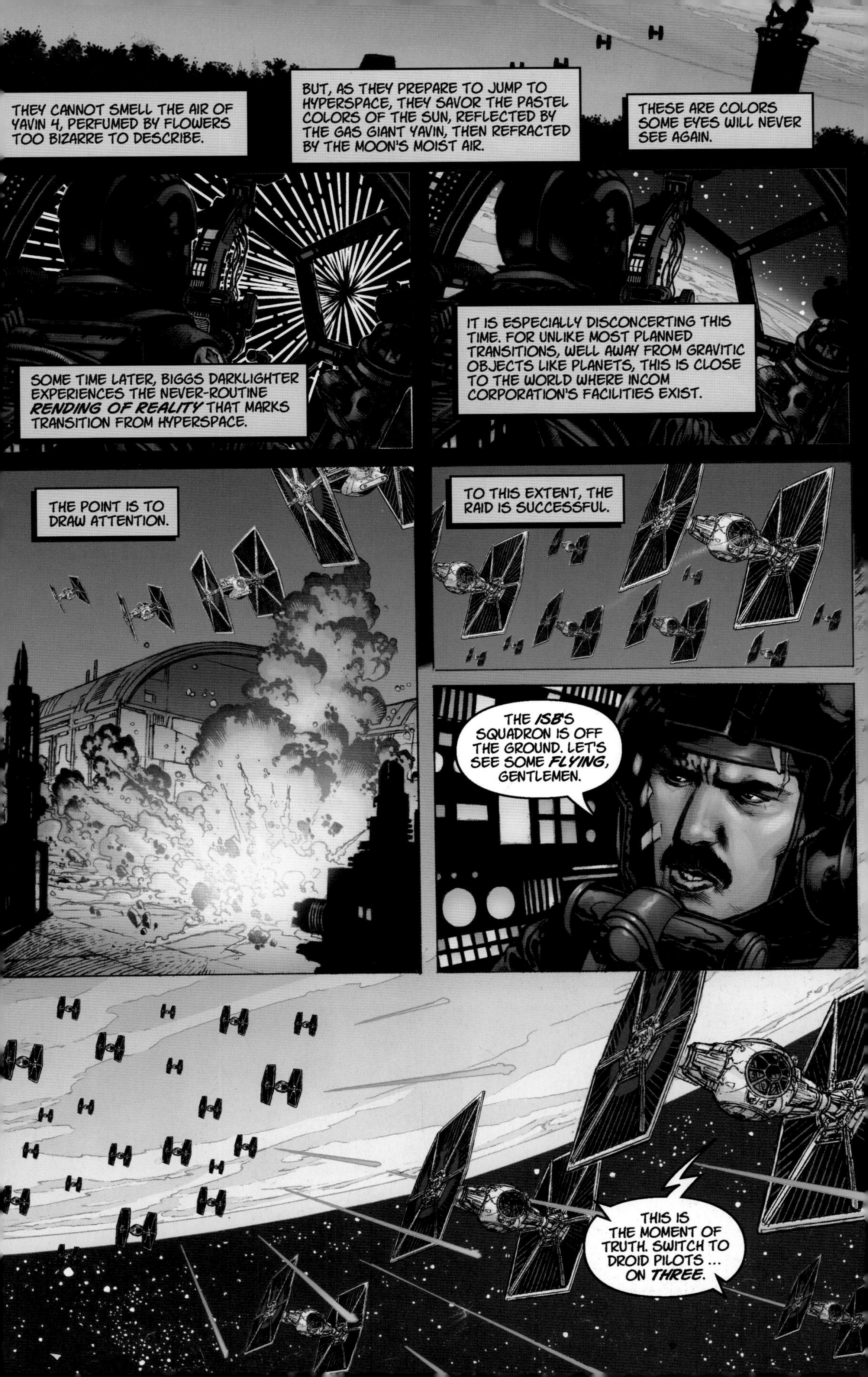
THEY CANNOT SMELL THE AIR OF YAVIN 4, PERFUMED BY FLOWERS TOO BIZARRE TO DESCRIBE.
BUT, AS THEY PREPARE TO JUMP TO HYPERSPACE, THEY SAVOR THE PASTEL COLORS OF THE SUN, REFLECTED BY THE GAS GIANT YAVIN, THEN REFRACTED BY THE MOON'S MOIST AIR.
THESE ARE COLORS SOME EYES WILL NEVER SEE AGAIN.
SOME TIME LATER, BIGGS DARKLIGHTER EXPERIENCES THE NEVER-ROUTINE *RENDING OF REALITY* THAT MARKS TRANSITION FROM HYPERSPACE.
IT IS ESPECIALLY DISCONCERTING THIS TIME. FOR UNLIKE MOST PLANNED TRANSITIONS, WELL AWAY FROM GRAVITIC OBJECTS LIKE PLANETS, THIS IS CLOSE TO THE WORLD WHERE INCOM CORPORATION'S FACILITIES EXIST.
THE POINT IS TO DRAW ATTENTION.
TO THIS EXTENT, THE RAID IS SUCCESSFUL.
THE *ISB*'S SQUADRON IS OFF THE GROUND. LET'S SEE SOME *FLYING*, GENTLEMEN.
THIS IS THE MOMENT OF TRUTH. SWITCH TO DROID PILOTS ... ON *THREE*.

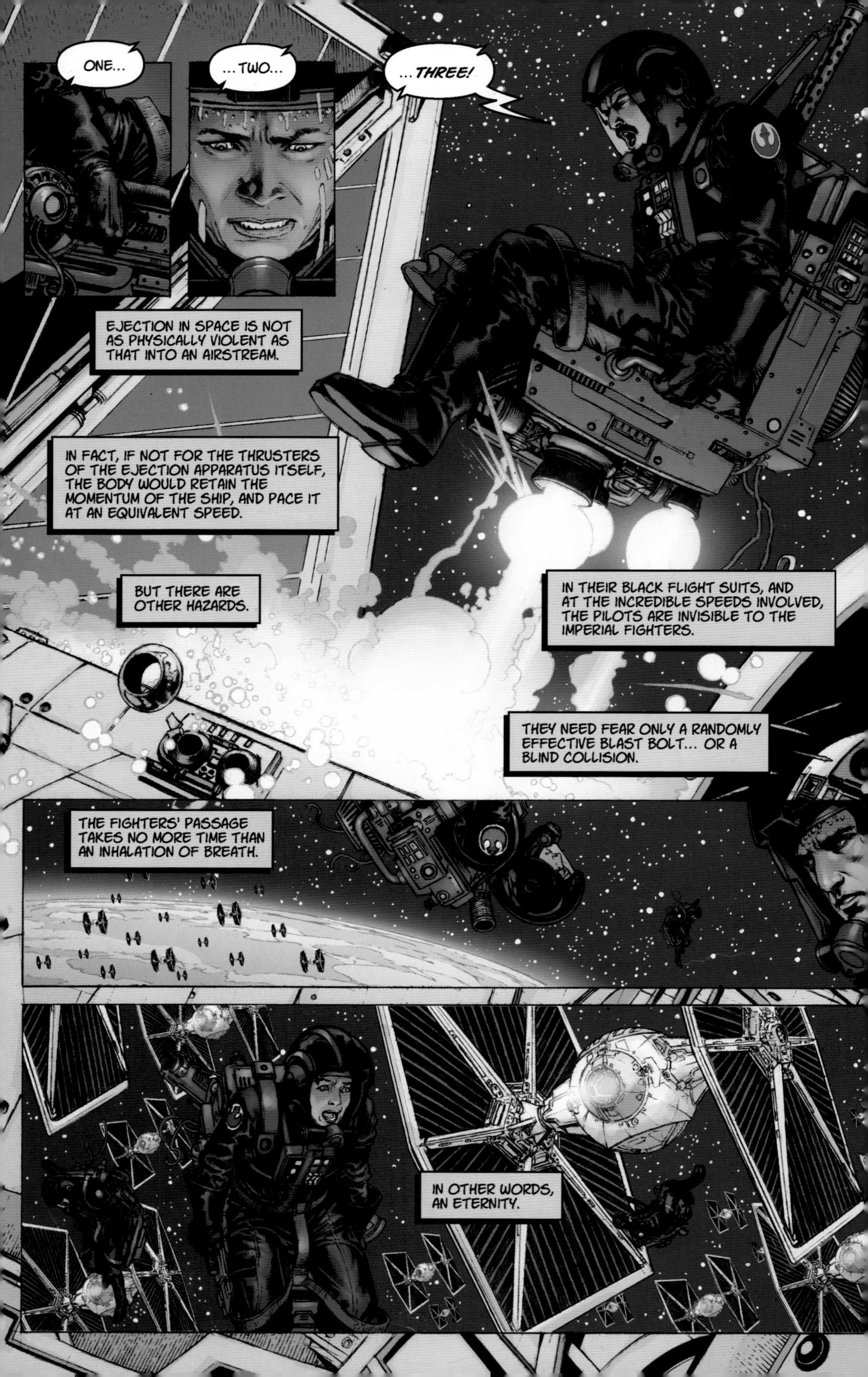
ONE...
...TWO...
...THREE!
EJECTION IN SPACE IS NOT AS PHYSICALLY VIOLENT AS THAT INTO AN AIRSTREAM.
IN FACT, IF NOT FOR THE THRUSTERS OF THE EJECTION APPARATUS ITSELF, THE BODY WOULD RETAIN THE MOMENTUM OF THE SHIP, AND PACE IT AT AN EQUIVALENT SPEED.
BUT THERE ARE OTHER HAZARDS.
IN THEIR BLACK FLIGHT SUITS, AND AT THE INCREDIBLE SPEEDS INVOLVED, THE PILOTS ARE INVISIBLE TO THE IMPERIAL FIGHTERS.
THEY NEED FEAR ONLY A RANDOMLY EFFECTIVE BLAST BOLT... OR A BLIND COLLISION.
THE FIGHTERS' PASSAGE TAKES NO MORE TIME THAN AN INHALATION OF BREATH.
IN OTHER WORDS, AN ETERNITY.

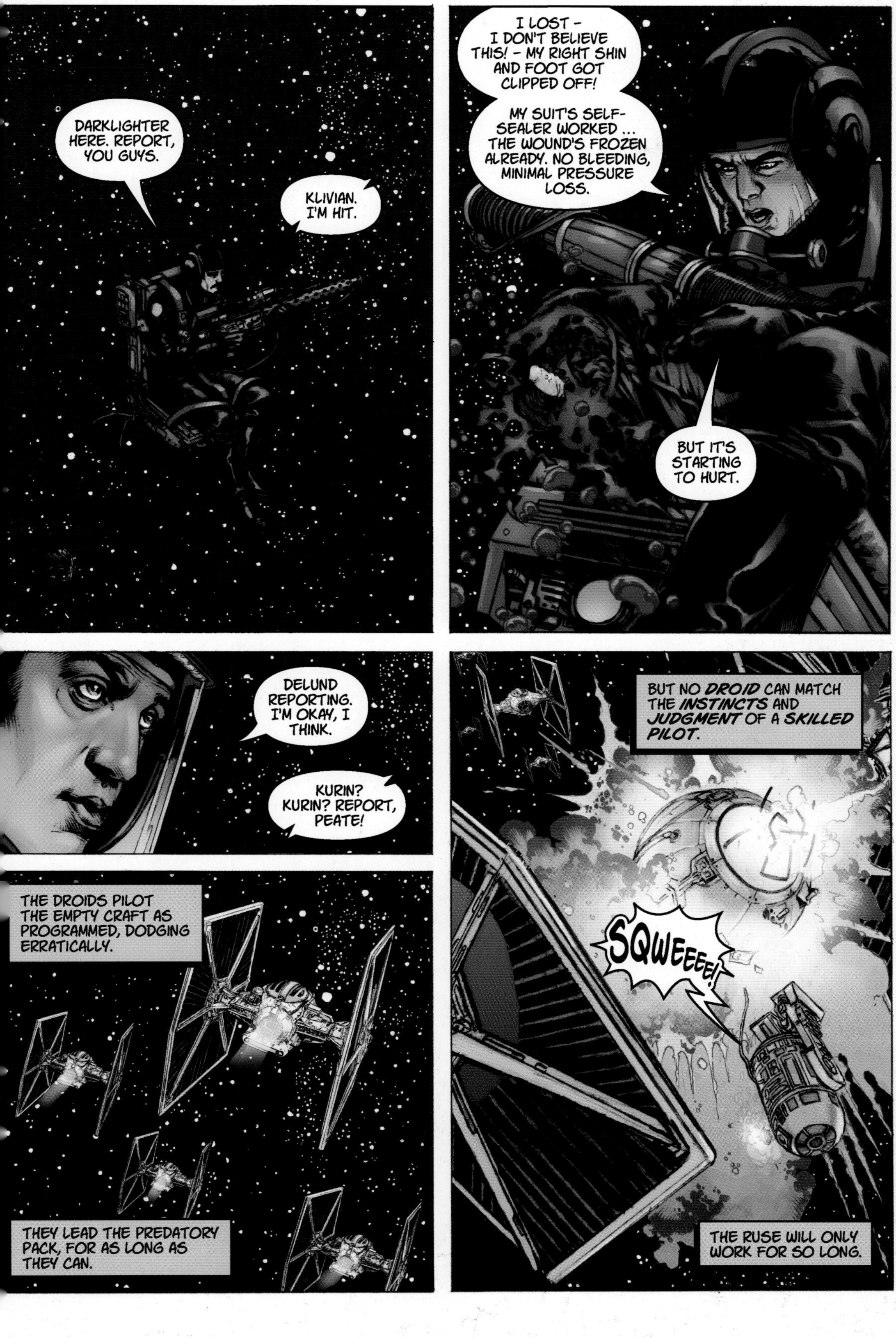
DARKLIGHTER HERE. REPORT, YOU GUYS.
KLIVIAN. I'M HIT.
I LOST - I DON'T BELIEVE THIS! - MY RIGHT SHIN AND FOOT GOT CLIPPED OFF!
MY SUIT'S SELF-SEALER WORKED ... THE WOUND'S FROZEN ALREADY. NO BLEEDING, MINIMAL PRESSURE LOSS.
BUT IT'S STARTING TO HURT.
DELUND REPORTING. I'M OKAY, I THINK.
KURIN? KURIN? REPORT, PEATE!
THE DROIDS PILOT THE EMPTY CRAFT AS PROGRAMMED, DODGING ERRATICALLY.
THEY LEAD THE PREDATORY PACK, FOR AS LONG AS THEY CAN.
BUT NO *DROID* CAN MATCH THE *INSTINCTS* AND *JUDGMENT* OF A *SKILLED PILOT*.
SQWEEEEE!
THE RUSE WILL ONLY WORK FOR SO LONG.

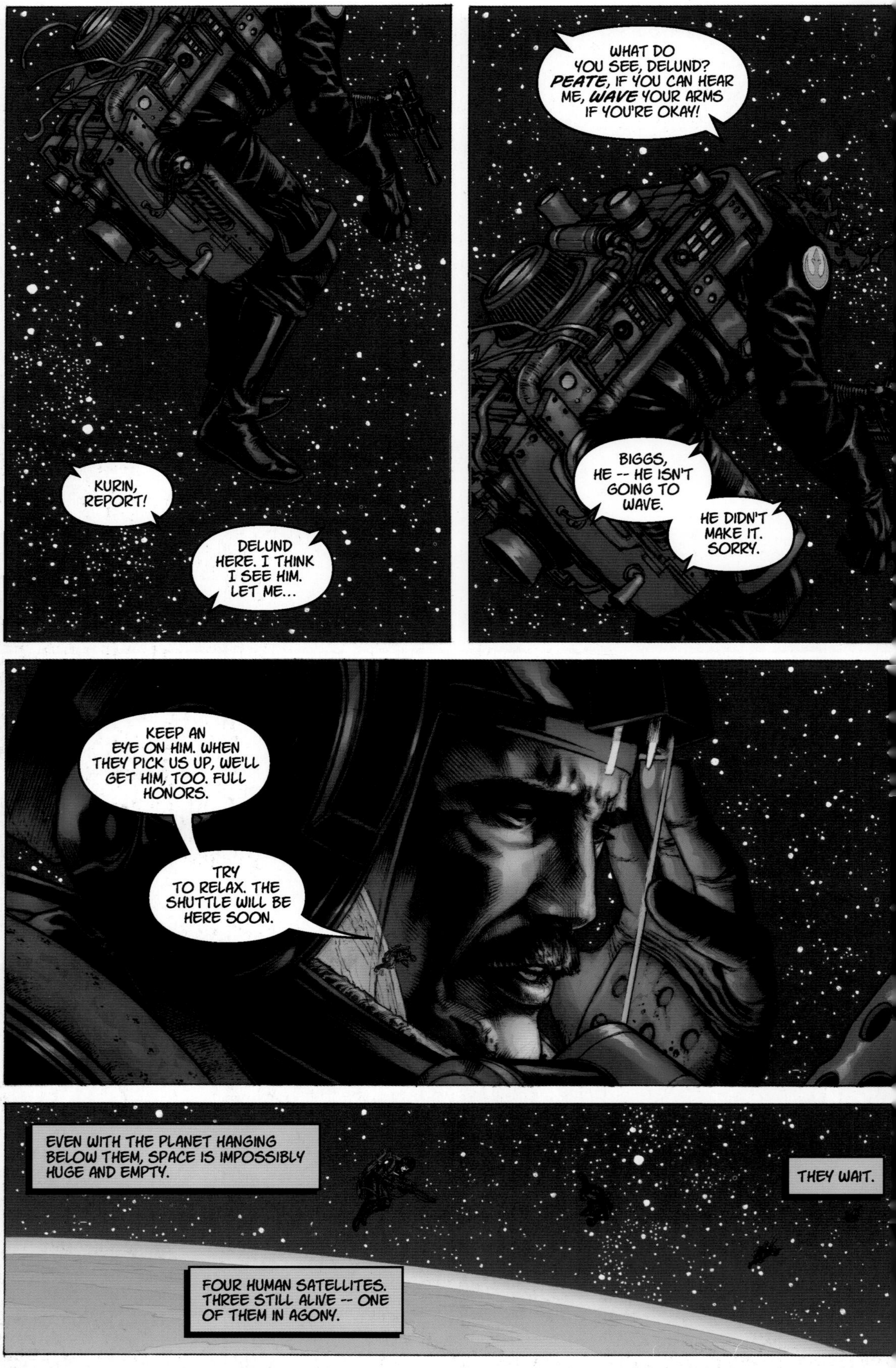
KURIN, REPORT!
DELUND HERE. I THINK I SEE HIM. LET ME...
WHAT DO YOU SEE, DELUND? PEATE, IF YOU CAN HEAR ME, WAVE YOUR ARMS IF YOU'RE OKAY!
BIGGS, HE -- HE ISN'T GOING TO WAVE.
HE DIDN'T MAKE IT. SORRY.
KEEP AN EYE ON HIM. WHEN THEY PICK US UP, WE'LL GET HIM, TOO. FULL HONORS.
TRY TO RELAX. THE SHUTTLE WILL BE HERE SOON.
EVEN WITH THE PLANET HANGING BELOW THEM, SPACE IS IMPOSSIBLY HUGE AND EMPTY.
THEY WAIT.
FOUR HUMAN SATELLITES. THREE STILL ALIVE -- ONE OF THEM IN AGONY.

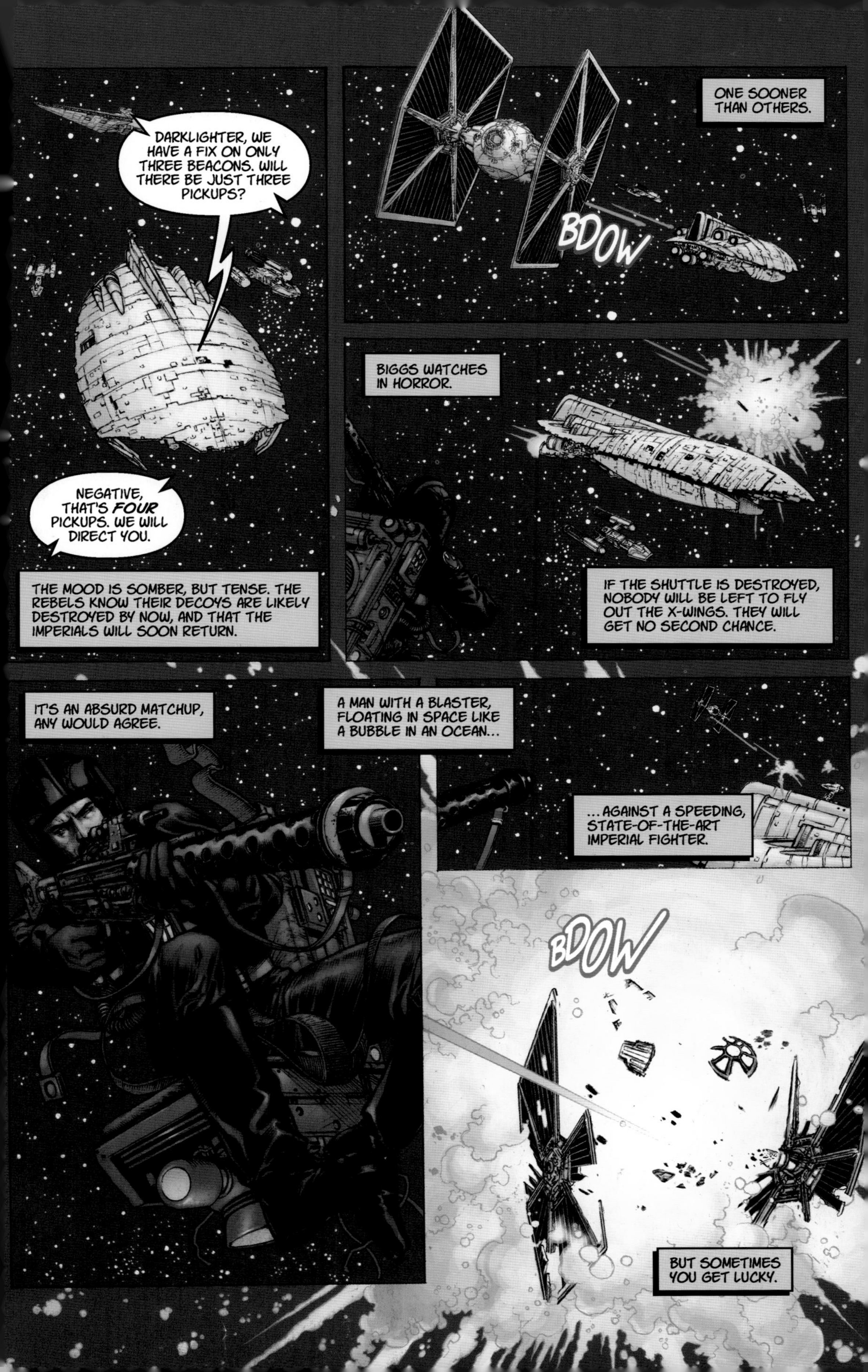
DARKLIGHTER, WE HAVE A FIX ON ONLY THREE BEACONS. WILL THERE BE JUST THREE PICKUPS?
NEGATIVE, THAT'S *FOUR* PICKUPS. WE WILL DIRECT YOU.
THE MOOD IS SOMBER, BUT TENSE. THE REBELS KNOW THEIR DECOYS ARE LIKELY DESTROYED BY NOW, AND THAT THE IMPERIALS WILL SOON RETURN.
ONE SOONER THAN OTHERS.
BDOW
BIGGS WATCHES IN HORROR.
IF THE SHUTTLE IS DESTROYED, NOBODY WILL BE LEFT TO FLY OUT THE X-WINGS. THEY WILL GET NO SECOND CHANCE.
IT'S AN ABSURD MATCHUP, ANY WOULD AGREE.
A MAN WITH A BLASTER, FLOATING IN SPACE LIKE A BUBBLE IN AN OCEAN...
...AGAINST A SPEEDING, STATE-OF-THE-ART IMPERIAL FIGHTER.
BDOW
BUT SOMETIMES YOU GET LUCKY.

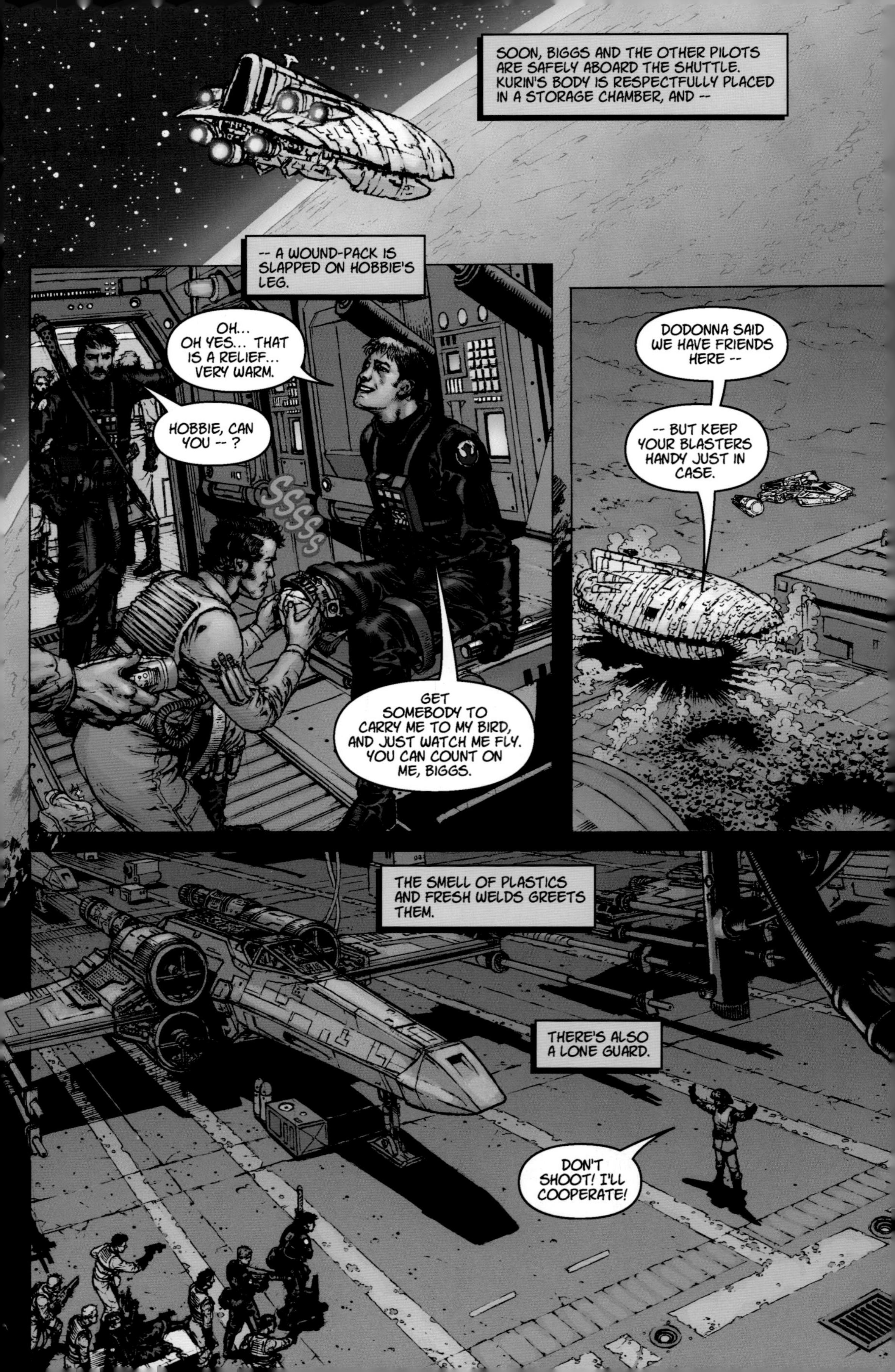
SOON, BIGGS AND THE OTHER PILOTS ARE SAFELY ABOARD THE SHUTTLE. KURIN'S BODY IS RESPECTFULLY PLACED IN A STORAGE CHAMBER, AND --
-- A WOUND-PACK IS SLAPPED ON HOBBIE'S LEG.
OH... OH YES... THAT IS A RELIEF... VERY WARM.
HOBBIE, CAN YOU -- ?
SSSSS
GET SOMEBODY TO CARRY ME TO MY BIRD, AND JUST WATCH ME FLY. YOU CAN COUNT ON ME, BIGGS.
DODONNA SAID WE HAVE FRIENDS HERE --
-- BUT KEEP YOUR BLASTERS HANDY JUST IN CASE.
THE SMELL OF PLASTICS AND FRESH WELDS GREETS THEM.
THERE'S ALSO A LONE GUARD.
DON'T SHOOT! I'LL COOPERATE!

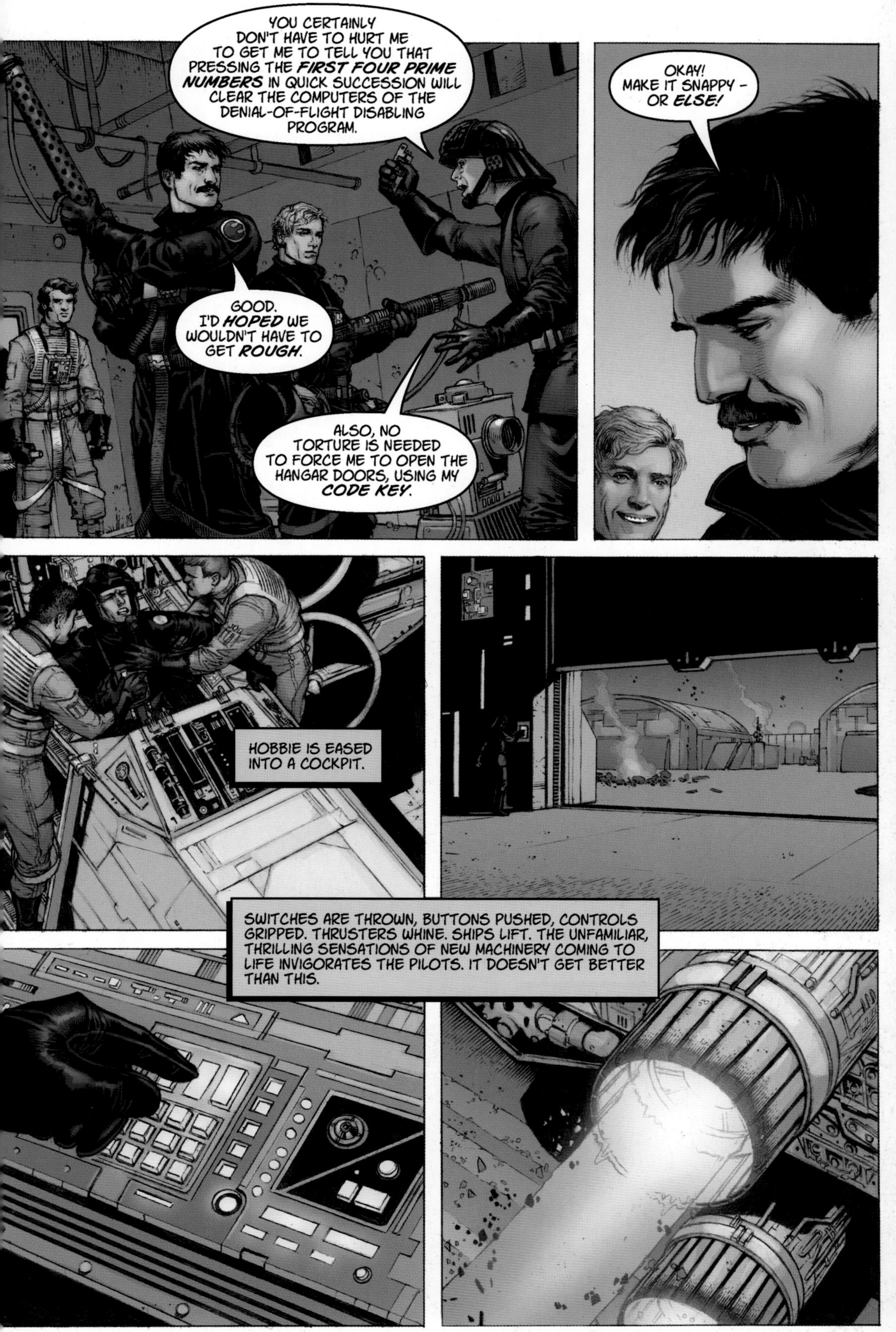
YOU CERTAINLY DON'T HAVE TO HURT ME TO GET ME TO TELL YOU THAT PRESSING THE FIRST FOUR PRIME NUMBERS IN QUICK SUCCESSION WILL CLEAR THE COMPUTERS OF THE DENIAL-OF-FLIGHT DISABLING PROGRAM.
GOOD. I'D HOPED WE WOULDN'T HAVE TO GET ROUGH.
ALSO, NO TORTURE IS NEEDED TO FORCE ME TO OPEN THE HANGAR DOORS, USING MY CODE KEY.
OKAY! MAKE IT SNAPPY - OR ELSE!
HOBBIE IS EASED INTO A COCKPIT.
SWITCHES ARE THROWN, BUTTONS PUSHED, CONTROLS GRIPPED. THRUSTERS WHINE. SHIPS LIFT. THE UNFAMILIAR, THRILLING SENSATIONS OF NEW MACHINERY COMING TO LIFE INVIGORATES THE PILOTS. IT DOESN'T GET BETTER THAN THIS.

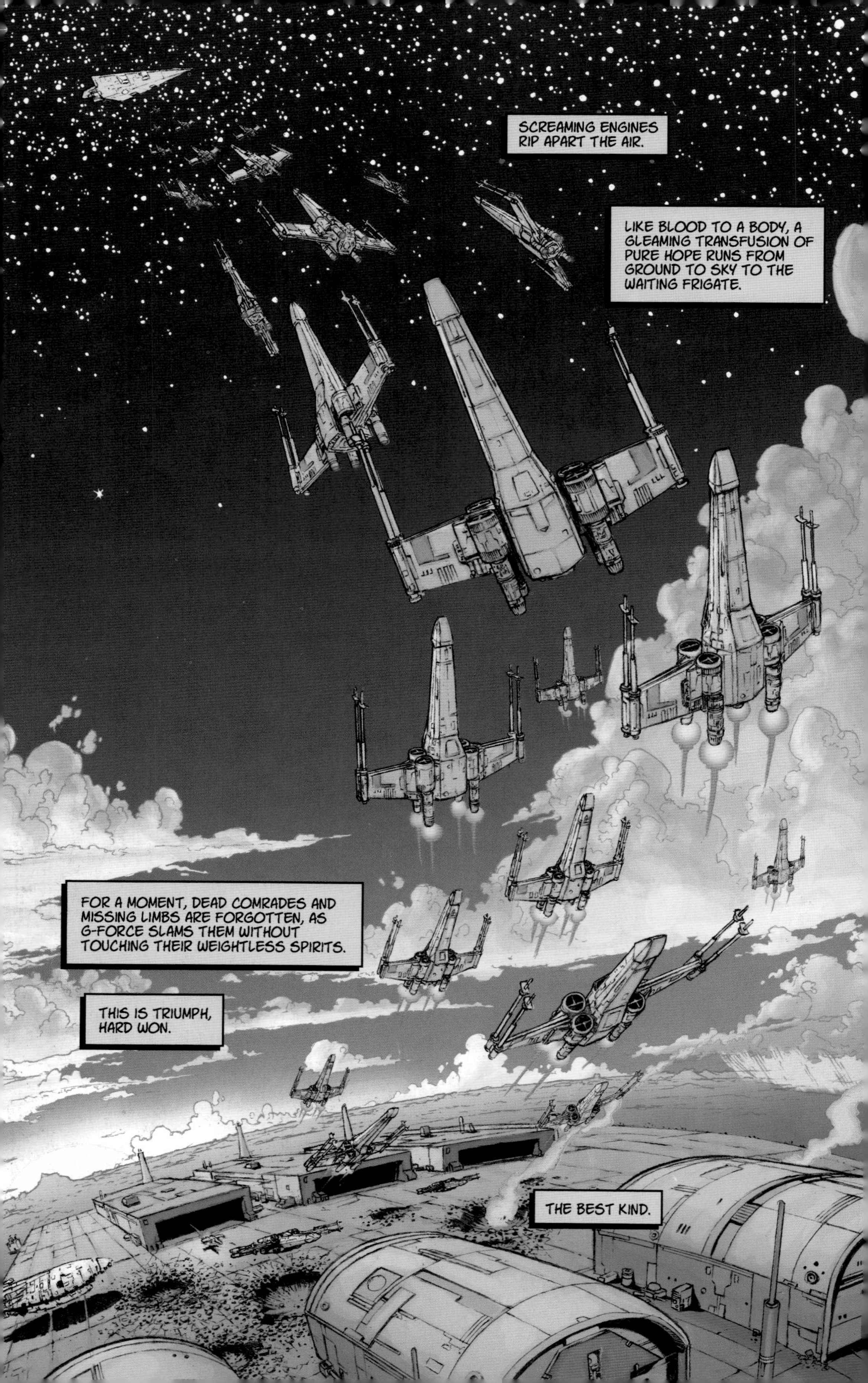
SCREAMING ENGINES RIP APART THE AIR.
LIKE BLOOD TO A BODY, A GLEAMING TRANSFUSION OF PURE HOPE RUNS FROM GROUND TO SKY TO THE WAITING FRIGATE.
FOR A MOMENT, DEAD COMRADES AND MISSING LIMBS ARE FORGOTTEN, AS G-FORCE SLAMS THEM WITHOUT TOUCHING THEIR WEIGHTLESS SPIRITS.
THIS IS TRIUMPH, HARD WON.
THE BEST KIND.

LATER...

I AM INFORMED YOU HAVE VISITORS, MASTER KLIVIAN. DO YOU WISH TO RECEIVE THEM?

SURE, LET 'EM IN.

HOW MANY?

JUST ME, WEDGE, DOC, AND JEK

WE'VE BEEN PRACTICING SOME MOVES. YOU GOTTA SEE THE X-WINGS IN ACTION, HOBBIE! ROGUE SQUADRON IS GOING TO GIVE THE EMPIRE SOME GRIEF!

WE GOTTA GET YOU BACK IN THE COCKPIT! WHAT'S THE DELAY?

WELL, APART FROM THE FACT THAT I'LL HAVE TO WAIT FOR A MECHNO LEG TO BE DELIVERED...

...SOME KIND OF INFECTION'S STARTED.

THEY THINK IT'S SOMETHING NATIVE TO YAVIN FOUR. RESISTANT TO TREATMENT SO FAR.

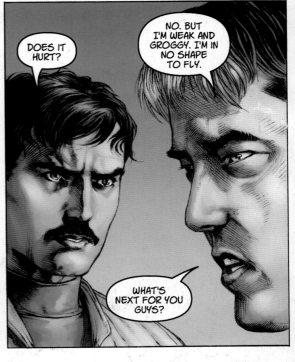

DOES IT HURT?

NO. BUT I'M WEAK AND GROGGY. I'M IN NO SHAPE TO FLY.

WHAT'S NEXT FOR YOU GUYS?

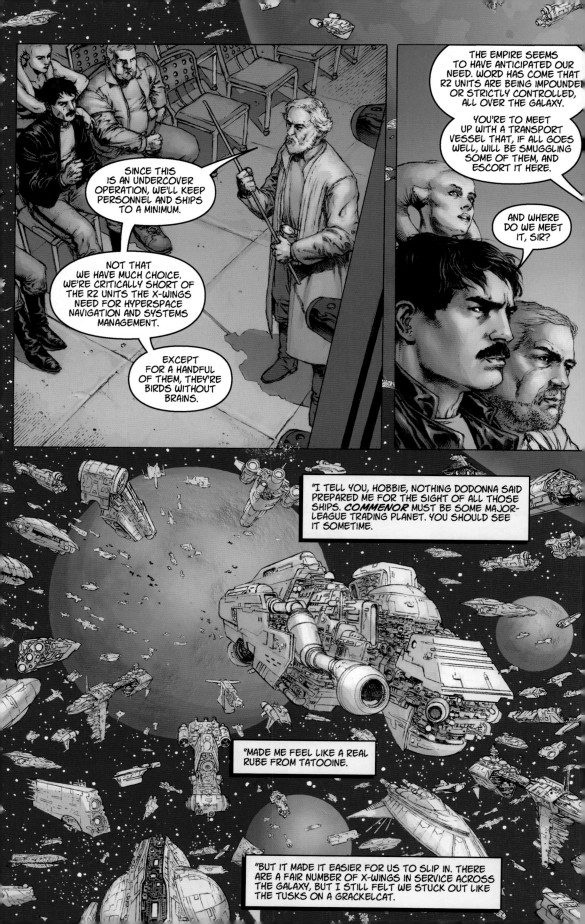

SINCE THIS IS AN UNDERCOVER OPERATION, WE'LL KEEP PERSONNEL AND SHIPS TO A MINIMUM.

NOT THAT WE HAVE MUCH CHOICE. WE'RE CRITICALLY SHORT OF THE R2 UNITS THE X-WINGS NEED FOR HYPERSPACE NAVIGATION AND SYSTEMS MANAGEMENT.

EXCEPT FOR A HANDFUL OF THEM, THEY'RE BIRDS WITHOUT BRAINS.

THE EMPIRE SEEMS TO HAVE ANTICIPATED OUR NEED. WORD HAS COME THAT R2 UNITS ARE BEING IMPOUNDED OR STRICTLY CONTROLLED, ALL OVER THE GALAXY.

YOU'RE TO MEET UP WITH A TRANSPORT VESSEL THAT, IF ALL GOES WELL, WILL BE SMUGGLING SOME OF THEM, AND ESCORT IT HERE.

AND WHERE DO WE MEET IT, SIR?

"I TELL YOU, HOBBIE, NOTHING DODONNA SAID PREPARED ME FOR THE SIGHT OF ALL THOSE SHIPS. *COMMENOR* MUST BE SOME MAJOR-LEAGUE TRADING PLANET. YOU SHOULD SEE IT SOMETIME.

"MADE ME FEEL LIKE A REAL RUBE FROM TATOOINE.

"BUT IT MADE IT EASIER FOR US TO SLIP IN. THERE ARE A FAIR NUMBER OF X-WINGS IN SERVICE ACROSS THE GALAXY, BUT I STILL FELT WE STUCK OUT LIKE THE TUSKS ON A GRACKELCAT.

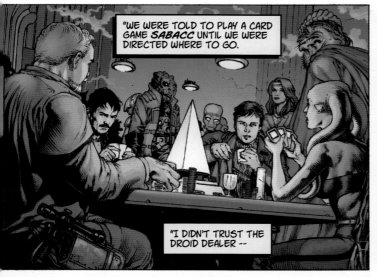

"WE WERE TOLD TO PLAY A CARD GAME *SABACC* UNTIL WE WERE DIRECTED WHERE TO GO.

"I DIDN'T TRUST THE DROID DEALER --

" -- UNTIL IT DEALT WEDGE A *CARD* THAT TOLD US THE *HANGAR* WHERE THE SMUGGLER'S *SHIP* WAS!

"THEN TROUBLE CAME. NOT IMPERIALS, THOUGH.

"SOME LOCAL TOUGHS PLANTED THEMSELVES ON OUR RENTED *LANDSPEEDER*, AND TRIED TO SHAKE US DOWN FOR A *'PROTECTION'* FEE!

"BUT THEY MADE A MISTAKE --

"--THEY MADE A *FAT JOKE* ABOUT JEK.

"HE LEFT A FEW FOR US TO KNOCK AROUND A BIT. I'M NOT USUALLY MUCH FOR BRAWLING, BUT IT FELT GOOD TO SEE THOSE PUNKS SPITTING TEETH ON THE DECK. AM I GETTING HARDENED, HOBBIE?

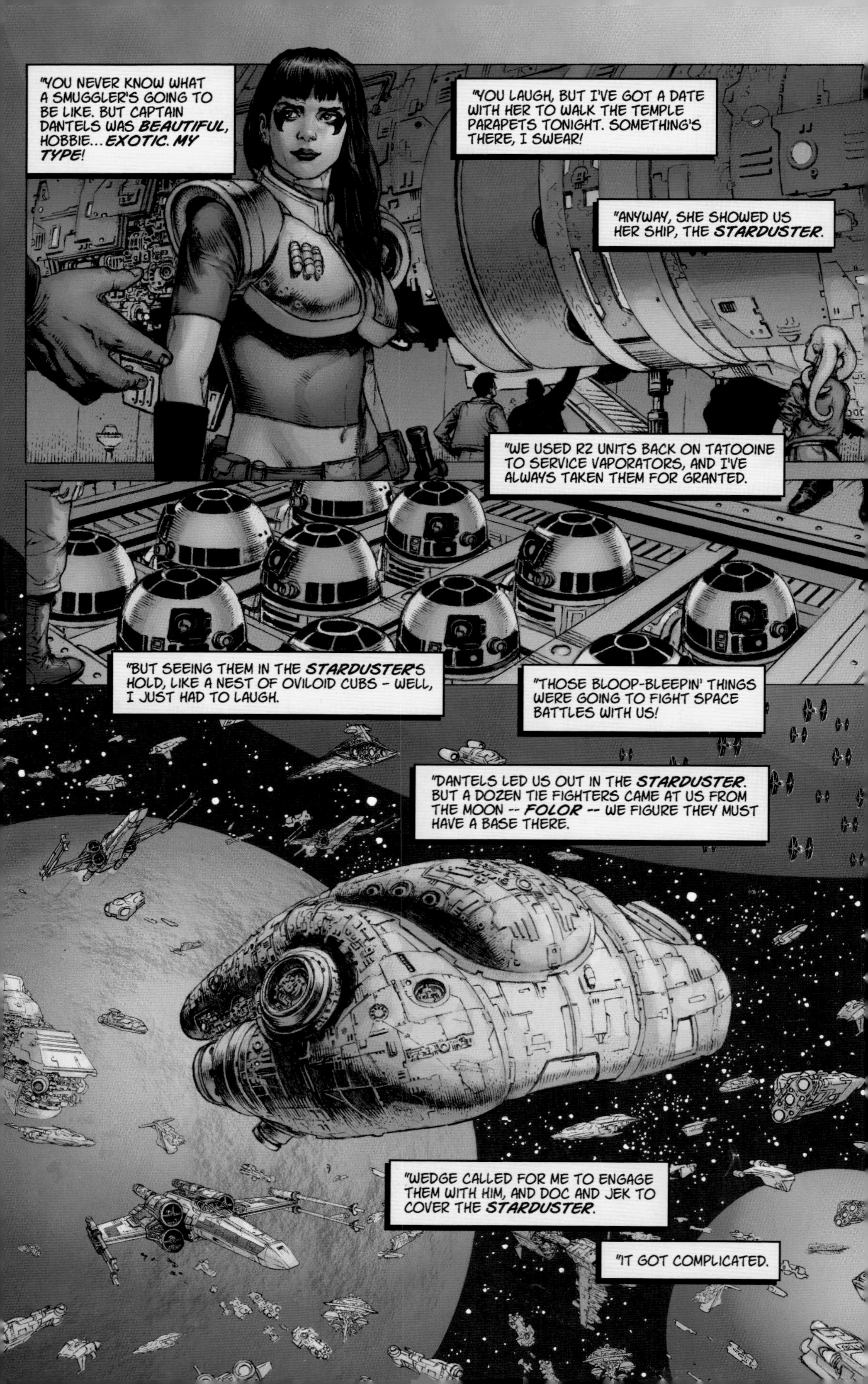
"YOU NEVER KNOW WHAT A SMUGGLER'S GOING TO BE LIKE. BUT CAPTAIN DANTELS WAS BEAUTIFUL, HOBBIE... EXOTIC. MY TYPE!
"YOU LAUGH, BUT I'VE GOT A DATE WITH HER TO WALK THE TEMPLE PARAPETS TONIGHT. SOMETHING'S THERE, I SWEAR!
"ANYWAY, SHE SHOWED US HER SHIP, THE STARDUSTER.
"WE USED R2 UNITS BACK ON TATOOINE TO SERVICE VAPORATORS, AND I'VE ALWAYS TAKEN THEM FOR GRANTED.
"BUT SEEING THEM IN THE STARDUSTER'S HOLD, LIKE A NEST OF OVILOID CUBS - WELL, I JUST HAD TO LAUGH.
"THOSE BLOOP-BLEEPIN' THINGS WERE GOING TO FIGHT SPACE BATTLES WITH US!
"DANTELS LED US OUT IN THE STARDUSTER. BUT A DOZEN TIE FIGHTERS CAME AT US FROM THE MOON -- FOLOR -- WE FIGURE THEY MUST HAVE A BASE THERE.
"WEDGE CALLED FOR ME TO ENGAGE THEM WITH HIM, AND DOC AND JEK TO COVER THE STARDUSTER.
"IT GOT COMPLICATED.

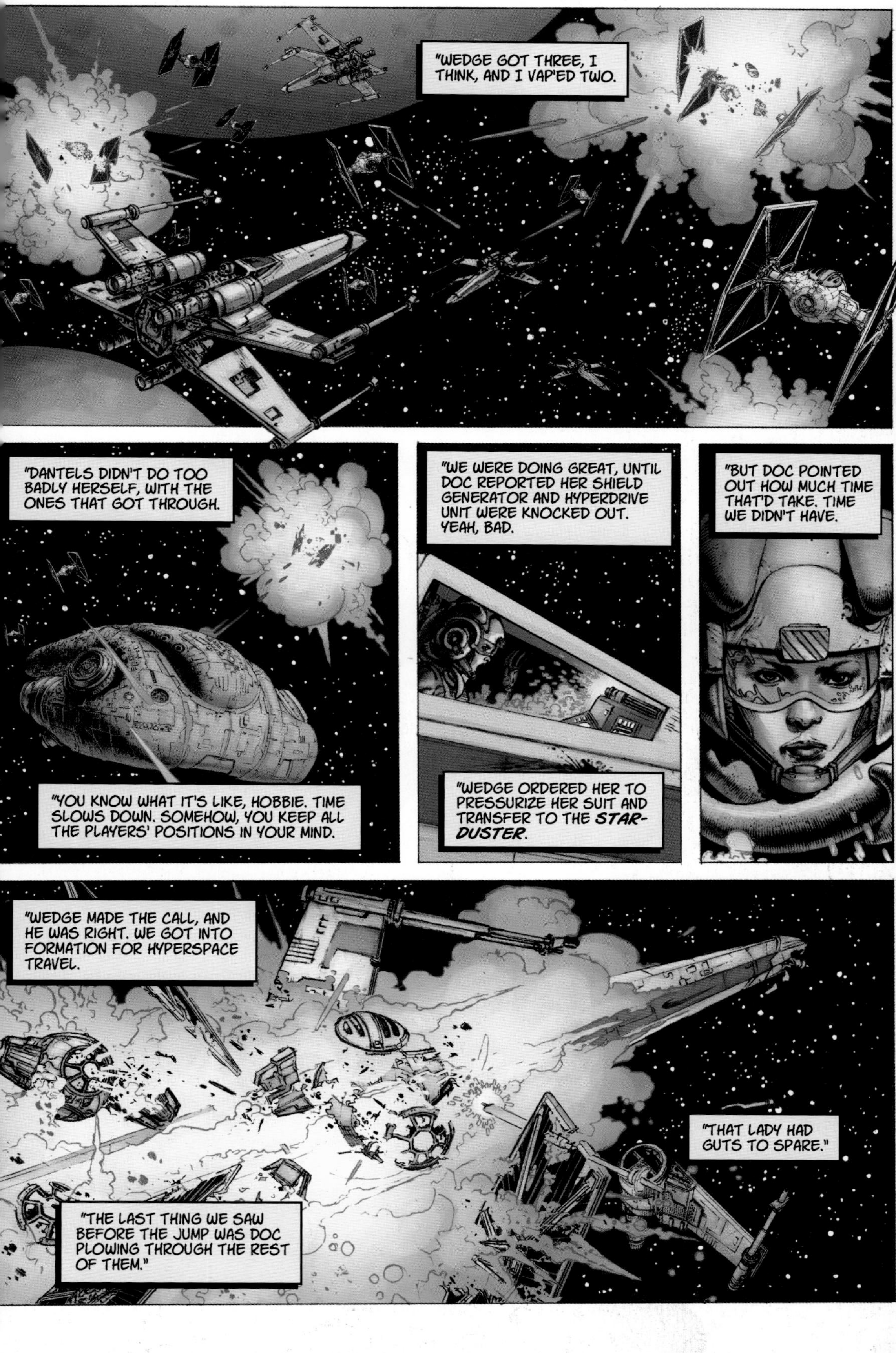
"WEDGE GOT THREE, I THINK, AND I VAP'ED TWO.
"DANTELS DIDN'T DO TOO BADLY HERSELF, WITH THE ONES THAT GOT THROUGH.
"YOU KNOW WHAT IT'S LIKE, HOBBIE. TIME SLOWS DOWN. SOMEHOW, YOU KEEP ALL THE PLAYERS' POSITIONS IN YOUR MIND.
"WE WERE DOING GREAT, UNTIL DOC REPORTED HER SHIELD GENERATOR AND HYPERDRIVE UNIT WERE KNOCKED OUT. YEAH, BAD.
"WEDGE ORDERED HER TO PRESSURIZE HER SUIT AND TRANSFER TO THE STAR-DUSTER.
"BUT DOC POINTED OUT HOW MUCH TIME THAT'D TAKE. TIME WE DIDN'T HAVE.
"WEDGE MADE THE CALL, AND HE WAS RIGHT. WE GOT INTO FORMATION FOR HYPERSPACE TRAVEL.
"THAT LADY HAD GUTS TO SPARE."
"THE LAST THING WE SAW BEFORE THE JUMP WAS DOC PLOWING THROUGH THE REST OF THEM."

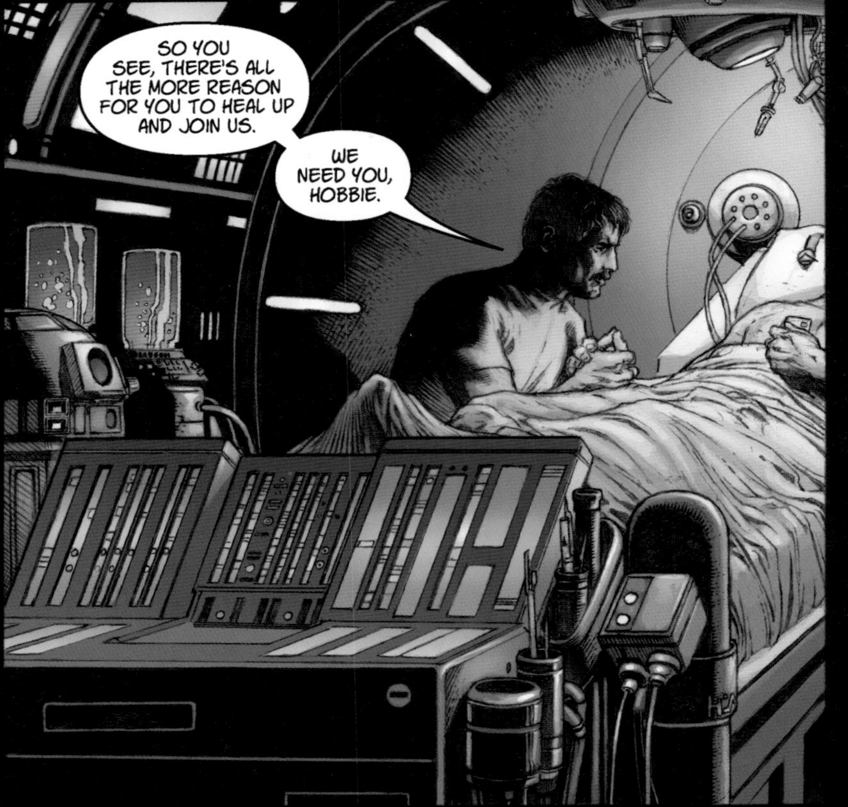
SO YOU SEE, THERE'S ALL THE MORE REASON FOR YOU TO HEAL UP AND JOIN US.
WE NEED YOU, HOBBIE.

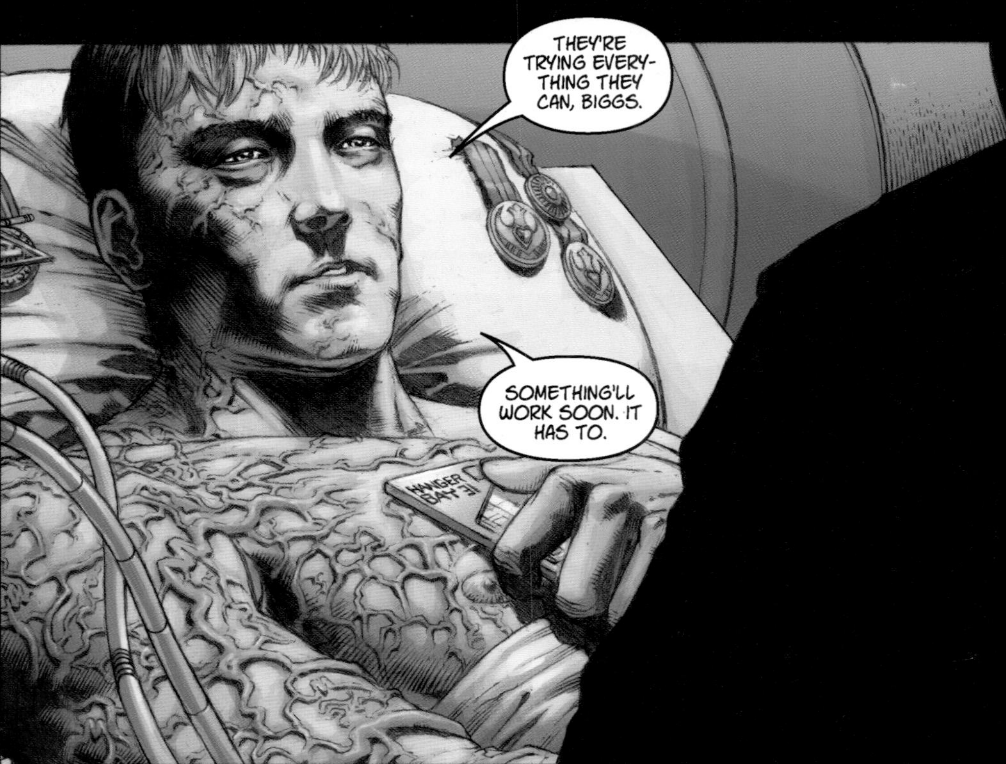
THEY'RE TRYING EVERY-THING THEY CAN, BIGGS.
SOMETHING'LL WORK SOON. IT HAS TO.
HANGER BAY 31

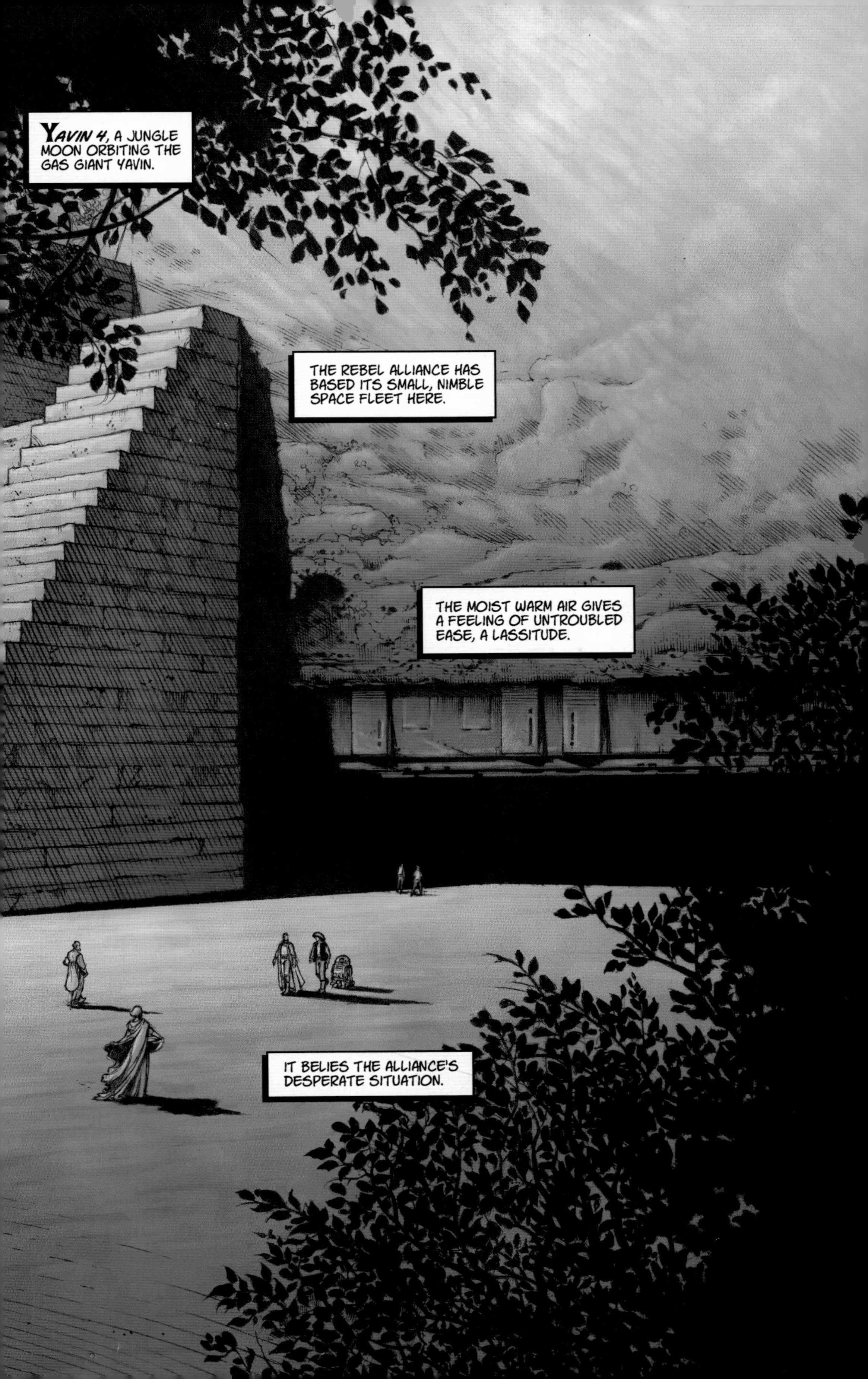
YAVIN 4, A JUNGLE MOON ORBITING THE GAS GIANT YAVIN.
THE REBEL ALLIANCE HAS BASED ITS SMALL, NIMBLE SPACE FLEET HERE.
THE MOIST WARM AIR GIVES A FEELING OF UNTROUBLED EASE, A LASSITUDE.
IT BELIES THE ALLIANCE'S DESPERATE SITUATION.

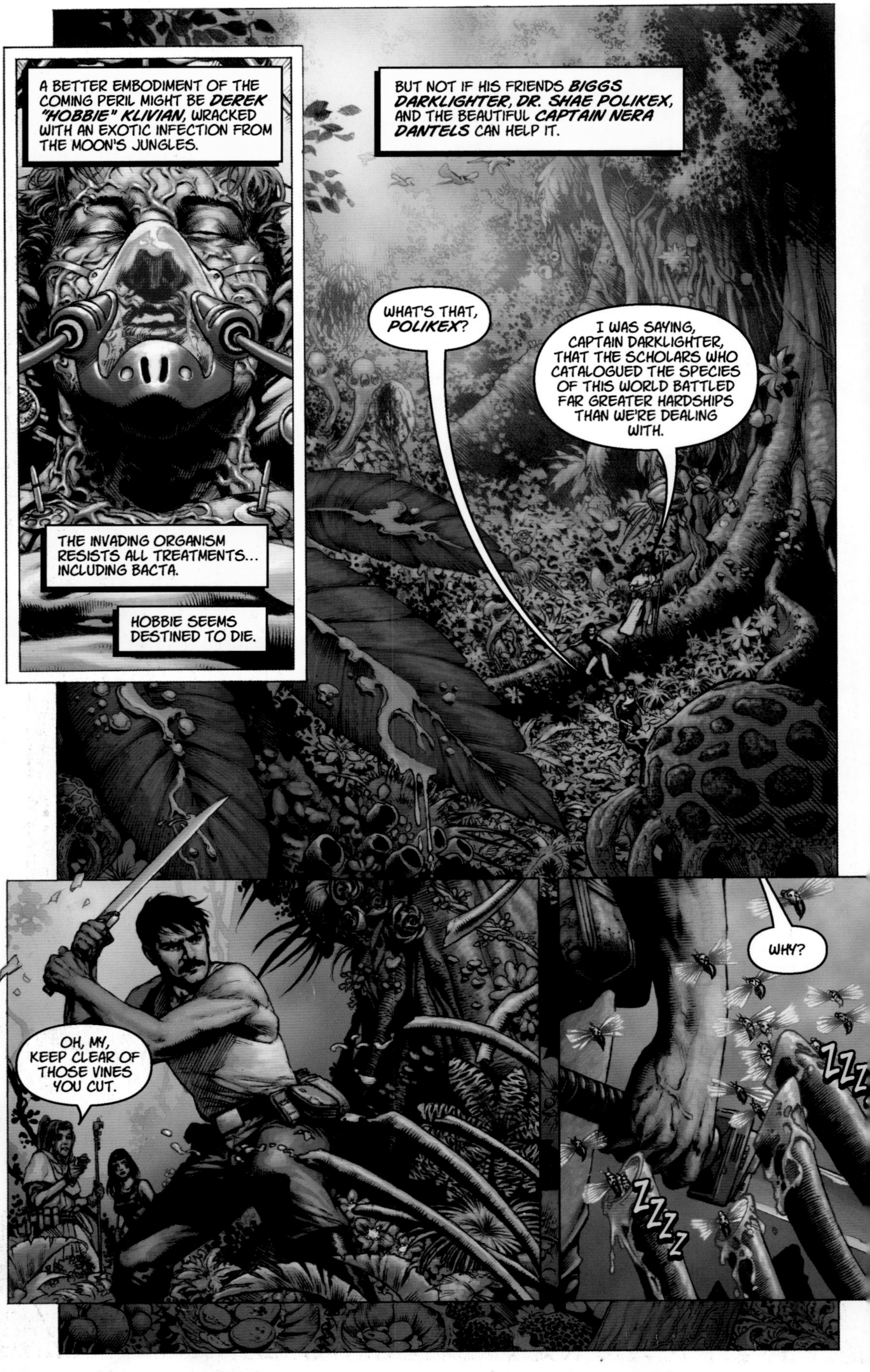
A BETTER EMBODIMENT OF THE COMING PERIL MIGHT BE DEREK "HOBBIE" KLIVIAN, WRACKED WITH AN EXOTIC INFECTION FROM THE MOON'S JUNGLES.
THE INVADING ORGANISM RESISTS ALL TREATMENTS... INCLUDING BACTA.
HOBBIE SEEMS DESTINED TO DIE.
BUT NOT IF HIS FRIENDS BIGGS DARKLIGHTER, DR. SHAE POLIKEX, AND THE BEAUTIFUL CAPTAIN NERA DANTELS CAN HELP IT.
WHAT'S THAT, POLIKEX?
I WAS SAYING, CAPTAIN DARKLIGHTER, THAT THE SCHOLARS WHO CATALOGUED THE SPECIES OF THIS WORLD BATTLED FAR GREATER HARDSHIPS THAN WE'RE DEALING WITH.
OH, MY, KEEP CLEAR OF THOSE VINES YOU CUT.
WHY?
ZZZ
ZZZZ

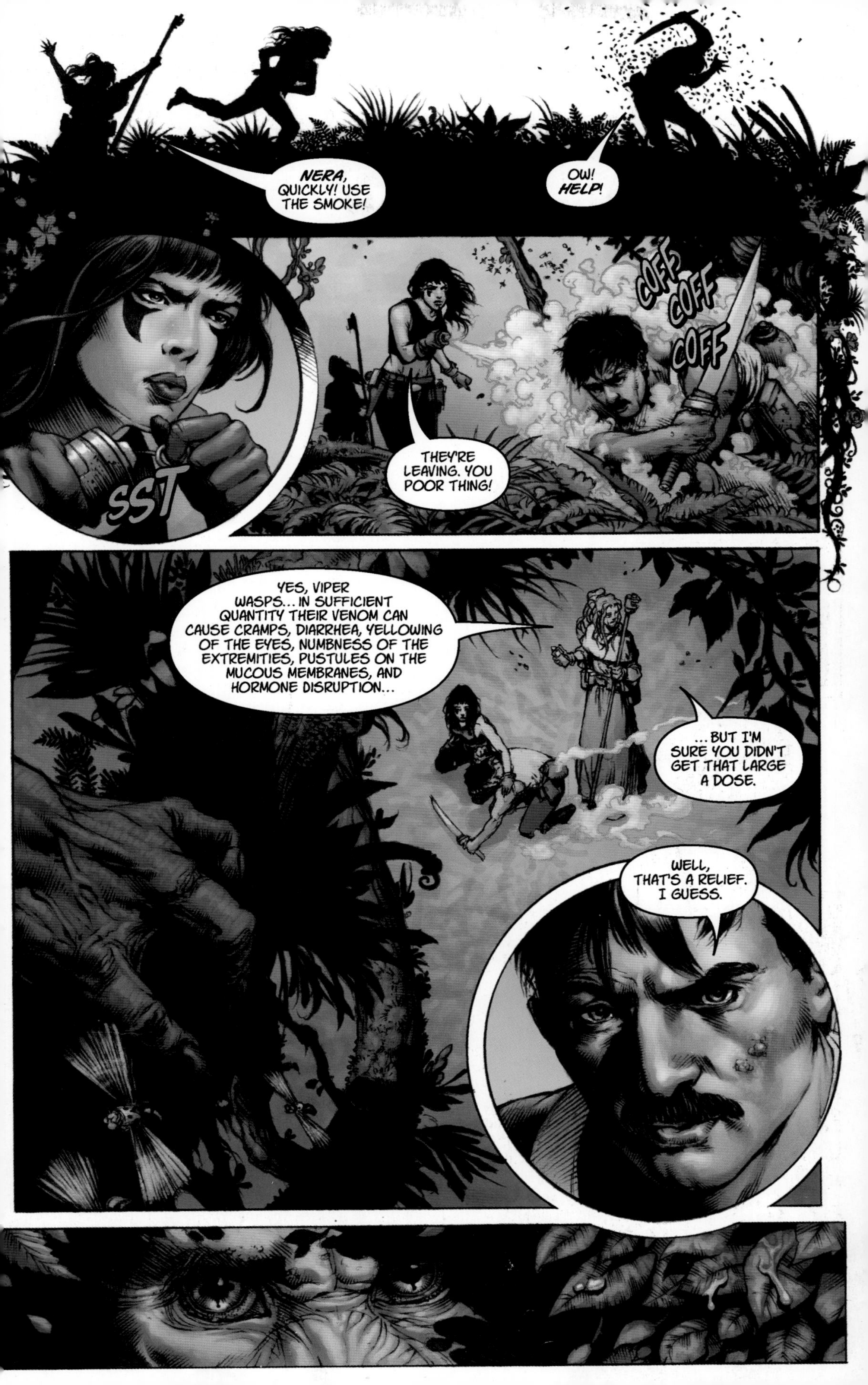
NERA, QUICKLY! USE THE SMOKE!
OW! HELP!
SST
THEY'RE LEAVING. YOU POOR THING!
COFF COFF COFF
YES, VIPER WASPS... IN SUFFICIENT QUANTITY THEIR VENOM CAN CAUSE CRAMPS, DIARRHEA, YELLOWING OF THE EYES, NUMBNESS OF THE EXTREMITIES, PUSTULES ON THE MUCOUS MEMBRANES, AND HORMONE DISRUPTION...
...BUT I'M SURE YOU DIDN'T GET THAT LARGE A DOSE.
WELL, THAT'S A RELIEF. I GUESS.

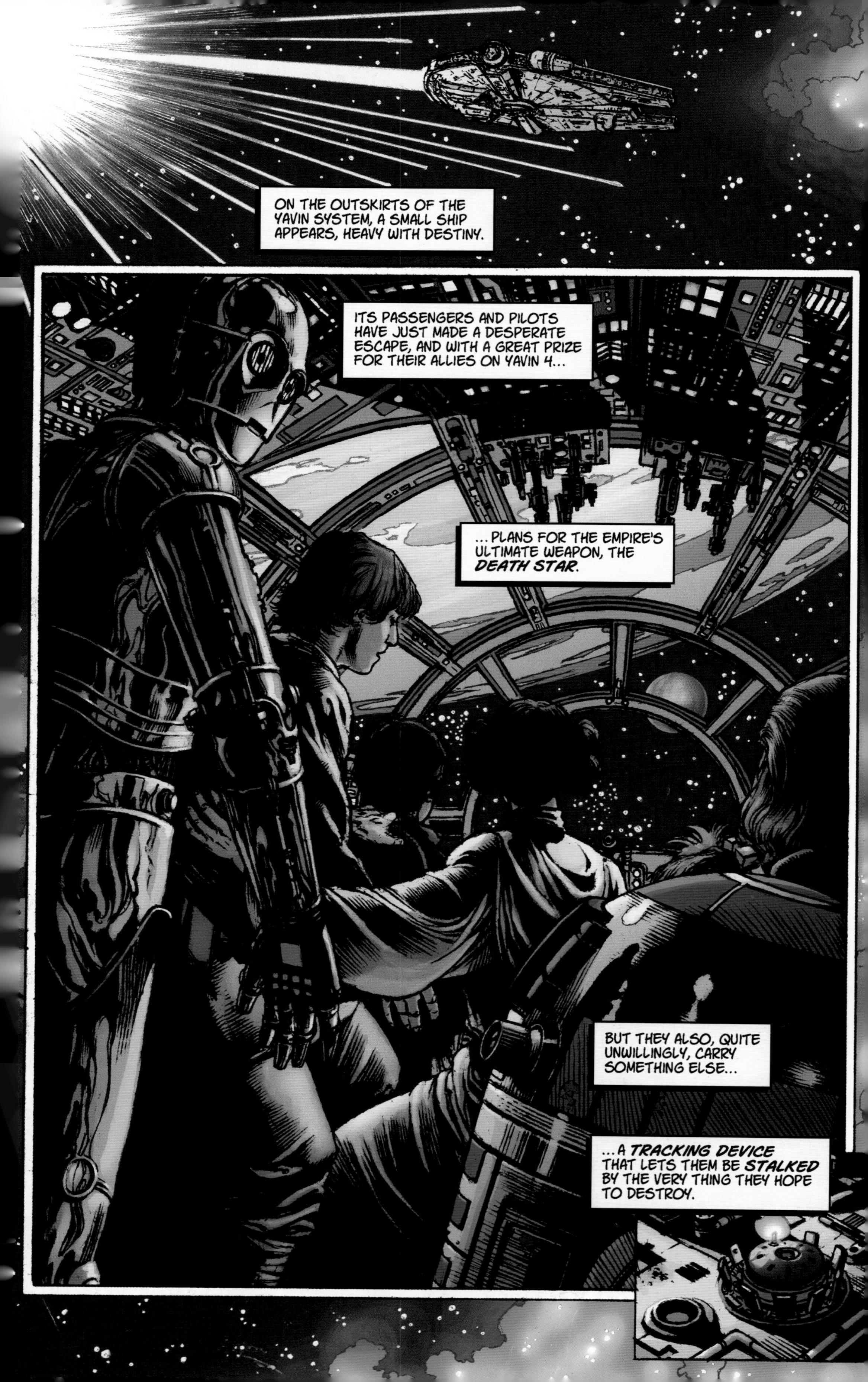
ON THE OUTSKIRTS OF THE YAVIN SYSTEM, A SMALL SHIP APPEARS, HEAVY WITH DESTINY.
ITS PASSENGERS AND PILOTS HAVE JUST MADE A DESPERATE ESCAPE, AND WITH A GREAT PRIZE FOR THEIR ALLIES ON YAVIN 4...
...PLANS FOR THE EMPIRE'S ULTIMATE WEAPON, THE *DEATH STAR*.
BUT THEY ALSO, QUITE UNWILLINGLY, CARRY SOMETHING ELSE...
...A *TRACKING DEVICE* THAT LETS THEM BE *STALKED* BY THE VERY THING THEY HOPE TO DESTROY.

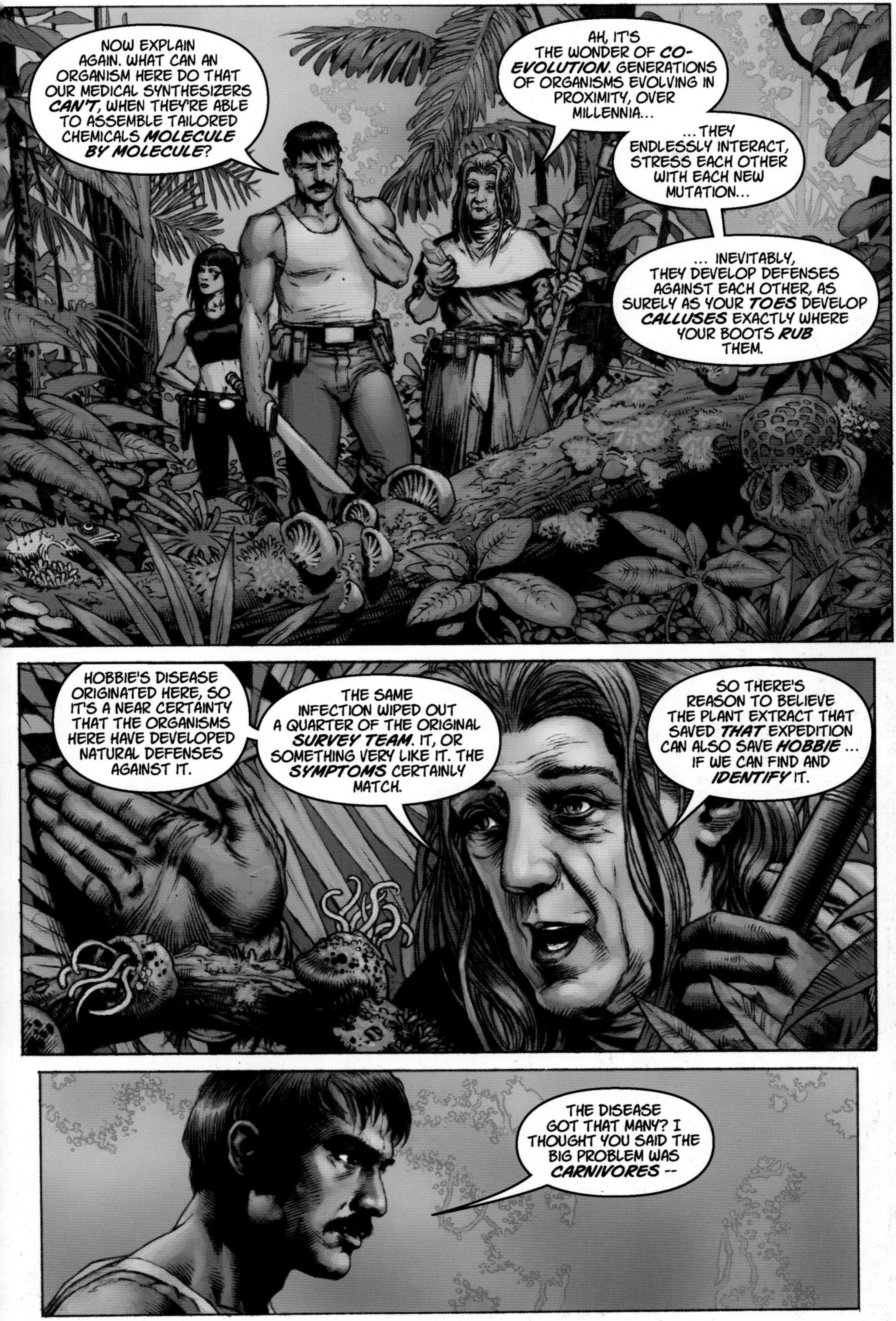
NOW EXPLAIN AGAIN. WHAT CAN AN ORGANISM HERE DO THAT OUR MEDICAL SYNTHESIZERS CAN'T, WHEN THEY'RE ABLE TO ASSEMBLE TAILORED CHEMICALS MOLECULE BY MOLECULE?
AH, IT'S THE WONDER OF CO-EVOLUTION. GENERATIONS OF ORGANISMS EVOLVING IN PROXIMITY, OVER MILLENNIA...
... THEY ENDLESSLY INTERACT, STRESS EACH OTHER WITH EACH NEW MUTATION...
... INEVITABLY, THEY DEVELOP DEFENSES AGAINST EACH OTHER, AS SURELY AS YOUR TOES DEVELOP CALLUSES EXACTLY WHERE YOUR BOOTS RUB THEM.
HOBBIE'S DISEASE ORIGINATED HERE, SO IT'S A NEAR CERTAINTY THAT THE ORGANISMS HERE HAVE DEVELOPED NATURAL DEFENSES AGAINST IT.
THE SAME INFECTION WIPED OUT A QUARTER OF THE ORIGINAL SURVEY TEAM. IT, OR SOMETHING VERY LIKE IT. THE SYMPTOMS CERTAINLY MATCH.
SO THERE'S REASON TO BELIEVE THE PLANT EXTRACT THAT SAVED THAT EXPEDITION CAN ALSO SAVE HOBBIE ... IF WE CAN FIND AND IDENTIFY IT.
THE DISEASE GOT THAT MANY? I THOUGHT YOU SAID THE BIG PROBLEM WAS CARNIVORES --

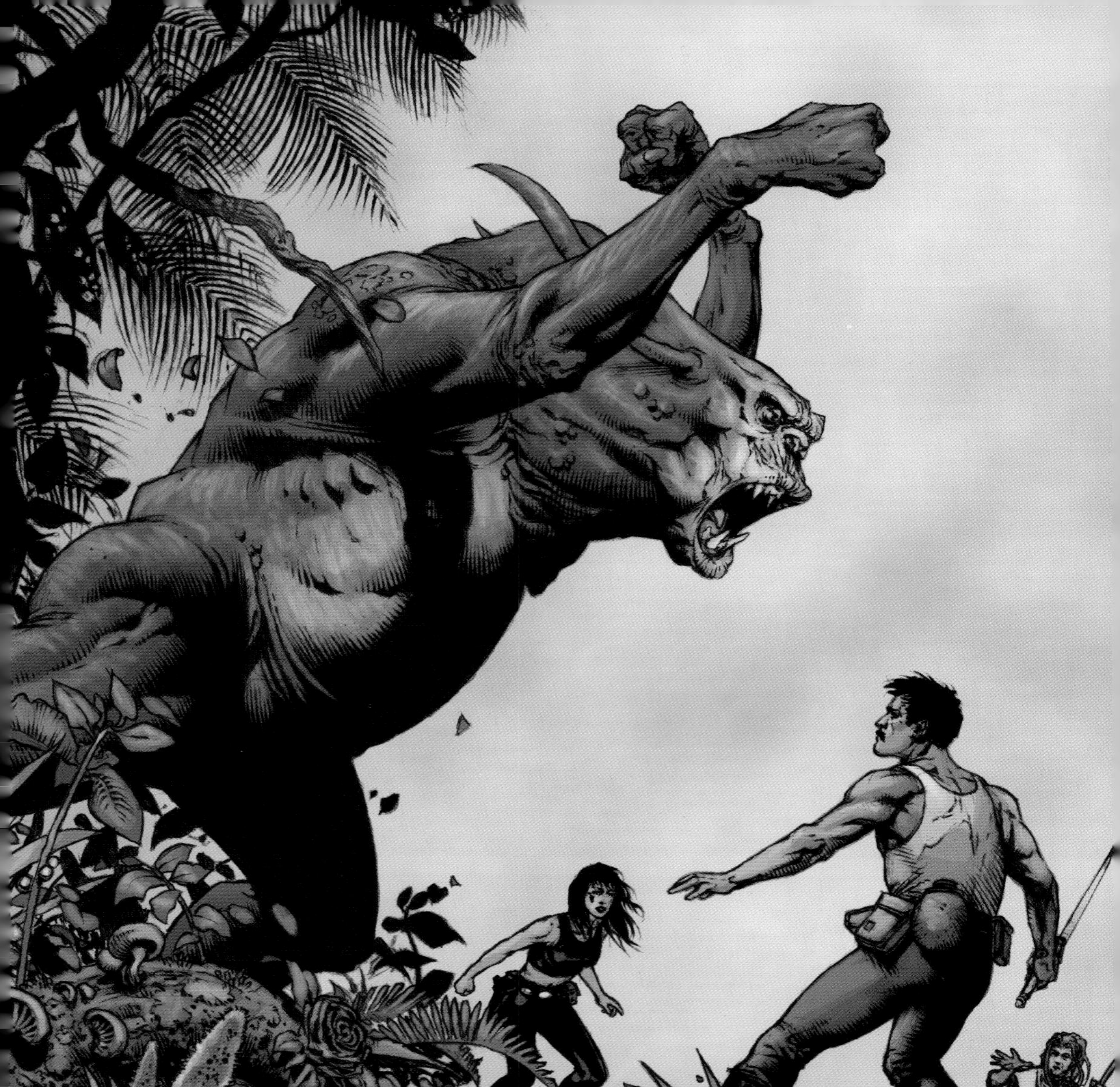
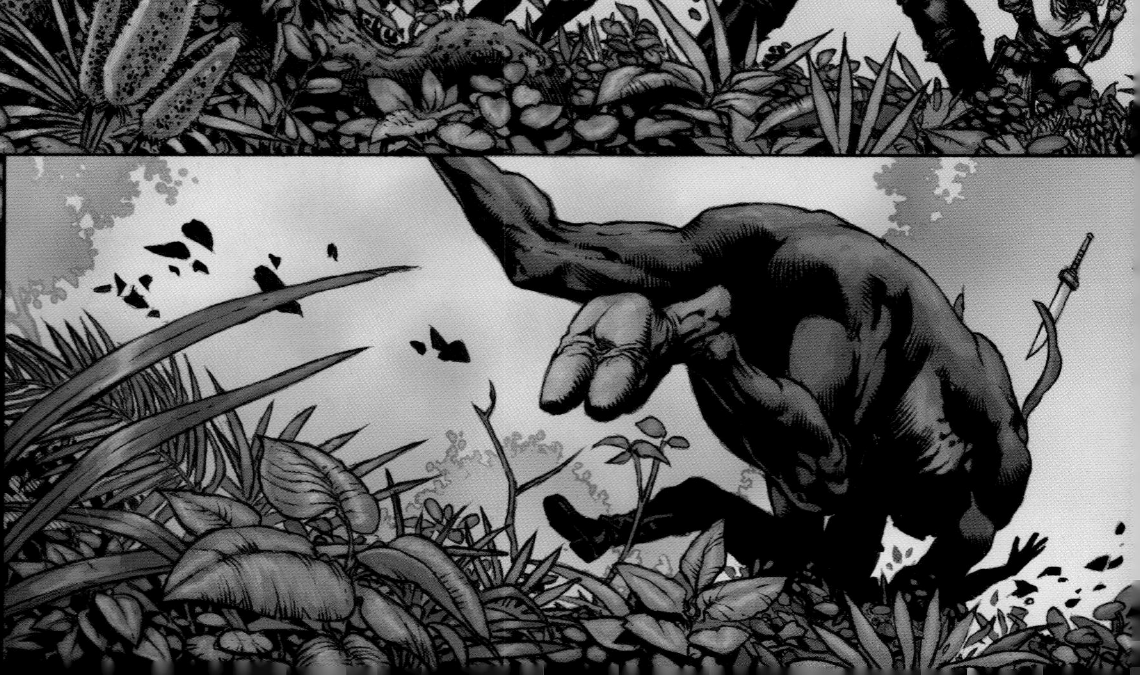

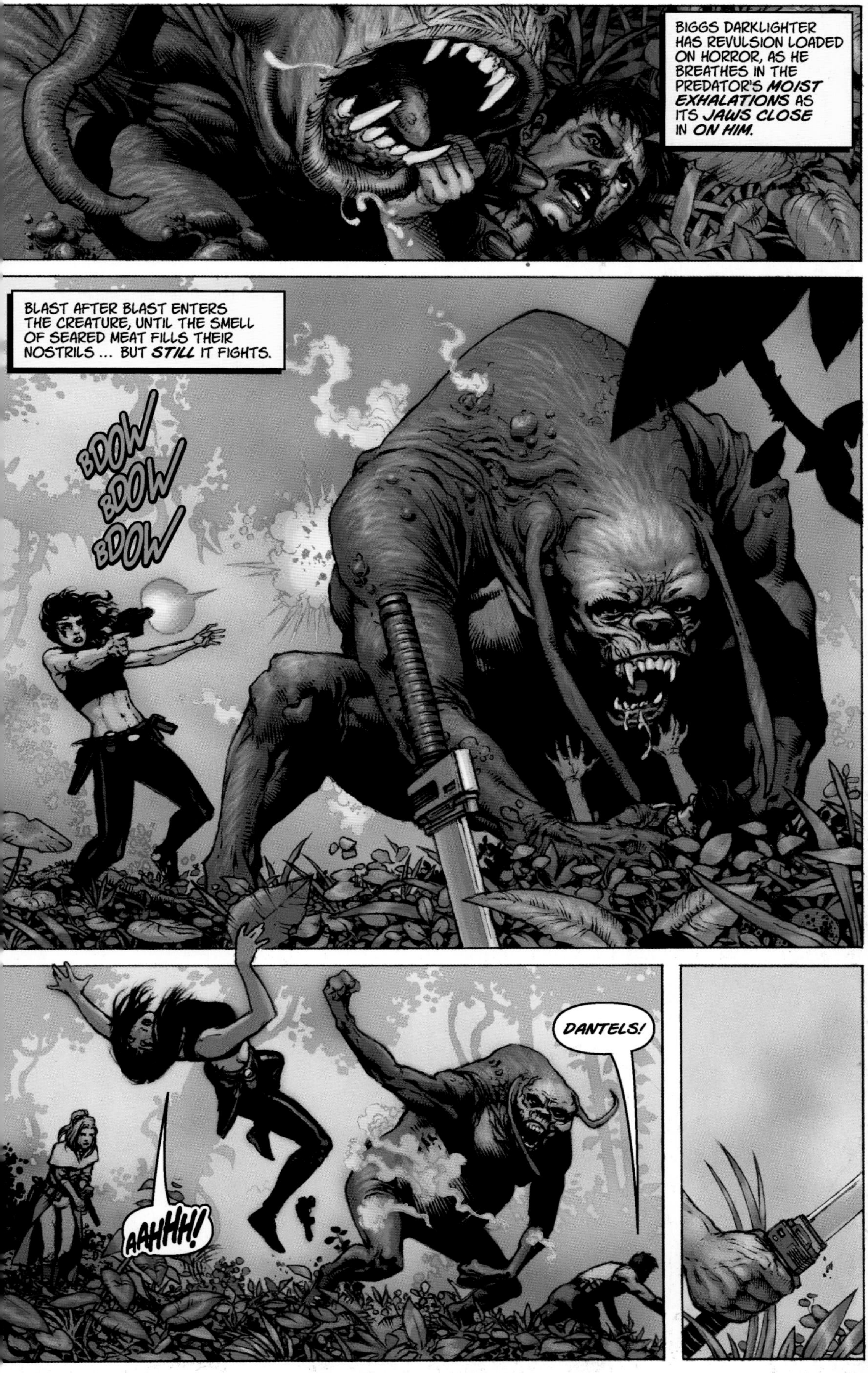

BIGGS DARKLIGHTER HAS REVULSION LOADED ON HORROR, AS HE BREATHES IN THE PREDATOR'S MOIST EXHALATIONS AS ITS JAWS CLOSE IN ON HIM.
BLAST AFTER BLAST ENTERS THE CREATURE, UNTIL THE SMELL OF SEARED MEAT FILLS THEIR NOSTRILS ... BUT STILL IT FIGHTS.
BDOW
BDOW
BDOW
DANTELS!
AAHHH!

FINALLY, BREATHING ENDS. AWARENESS DEPARTS FROM ITS EYES.

THUK

BIGGS EXPERIENCES A WEIRD INTIMACY WITH THIS DYING, SEMI-INTELLIGENT BEING... *HE FEELS THE DEATH HIMSELF.*

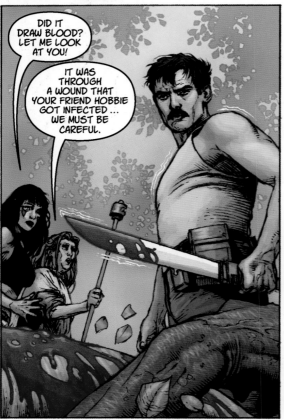

DID IT DRAW BLOOD? LET ME LOOK AT YOU!

IT WAS THROUGH A WOUND THAT YOUR FRIEND HOBBIE GOT INFECTED ... WE MUST BE CAREFUL.

DEEPLY SHAKEN, BIGGS IS AWASH IN THOUGHTS OF LIFE AND DEATH AND FEELINGS HE COULD NEVER PUT INTO WORDS.

I'M OKAY. IT DIDN'T GET TO ME.

NOT PHYSICALLY, ANYWAY.

IT'S WEIRD. I FEEL LIKE... AS THE CREATURE WAS DYING ... I LOOKED THROUGH A DOOR THAT OPENED. AND MAYBE I STILL SEE A LITTLE THROUGH IT, SOMEHOW.

TO EVERYTHING. TO FOREVER...

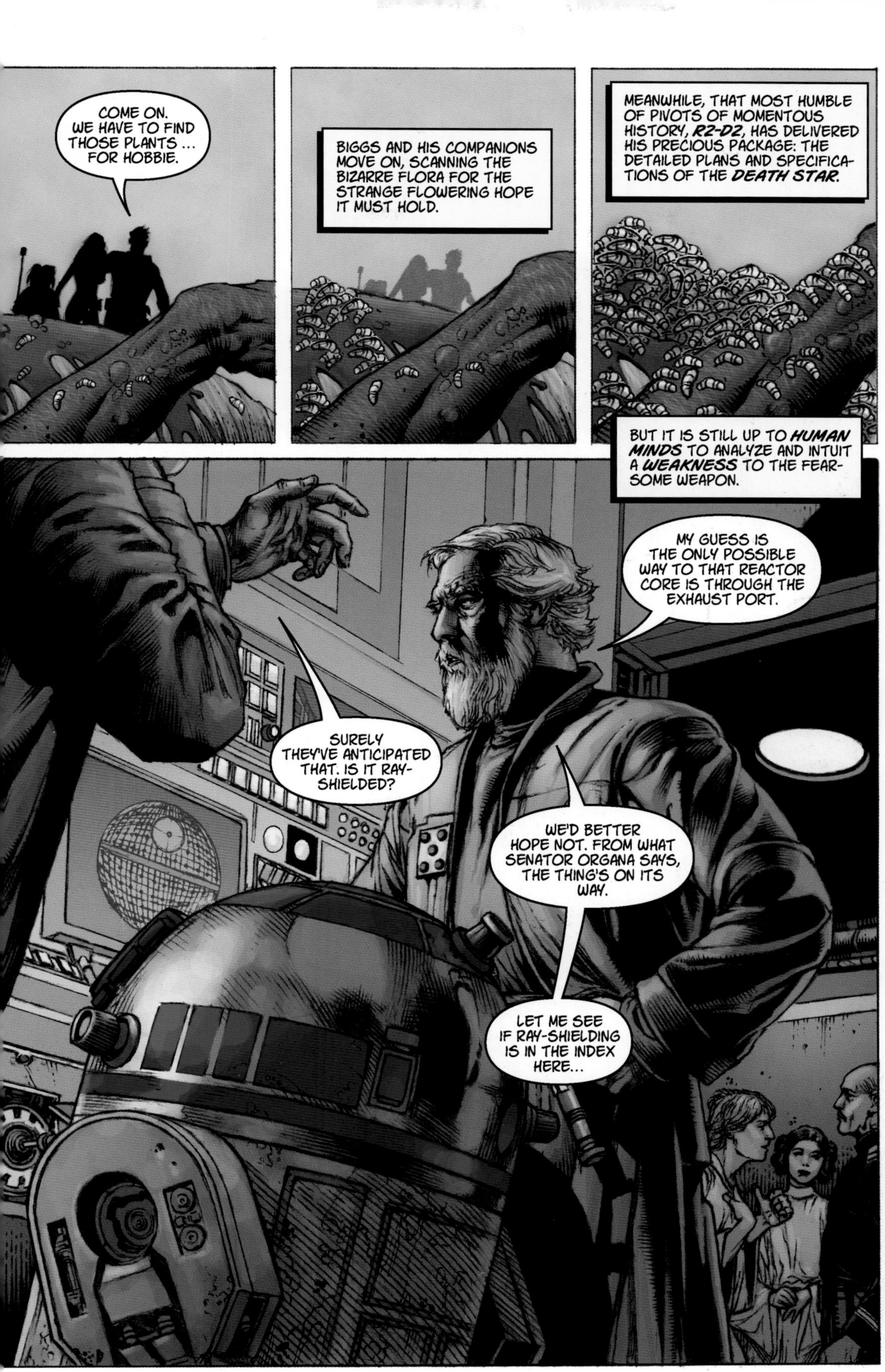
COME ON. WE HAVE TO FIND THOSE PLANTS ... FOR HOBBIE.
BIGGS AND HIS COMPANIONS MOVE ON, SCANNING THE BIZARRE FLORA FOR THE STRANGE FLOWERING HOPE IT MUST HOLD.
MEANWHILE, THAT MOST HUMBLE OF PIVOTS OF MOMENTOUS HISTORY, R2-D2, HAS DELIVERED HIS PRECIOUS PACKAGE: THE DETAILED PLANS AND SPECIFICATIONS OF THE DEATH STAR.
BUT IT IS STILL UP TO HUMAN MINDS TO ANALYZE AND INTUIT A WEAKNESS TO THE FEARSOME WEAPON.
MY GUESS IS THE ONLY POSSIBLE WAY TO THAT REACTOR CORE IS THROUGH THE EXHAUST PORT.
SURELY THEY'VE ANTICIPATED THAT. IS IT RAY-SHIELDED?
WE'D BETTER HOPE NOT. FROM WHAT SENATOR ORGANA SAYS, THE THING'S ON ITS WAY.
LET ME SEE IF RAY-SHIELDING IS IN THE INDEX HERE...

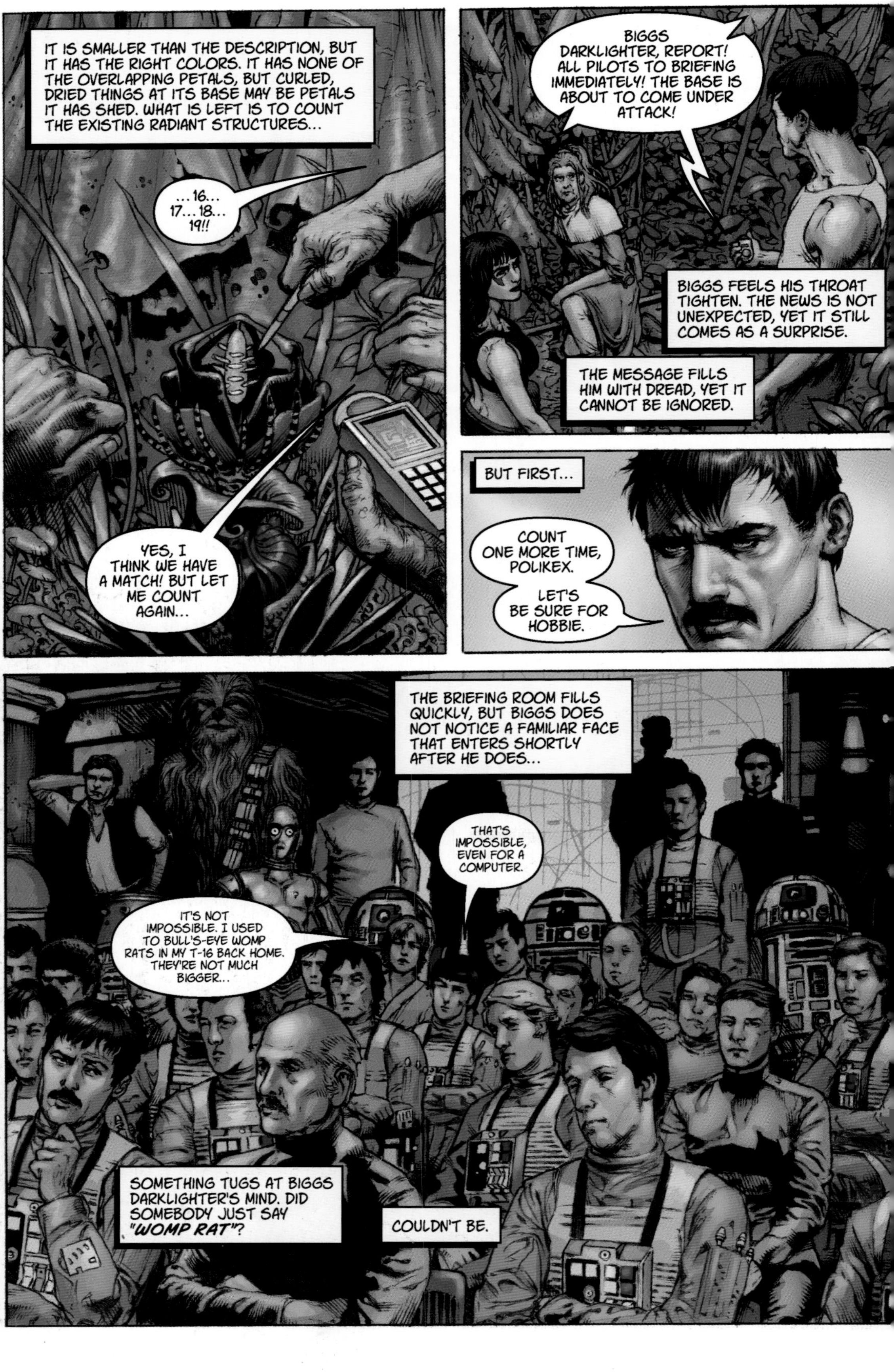
IT IS SMALLER THAN THE DESCRIPTION, BUT IT HAS THE RIGHT COLORS. IT HAS NONE OF THE OVERLAPPING PETALS, BUT CURLED, DRIED THINGS AT ITS BASE MAY BE PETALS IT HAS SHED. WHAT IS LEFT IS TO COUNT THE EXISTING RADIANT STRUCTURES...
...16... 17...18... 19!!
YES, I THINK WE HAVE A MATCH! BUT LET ME COUNT AGAIN...
BIGGS DARKLIGHTER, REPORT! ALL PILOTS TO BRIEFING IMMEDIATELY! THE BASE IS ABOUT TO COME UNDER ATTACK!
BIGGS FEELS HIS THROAT TIGHTEN. THE NEWS IS NOT UNEXPECTED, YET IT STILL COMES AS A SURPRISE.
THE MESSAGE FILLS HIM WITH DREAD, YET IT CANNOT BE IGNORED.
BUT FIRST...
COUNT ONE MORE TIME, POLIKEX.
LET'S BE SURE FOR HOBBIE.
THE BRIEFING ROOM FILLS QUICKLY, BUT BIGGS DOES NOT NOTICE A FAMILIAR FACE THAT ENTERS SHORTLY AFTER HE DOES...
THAT'S IMPOSSIBLE, EVEN FOR A COMPUTER.
IT'S NOT IMPOSSIBLE. I USED TO BULL'S-EYE WOMP RATS IN MY T-16 BACK HOME. THEY'RE NOT MUCH BIGGER...
SOMETHING TUGS AT BIGGS DARKLIGHTER'S MIND. DID SOMEBODY JUST SAY "*WOMP RAT*"?
COULDN'T BE.

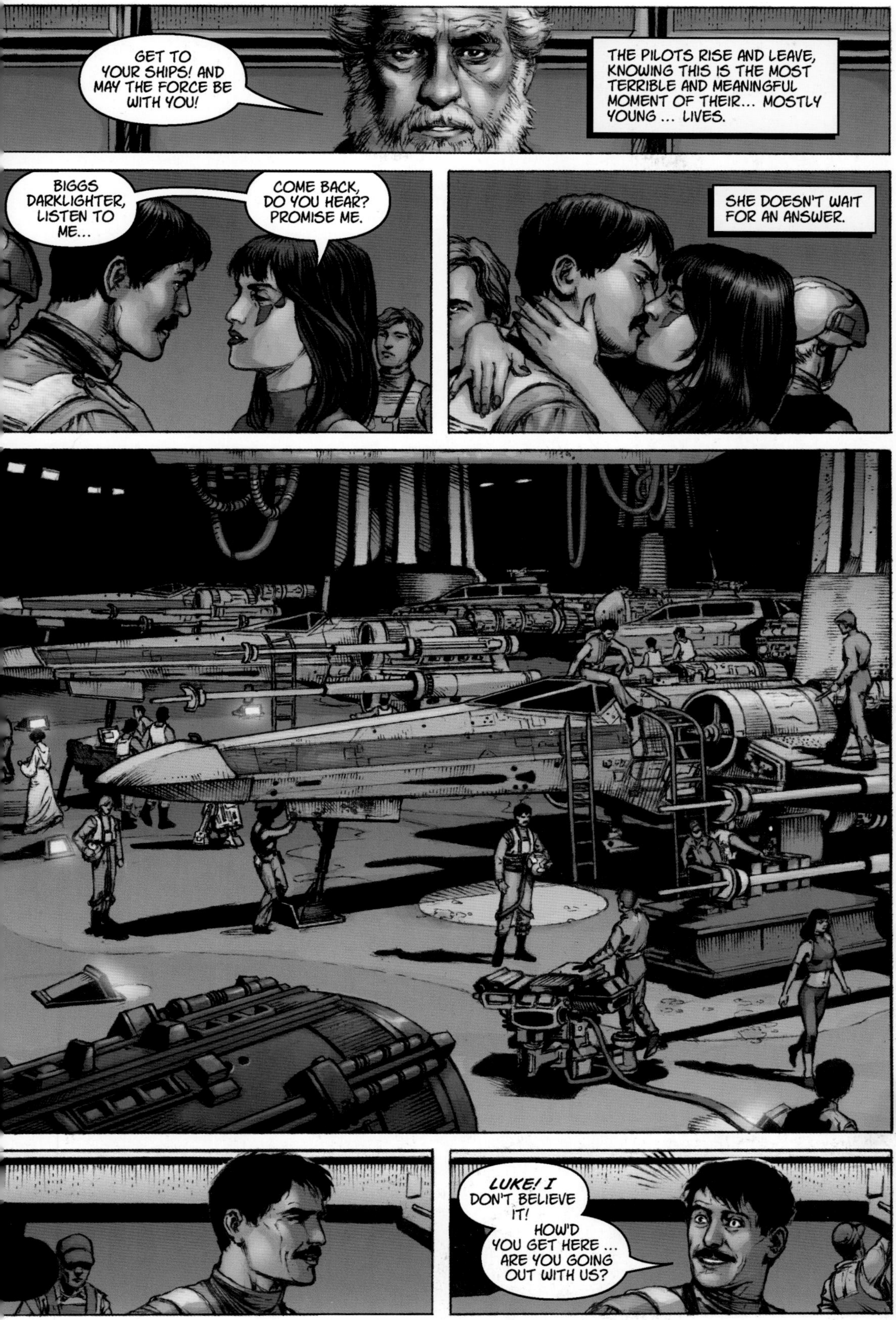
GET TO YOUR SHIPS! AND MAY THE FORCE BE WITH YOU!
THE PILOTS RISE AND LEAVE, KNOWING THIS IS THE MOST TERRIBLE AND MEANINGFUL MOMENT OF THEIR... MOSTLY YOUNG ... LIVES.
BIGGS DARKLIGHTER, LISTEN TO ME...
COME BACK, DO YOU HEAR? PROMISE ME.
SHE DOESN'T WAIT FOR AN ANSWER.
LUKE! I DON'T BELIEVE IT!
HOW'D YOU GET HERE ... ARE YOU GOING OUT WITH US?

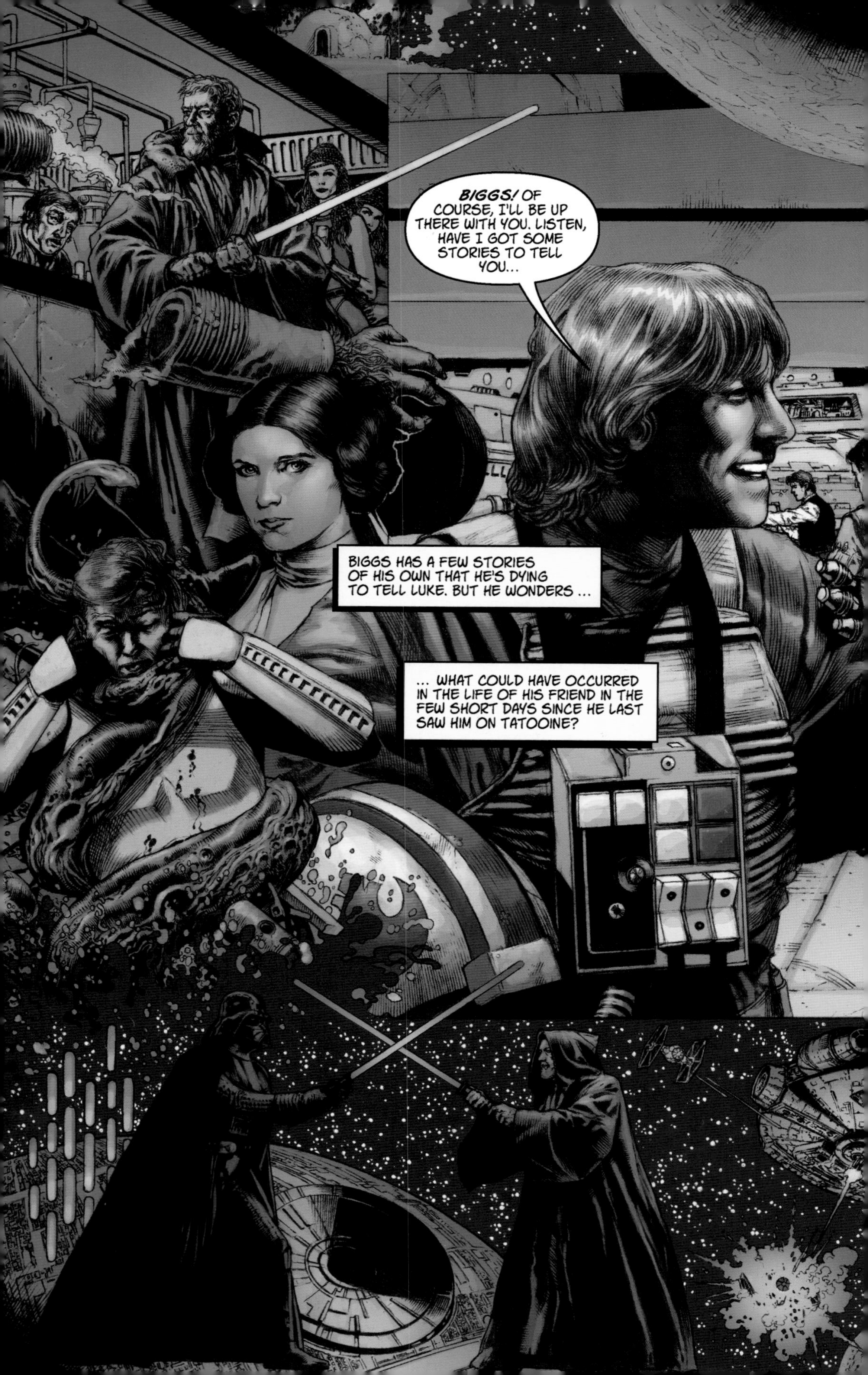
BIGGS! OF COURSE, I'LL BE UP THERE WITH YOU. LISTEN, HAVE I GOT SOME STORIES TO TELL YOU...
BIGGS HAS A FEW STORIES OF HIS OWN THAT HE'S DYING TO TELL LUKE. BUT HE WONDERS ...
... WHAT COULD HAVE OCCURRED IN THE LIFE OF HIS FRIEND IN THE FEW SHORT DAYS SINCE HE LAST SAW HIM ON TATOOINE?

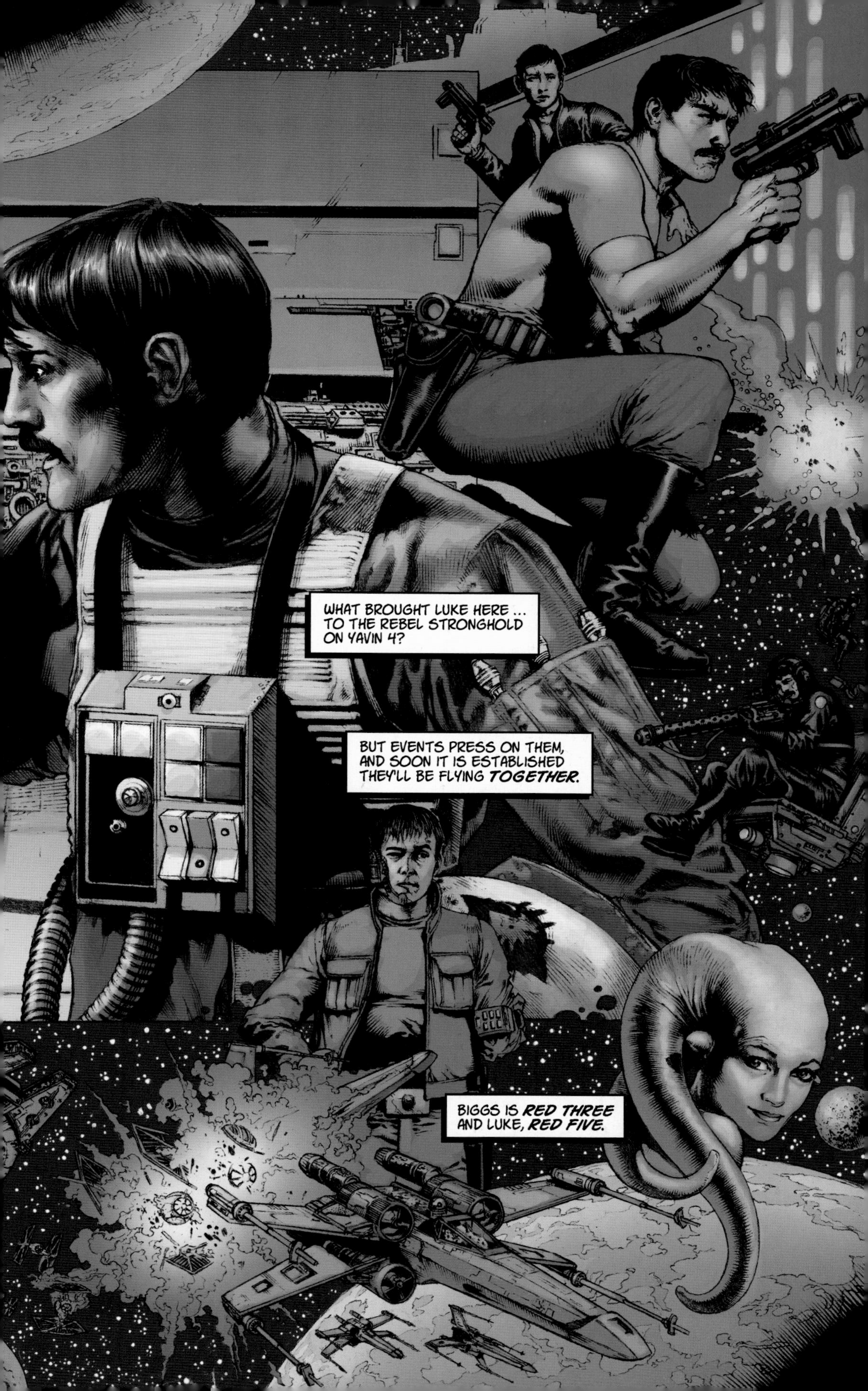
WHAT BROUGHT LUKE HERE ... TO THE REBEL STRONGHOLD ON YAVIN 4?
BUT EVENTS PRESS ON THEM, AND SOON IT IS ESTABLISHED THEY'LL BE FLYING *TOGETHER*.
BIGGS IS *RED THREE* AND LUKE, *RED FIVE*.

IN ANOTHER PART OF THE BASE, A FAR QUIETER, BUT NO LESS FATEFUL DRAMA IS UNFOLDING.

I DON'T KNOW IF YOU CAN HEAR ME, HOBBIE, BUT WE THINK THIS WILL HELP YOU.

YOUR FRIEND BIGGS HAD SOME MOST UNPLEASANT ADVENTURES ON OUR LITTLE EXPEDITION; I BET HE'LL LOVE TO TELL YOU ABOUT THEM.

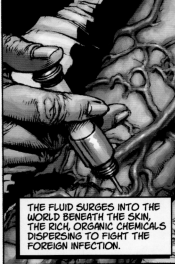

THE FLUID SURGES INTO THE WORLD BENEATH THE SKIN, THE RICH, ORGANIC CHEMICALS DISPERSING TO FIGHT THE FOREIGN INFECTION.

THE REBEL CRAFT SURGE INTO INFINITE SPACE, TOWARDS A RENDEZVOUS WITH A MUCH LARGER INVADER.

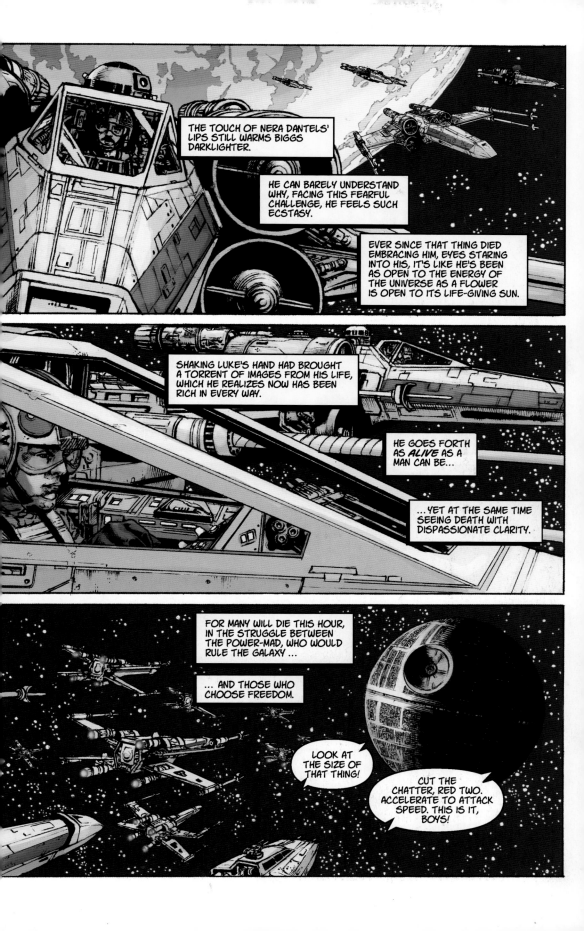

THE TOUCH OF NERA DANTELS' LIPS STILL WARMS BIGGS DARKLIGHTER.

HE CAN BARELY UNDERSTAND WHY, FACING THIS FEARFUL CHALLENGE, HE FEELS SUCH ECSTASY.

EVER SINCE THAT THING DIED EMBRACING HIM, EYES STARING INTO HIS, IT'S LIKE HE'S BEEN AS OPEN TO THE ENERGY OF THE UNIVERSE AS A FLOWER IS OPEN TO ITS LIFE-GIVING SUN.

SHAKING LUKE'S HAND HAD BROUGHT A TORRENT OF IMAGES FROM HIS LIFE, WHICH HE REALIZES NOW HAS BEEN RICH IN EVERY WAY.

HE GOES FORTH AS *ALIVE* AS A MAN CAN BE...

...YET AT THE SAME TIME SEEING DEATH WITH DISPASSIONATE CLARITY.

FOR MANY WILL DIE THIS HOUR, IN THE STRUGGLE BETWEEN THE POWER-MAD, WHO WOULD RULE THE GALAXY ...

... AND THOSE WHO CHOOSE FREEDOM.

LOOK AT THE SIZE OF THAT THING!

CUT THE CHATTER, RED TWO. ACCELERATE TO ATTACK SPEED. THIS IS IT, BOYS!

BIGGS' MIND ENTERS THE PILOT'S SPECIAL STATE, WITH AN ALMOST MYSTICAL SENSE OF WHERE HIS FELLOW PILOTS ARE, THEIR SPEED, THEIR TIME OF ARRIVAL.

HE CAN'T BELIEVE HE'S FLYING WITH HIS OLD FRIEND, WHO, NOT SO LONG AGO, BIGGS SHOWED WHERE TO PUT HIS HANDS AND FEET IN A SKYHOPPER'S COCKPIT.

LUKE'S NO WALLFLOWER, HE OBSERVES, AS HE SEES *RED FIVE* DIVE FOR THE SURFACE OF THE ARTIFICIAL PLANET.

AND TO THINK, JUST DAYS AGO, HE LIED TO LUKE ABOUT HIS OWN INVOLVEMENT WITH THE REBELLION ... HOPING TO PROTECT HIS FRIEND FROM THE DANGERS OF CONFRONTING THE EMPIRE.

BUT LUKE IS MAYBE *TOO* EAGER...

LUKE! PULL OUT!

ARE YOU ALL RIGHT?

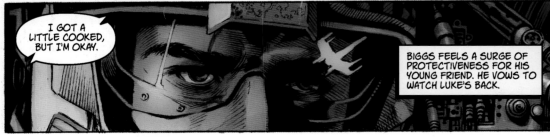

I GOT A LITTLE COOKED, BUT I'M OKAY.

BIGGS FEELS A SURGE OF PROTECTIVENESS FOR HIS YOUNG FRIEND. HE VOWS TO WATCH LUKE'S BACK.

SOON THERE IS MORE THAN *GUN TURRETS* FOR THE REBELS TO FEAR.

AMONG THE TIE FIGHTERS IS A SLEEK NEW CRAFT NONE HAVE EVER SEEN BEFORE. IT RADIATES A SPECIAL MALEVOLENCE WHICH BIGGS, IN HIS STRANGELY RECEPTIVE STATE, FEELS LIKE THE LIGHTLESS HEAT OF A GIGANTIC BLACK STAR.

A THOUGHT COMES, IRRATIONAL, INTUITIVE ... IT HAS SOMETHING TO DO WITH LUKE.

HE WILL NOT LET THE MYSTERY CRAFT GET NEAR HIS FRIEND.

BUT IT IS NOT THE ONLY THREAT...

BIGGS! YOU'VE PICKED ONE UP! WATCH IT!

I CAN'T *SEE* IT! WHERE IS HE?!

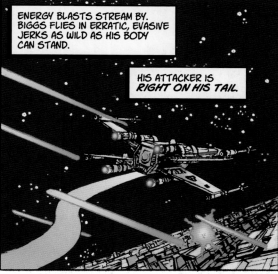

ENERGY BLASTS STREAM BY. BIGGS FLIES IN ERRATIC, EVASIVE JERKS AS WILD AS HIS BODY CAN STAND.

HIS ATTACKER IS *RIGHT ON HIS TAIL.*

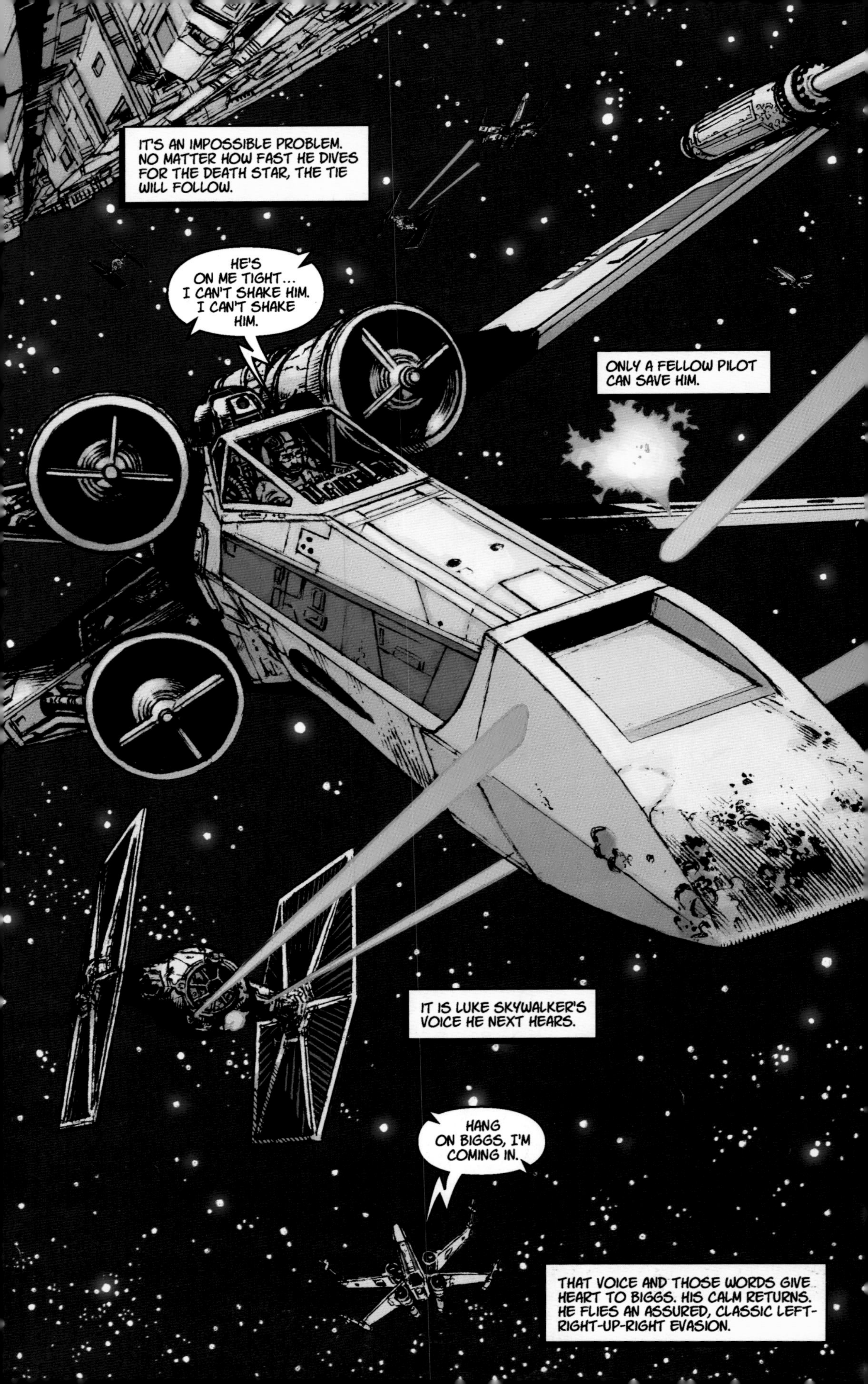
IT'S AN IMPOSSIBLE PROBLEM. NO MATTER HOW FAST HE DIVES FOR THE DEATH STAR, THE TIE WILL FOLLOW.
HE'S ON ME TIGHT... I CAN'T SHAKE HIM. I CAN'T SHAKE HIM.
ONLY A FELLOW PILOT CAN SAVE HIM.
IT IS LUKE SKYWALKER'S VOICE HE NEXT HEARS.
HANG ON BIGGS, I'M COMING IN.
THAT VOICE AND THOSE WORDS GIVE HEART TO BIGGS. HIS CALM RETURNS. HE FLIES AN ASSURED, CLASSIC LEFT-RIGHT-UP-RIGHT EVASION.

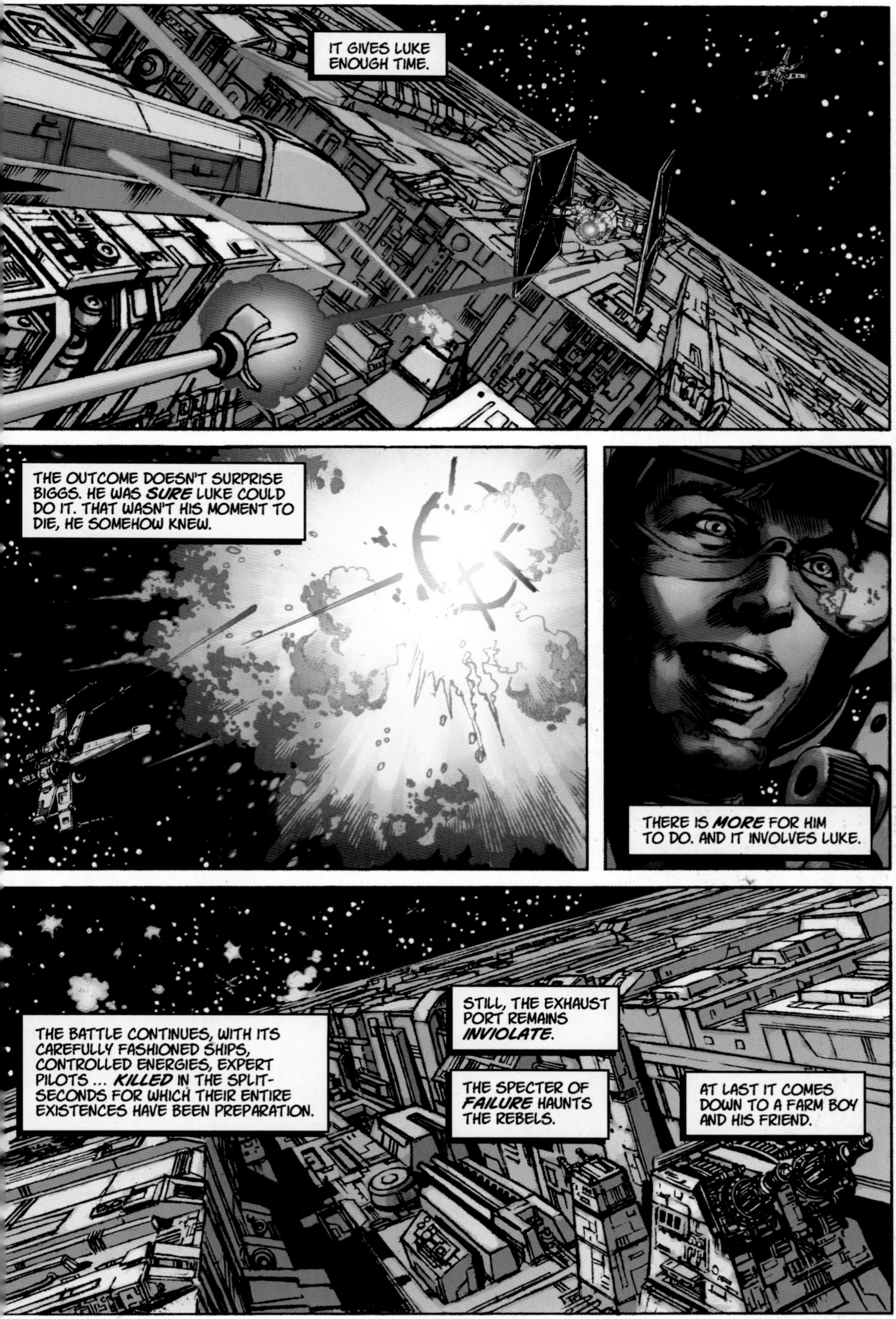
IT GIVES LUKE ENOUGH TIME.
THE OUTCOME DOESN'T SURPRISE BIGGS. HE WAS SURE LUKE COULD DO IT. THAT WASN'T HIS MOMENT TO DIE, HE SOMEHOW KNEW.
THERE IS MORE FOR HIM TO DO. AND IT INVOLVES LUKE.
THE BATTLE CONTINUES, WITH ITS CAREFULLY FASHIONED SHIPS, CONTROLLED ENERGIES, EXPERT PILOTS ... KILLED IN THE SPLIT-SECONDS FOR WHICH THEIR ENTIRE EXISTENCES HAVE BEEN PREPARATION.
STILL, THE EXHAUST PORT REMAINS INVIOLATE.
THE SPECTER OF FAILURE HAUNTS THE REBELS.
AT LAST IT COMES DOWN TO A FARM BOY AND HIS FRIEND.

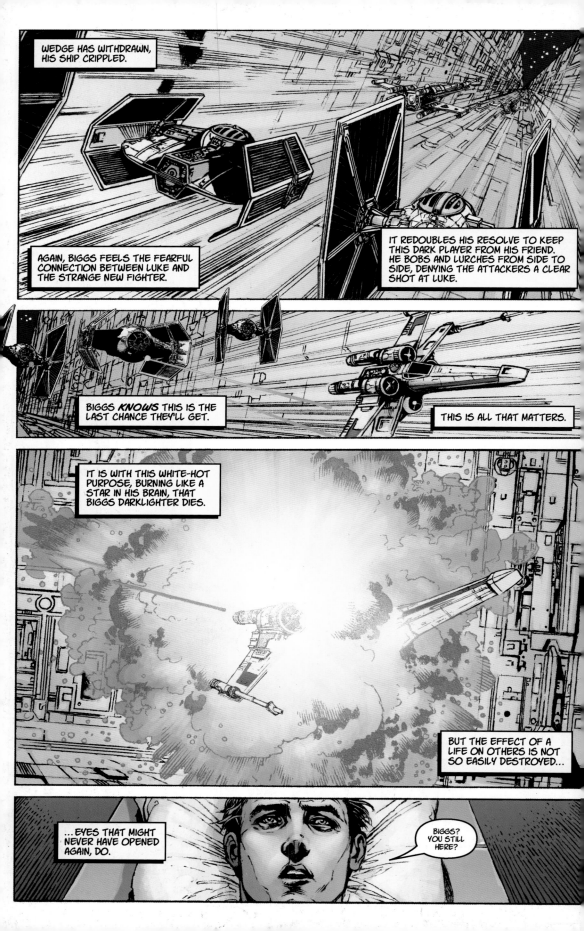

WEDGE HAS WITHDRAWN, HIS SHIP CRIPPLED.

AGAIN, BIGGS FEELS THE FEARFUL CONNECTION BETWEEN LUKE AND THE STRANGE NEW FIGHTER.

IT REDOUBLES HIS RESOLVE TO KEEP THIS DARK PLAYER FROM HIS FRIEND. HE BOBS AND LURCHES FROM SIDE TO SIDE, DENYING THE ATTACKERS A CLEAR SHOT AT LUKE.

BIGGS *KNOWS* THIS IS THE LAST CHANCE THEY'LL GET.

THIS IS ALL THAT MATTERS.

IT IS WITH THIS WHITE-HOT PURPOSE, BURNING LIKE A STAR IN HIS BRAIN, THAT BIGGS DARKLIGHTER DIES.

BUT THE EFFECT OF A LIFE ON OTHERS IS NOT SO EASILY DESTROYED...

...EYES THAT MIGHT NEVER HAVE OPENED AGAIN, DO.

BIGGS? YOU STILL HERE?

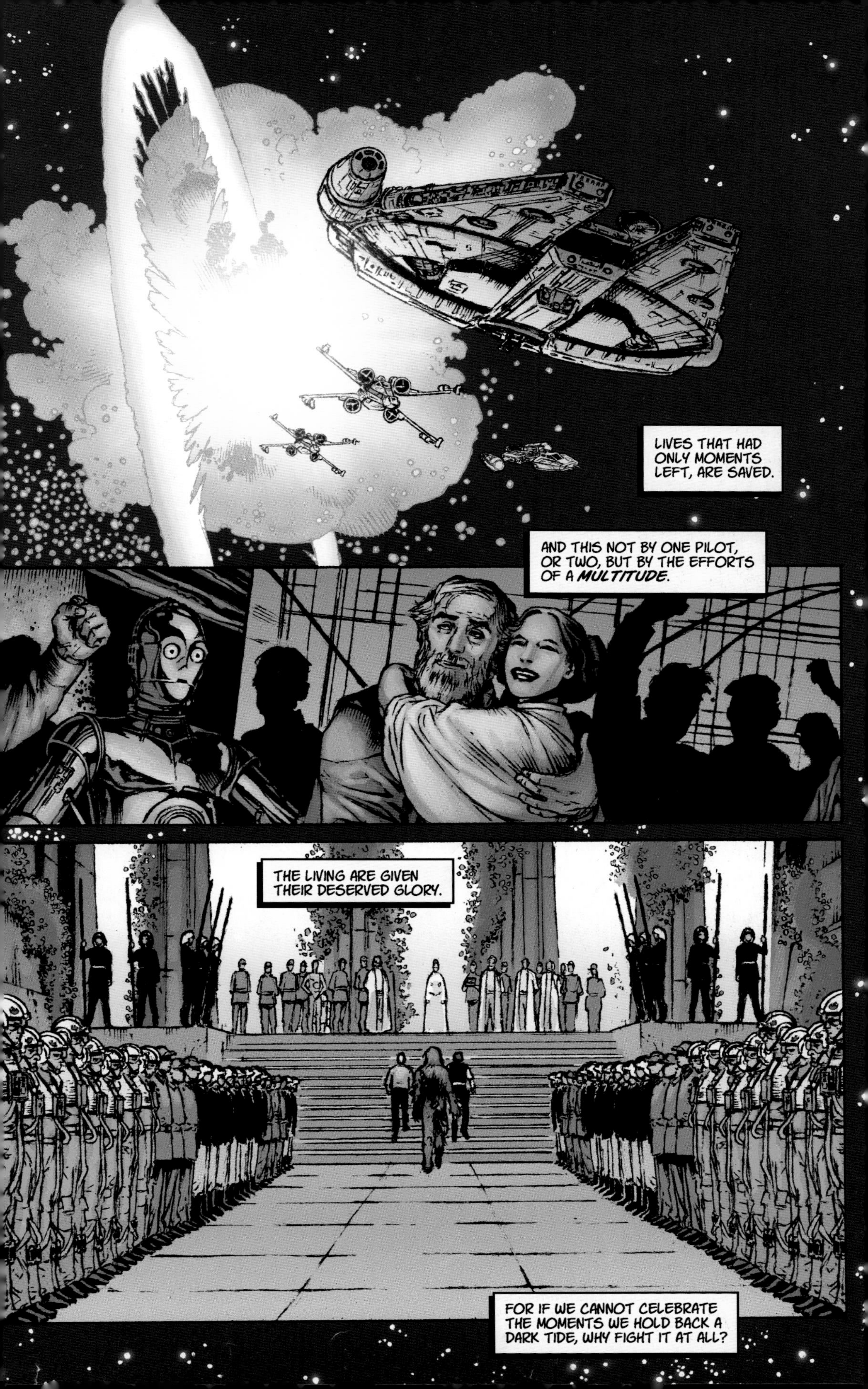

LIVES THAT HAD ONLY MOMENTS LEFT, ARE SAVED.
AND THIS NOT BY ONE PILOT, OR TWO, BUT BY THE EFFORTS OF A *MULTITUDE*.
THE LIVING ARE GIVEN THEIR DESERVED GLORY.
FOR IF WE CANNOT CELEBRATE THE MOMENTS WE HOLD BACK A DARK TIDE, WHY FIGHT IT AT ALL?

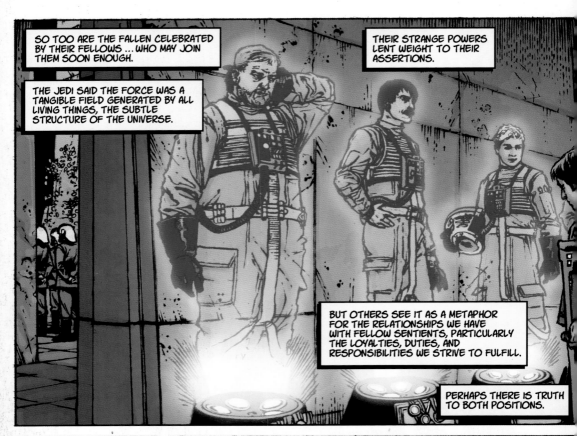

SO TOO ARE THE FALLEN CELEBRATED BY THEIR FELLOWS ... WHO MAY JOIN THEM SOON ENOUGH.

THE JEDI SAID THE FORCE WAS A TANGIBLE FIELD GENERATED BY ALL LIVING THINGS, THE SUBTLE STRUCTURE OF THE UNIVERSE.

THEIR STRANGE POWERS LENT WEIGHT TO THEIR ASSERTIONS.

BUT OTHERS SEE IT AS A METAPHOR FOR THE RELATIONSHIPS WE HAVE WITH FELLOW SENTIENTS, PARTICULARLY THE LOYALTIES, DUTIES, AND RESPONSIBILITIES WE STRIVE TO FULFILL.

PERHAPS THERE IS TRUTH TO BOTH POSITIONS.

FOR HUMAN BEINGS ARE NOT SOLITARY ANIMALS. IT NOT JUST OUR BRAINS AND MINDS ... GENES AND EXPERIENCES ... THAT MAKE US HUMAN.

IT IS OUR ALTRUISM AND LOYALTY, OUR RESTRAINT AND SELF-SACRIFICE...

THANKS, BIGGS.

... THAT ARE THE BEST, AND MOST HUMAN, OF WHAT WE ARE.

THE END

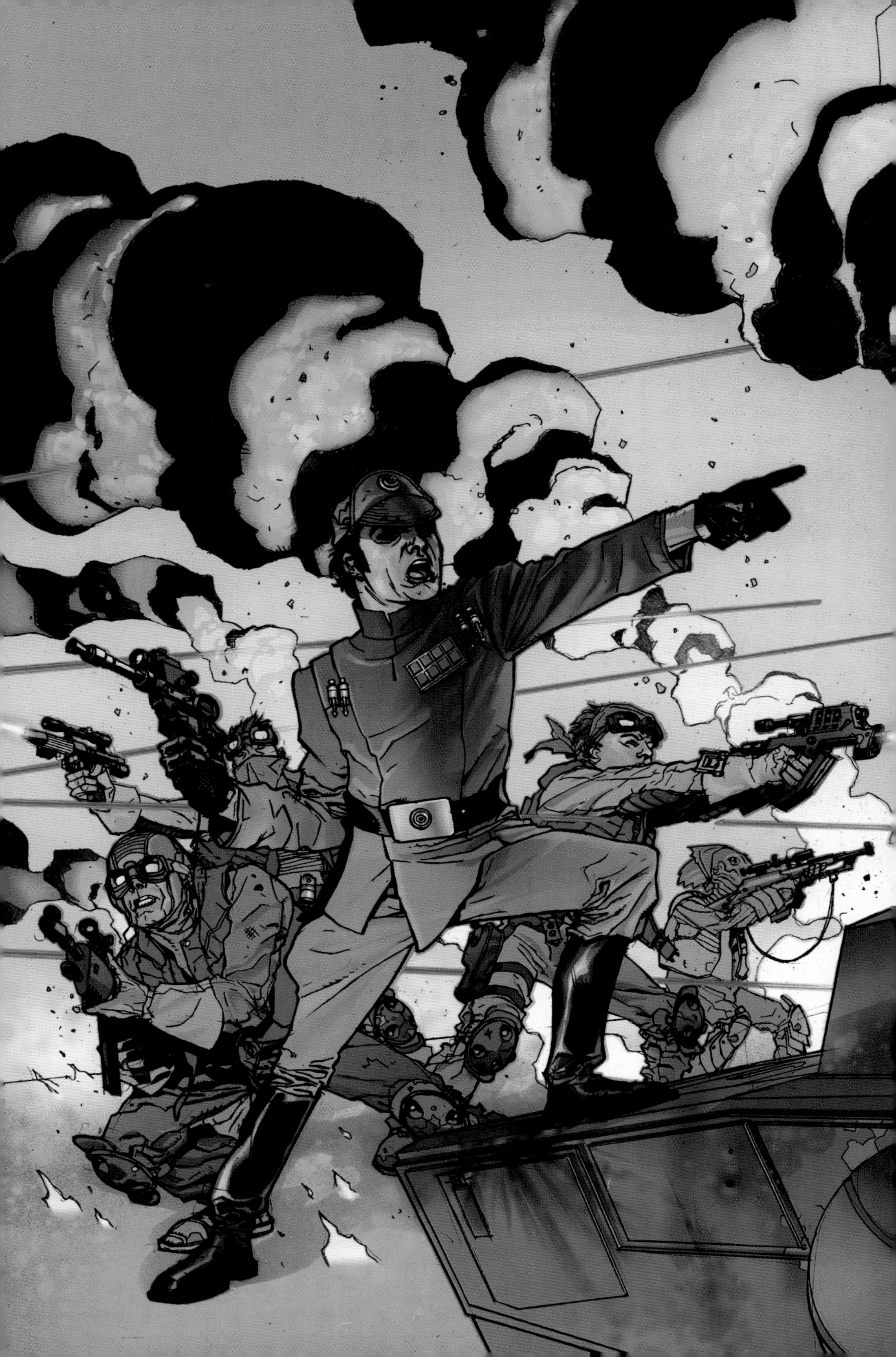

THE SHORT, HAPPY LIFE OF ROONS SEWELL

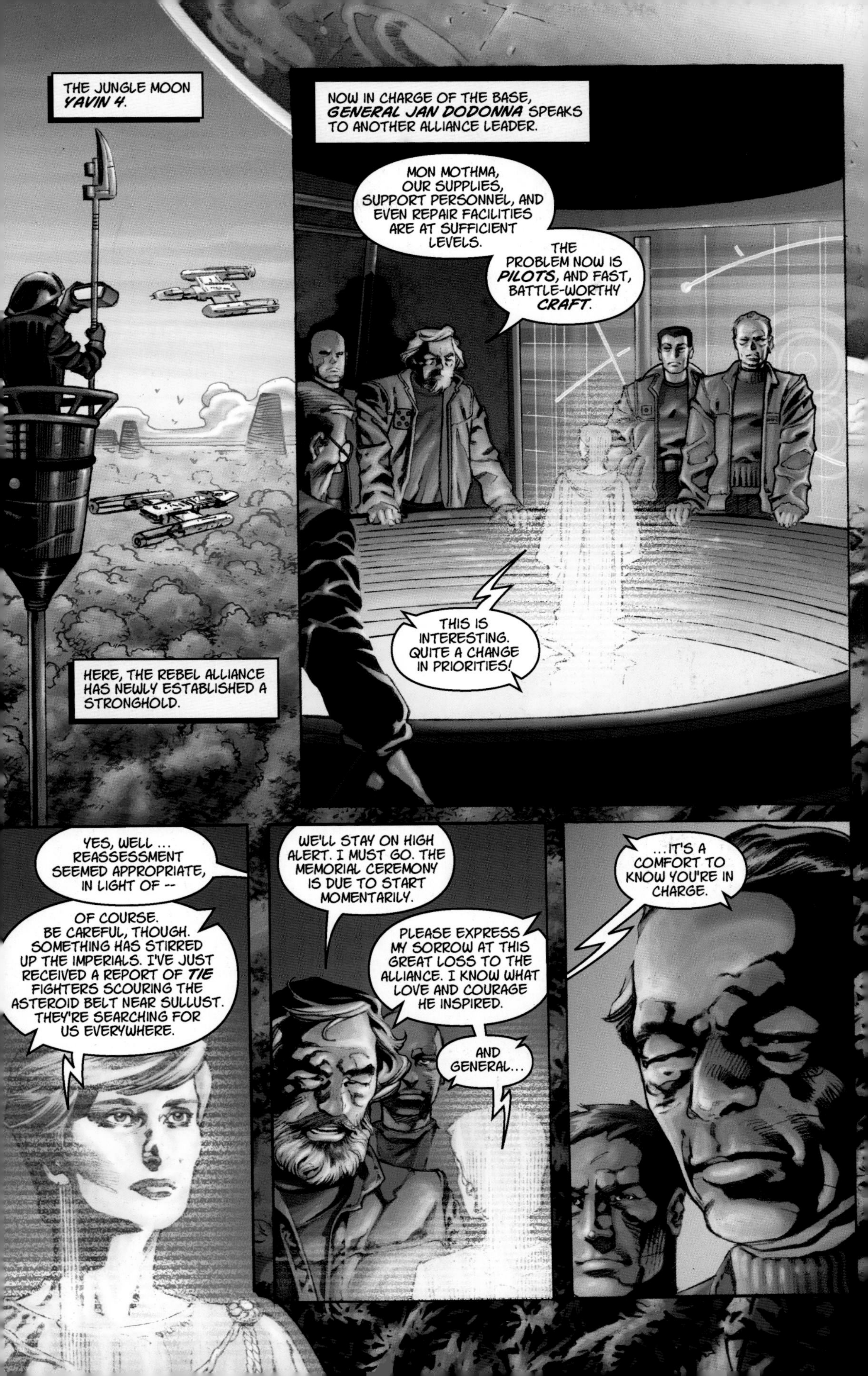
THE JUNGLE MOON *YAVIN 4*.
HERE, THE REBEL ALLIANCE HAS NEWLY ESTABLISHED A STRONGHOLD.
NOW IN CHARGE OF THE BASE, *GENERAL JAN DODONNA* SPEAKS TO ANOTHER ALLIANCE LEADER.
MON MOTHMA, OUR SUPPLIES, SUPPORT PERSONNEL, AND EVEN REPAIR FACILITIES ARE AT SUFFICIENT LEVELS.
THE PROBLEM NOW IS *PILOTS*, AND FAST, BATTLE-WORTHY *CRAFT*.
THIS IS INTERESTING. QUITE A CHANGE IN PRIORITIES!
YES, WELL ... REASSESSMENT SEEMED APPROPRIATE, IN LIGHT OF --
OF COURSE. BE CAREFUL, THOUGH. SOMETHING HAS STIRRED UP THE IMPERIALS. I'VE JUST RECEIVED A REPORT OF *TIE* FIGHTERS SCOURING THE ASTEROID BELT NEAR SULLUST. THEY'RE SEARCHING FOR US EVERYWHERE.
WE'LL STAY ON HIGH ALERT. I MUST GO. THE MEMORIAL CEREMONY IS DUE TO START MOMENTARILY.
PLEASE EXPRESS MY SORROW AT THIS GREAT LOSS TO THE ALLIANCE. I KNOW WHAT LOVE AND COURAGE HE INSPIRED.
AND GENERAL...
...IT'S A COMFORT TO KNOW YOU'RE IN CHARGE.

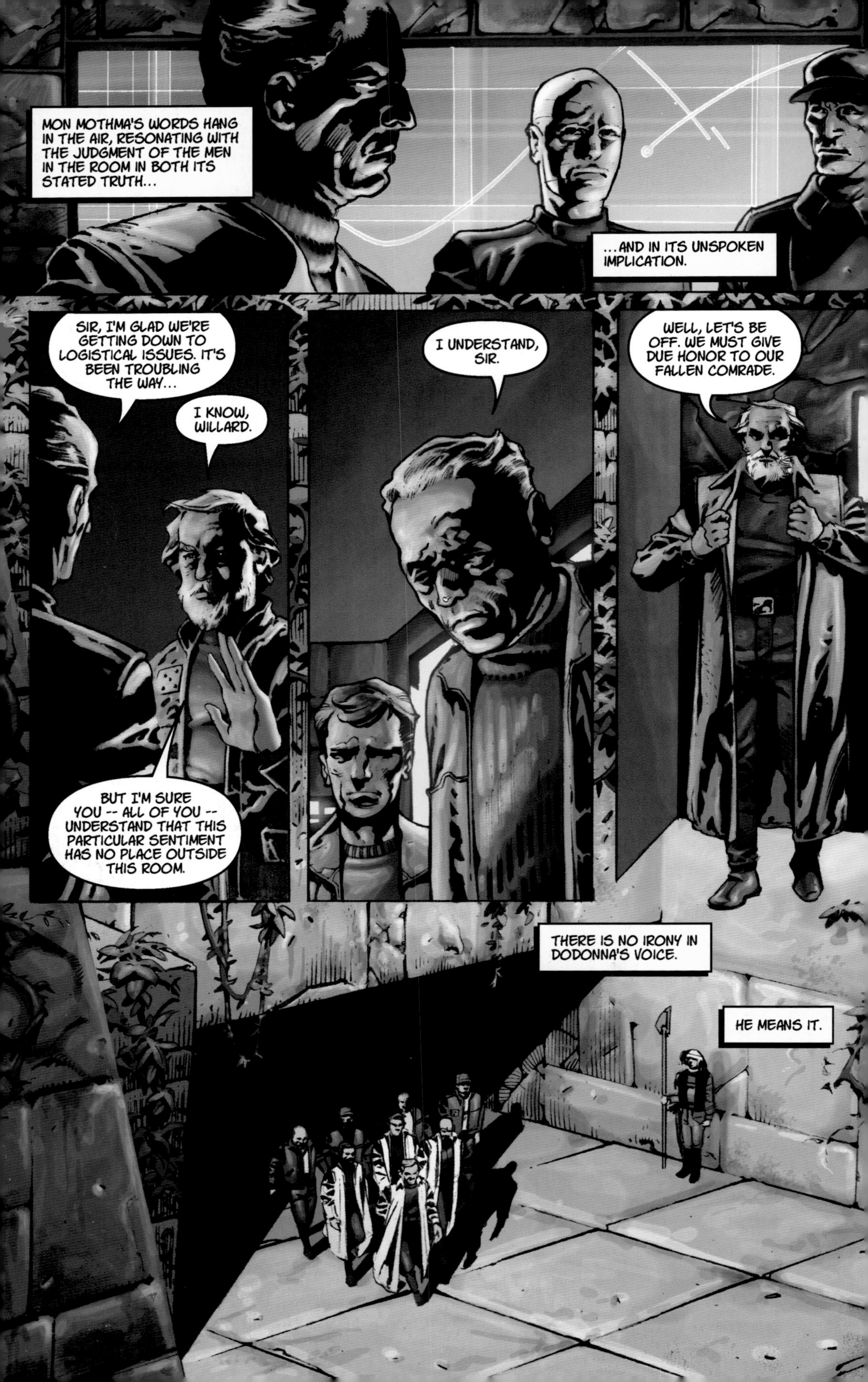
MON MOTHMA'S WORDS HANG IN THE AIR, RESONATING WITH THE JUDGMENT OF THE MEN IN THE ROOM IN BOTH ITS STATED TRUTH...
...AND IN ITS UNSPOKEN IMPLICATION.
SIR, I'M GLAD WE'RE GETTING DOWN TO LOGISTICAL ISSUES. IT'S BEEN TROUBLING THE WAY...
I KNOW, WILLARD.
BUT I'M SURE YOU -- ALL OF YOU -- UNDERSTAND THAT THIS PARTICULAR SENTIMENT HAS NO PLACE OUTSIDE THIS ROOM.
I UNDERSTAND, SIR.
WELL, LET'S BE OFF. WE MUST GIVE DUE HONOR TO OUR FALLEN COMRADE.
THERE IS NO IRONY IN DODONNA'S VOICE.
HE MEANS IT.

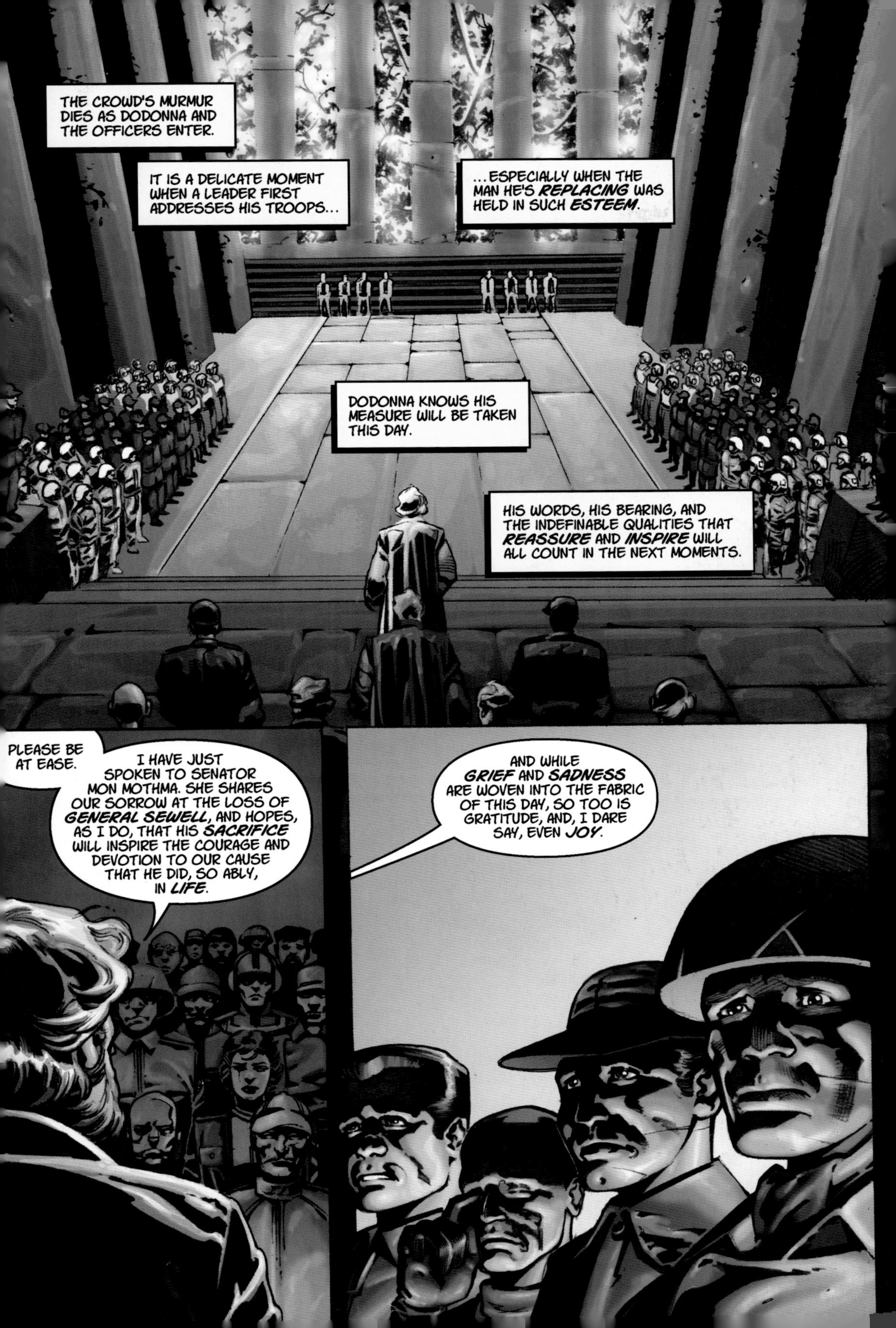
THE CROWD'S MURMUR DIES AS DODONNA AND THE OFFICERS ENTER.
IT IS A DELICATE MOMENT WHEN A LEADER FIRST ADDRESSES HIS TROOPS...
...ESPECIALLY WHEN THE MAN HE'S REPLACING WAS HELD IN SUCH ESTEEM.
DODONNA KNOWS HIS MEASURE WILL BE TAKEN THIS DAY.
HIS WORDS, HIS BEARING, AND THE INDEFINABLE QUALITIES THAT REASSURE AND INSPIRE WILL ALL COUNT IN THE NEXT MOMENTS.
PLEASE BE AT EASE.
I HAVE JUST SPOKEN TO SENATOR MON MOTHMA. SHE SHARES OUR SORROW AT THE LOSS OF GENERAL SEWELL, AND HOPES, AS I DO, THAT HIS SACRIFICE WILL INSPIRE THE COURAGE AND DEVOTION TO OUR CAUSE THAT HE DID, SO ABLY, IN LIFE.
AND WHILE GRIEF AND SADNESS ARE WOVEN INTO THE FABRIC OF THIS DAY, SO TOO IS GRATITUDE, AND, I DARE SAY, EVEN JOY.

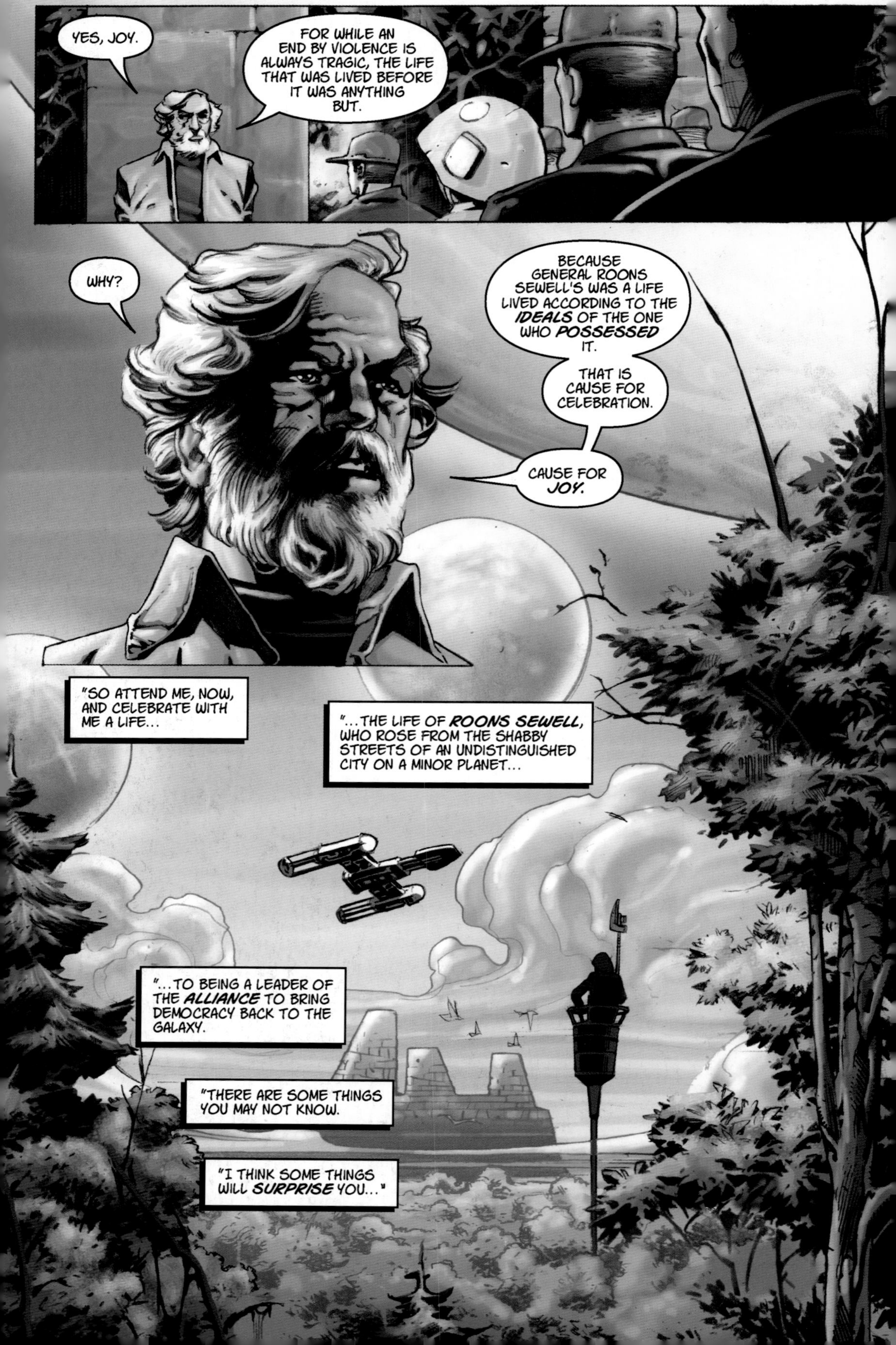

YES, JOY.
FOR WHILE AN END BY VIOLENCE IS ALWAYS TRAGIC, THE LIFE THAT WAS LIVED BEFORE IT WAS ANYTHING BUT.
WHY?
BECAUSE GENERAL ROONS SEWELL'S WAS A LIFE LIVED ACCORDING TO THE IDEALS OF THE ONE WHO POSSESSED IT.
THAT IS CAUSE FOR CELEBRATION.
CAUSE FOR JOY.
"SO ATTEND ME, NOW, AND CELEBRATE WITH ME A LIFE...
"...THE LIFE OF ROONS SEWELL, WHO ROSE FROM THE SHABBY STREETS OF AN UNDISTINGUISHED CITY ON A MINOR PLANET...
"...TO BEING A LEADER OF THE ALLIANCE TO BRING DEMOCRACY BACK TO THE GALAXY.
"THERE ARE SOME THINGS YOU MAY NOT KNOW.
"I THINK SOME THINGS WILL SURPRISE YOU..."

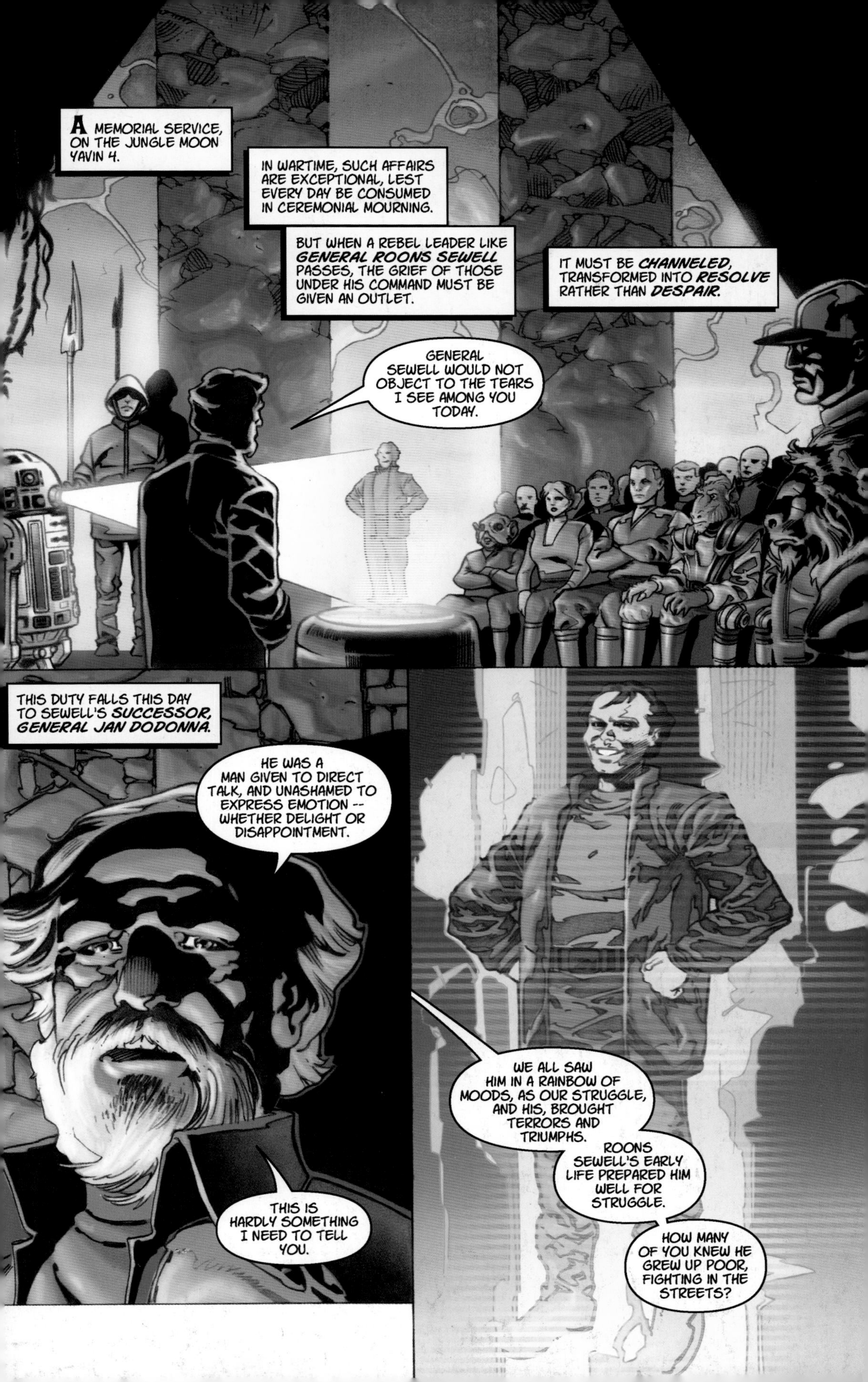
A MEMORIAL SERVICE, ON THE JUNGLE MOON YAVIN 4.
IN WARTIME, SUCH AFFAIRS ARE EXCEPTIONAL, LEST EVERY DAY BE CONSUMED IN CEREMONIAL MOURNING.
BUT WHEN A REBEL LEADER LIKE GENERAL ROONS SEWELL PASSES, THE GRIEF OF THOSE UNDER HIS COMMAND MUST BE GIVEN AN OUTLET.
IT MUST BE CHANNELED, TRANSFORMED INTO RESOLVE RATHER THAN DESPAIR.
GENERAL SEWELL WOULD NOT OBJECT TO THE TEARS I SEE AMONG YOU TODAY.
THIS DUTY FALLS THIS DAY TO SEWELL'S SUCCESSOR, GENERAL JAN DODONNA.
HE WAS A MAN GIVEN TO DIRECT TALK, AND UNASHAMED TO EXPRESS EMOTION -- WHETHER DELIGHT OR DISAPPOINTMENT.
THIS IS HARDLY SOMETHING I NEED TO TELL YOU.
WE ALL SAW HIM IN A RAINBOW OF MOODS, AS OUR STRUGGLE, AND HIS, BROUGHT TERRORS AND TRIUMPHS.
ROONS SEWELL'S EARLY LIFE PREPARED HIM WELL FOR STRUGGLE.
HOW MANY OF YOU KNEW HE GREW UP POOR, FIGHTING IN THE STREETS?

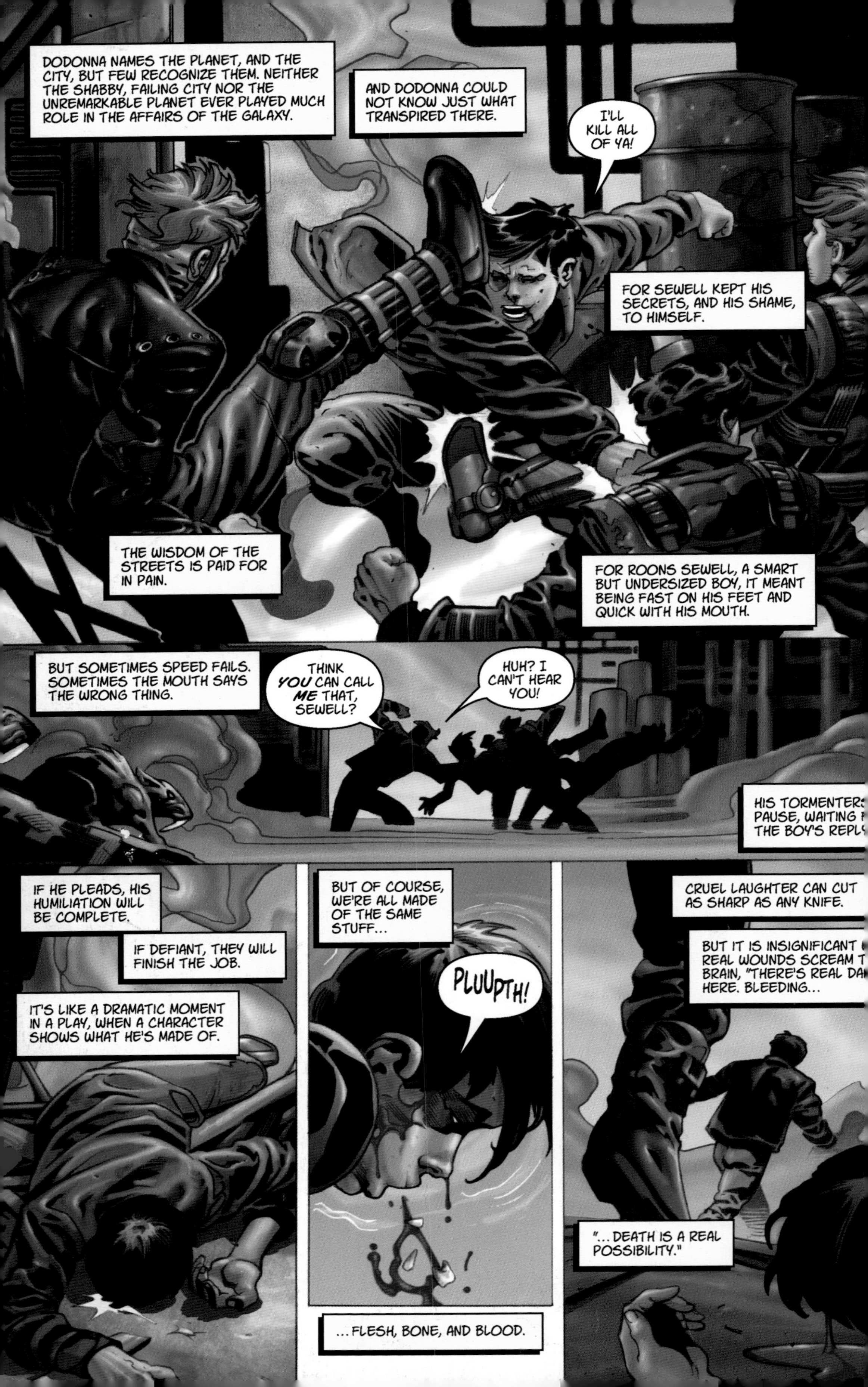
DODONNA NAMES THE PLANET, AND THE CITY, BUT FEW RECOGNIZE THEM. NEITHER THE SHABBY, FAILING CITY NOR THE UNREMARKABLE PLANET EVER PLAYED MUCH ROLE IN THE AFFAIRS OF THE GALAXY.
AND DODONNA COULD NOT KNOW JUST WHAT TRANSPIRED THERE.
I'LL KILL ALL OF YA!
FOR SEWELL KEPT HIS SECRETS, AND HIS SHAME, TO HIMSELF.
THE WISDOM OF THE STREETS IS PAID FOR IN PAIN.
FOR ROONS SEWELL, A SMART BUT UNDERSIZED BOY, IT MEANT BEING FAST ON HIS FEET AND QUICK WITH HIS MOUTH.
BUT SOMETIMES SPEED FAILS. SOMETIMES THE MOUTH SAYS THE WRONG THING.
THINK YOU CAN CALL ME THAT, SEWELL?
HUH? I CAN'T HEAR YOU!
HIS TORMENTERS PAUSE, WAITING F THE BOY'S REPL
IF HE PLEADS, HIS HUMILIATION WILL BE COMPLETE.
IF DEFIANT, THEY WILL FINISH THE JOB.
IT'S LIKE A DRAMATIC MOMENT IN A PLAY, WHEN A CHARACTER SHOWS WHAT HE'S MADE OF.
BUT OF COURSE, WE'RE ALL MADE OF THE SAME STUFF...
PLUUPTH!
...FLESH, BONE, AND BLOOD.
CRUEL LAUGHTER CAN CUT AS SHARP AS ANY KNIFE.
BUT IT IS INSIGNIFICANT REAL WOUNDS SCREAM T BRAIN, "THERE'S REAL DA HERE. BLEEDING...
"...DEATH IS A REAL POSSIBILITY."

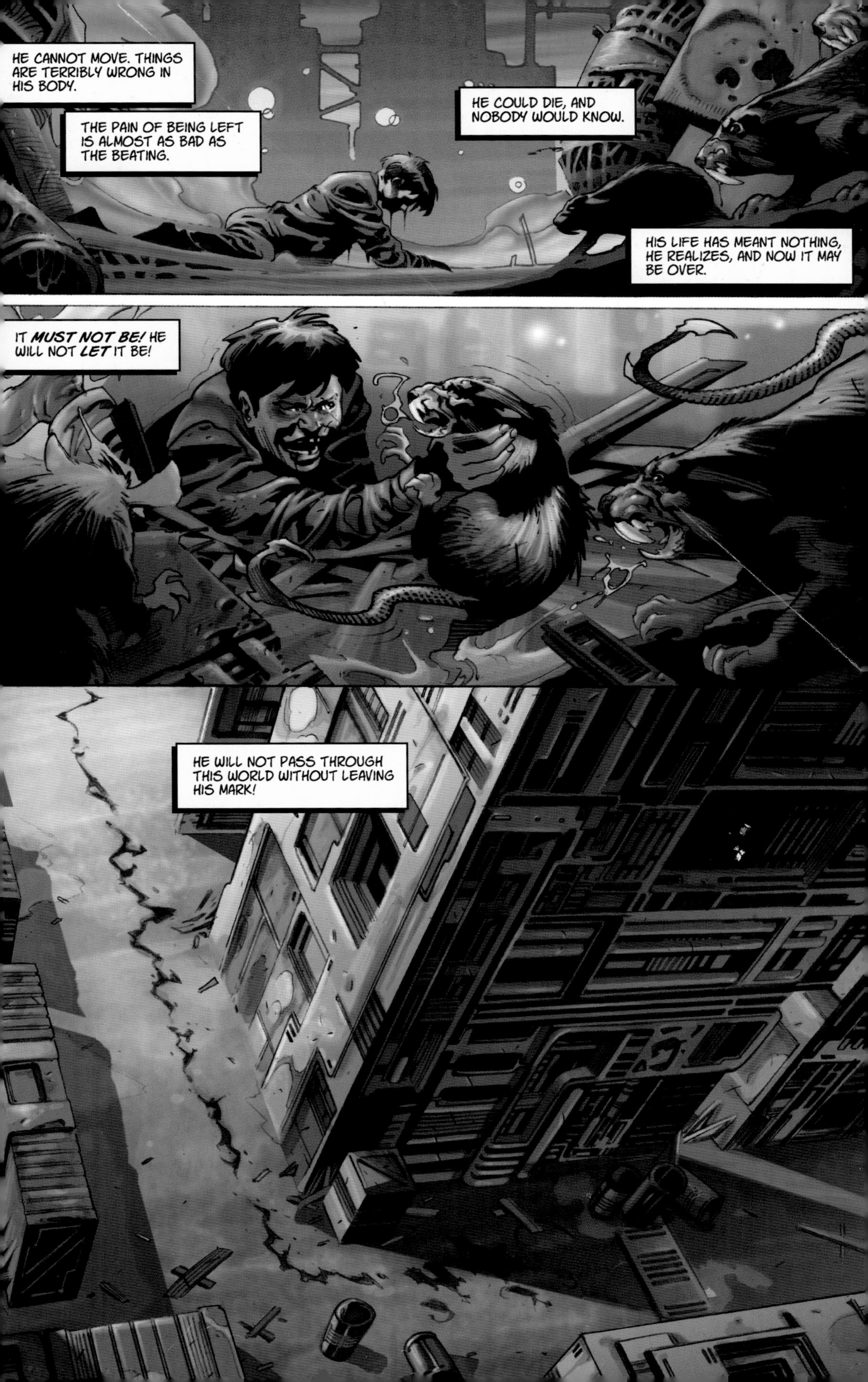
HE CANNOT MOVE. THINGS ARE TERRIBLY WRONG IN HIS BODY.
THE PAIN OF BEING LEFT IS ALMOST AS BAD AS THE BEATING.
HE COULD DIE, AND NOBODY WOULD KNOW.
HIS LIFE HAS MEANT NOTHING, HE REALIZES, AND NOW IT MAY BE OVER.
IT MUST NOT BE! HE WILL NOT LET IT BE!
HE WILL NOT PASS THROUGH THIS WORLD WITHOUT LEAVING HIS MARK!

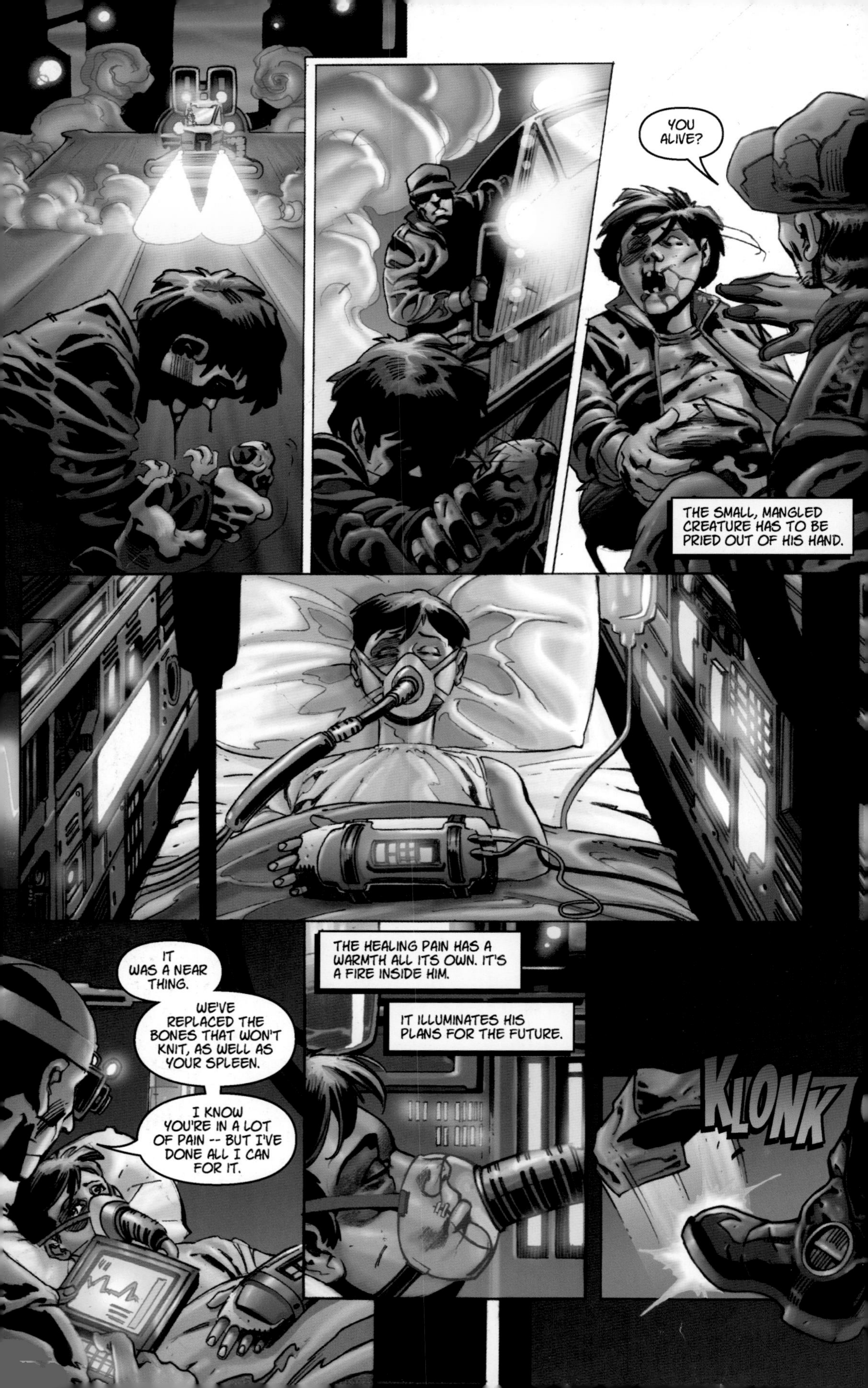
YOU ALIVE?
THE SMALL, MANGLED CREATURE HAS TO BE PRIED OUT OF HIS HAND.
IT WAS A NEAR THING.
WE'VE REPLACED THE BONES THAT WON'T KNIT, AS WELL AS YOUR SPLEEN.
I KNOW YOU'RE IN A LOT OF PAIN -- BUT I'VE DONE ALL I CAN FOR IT.
THE HEALING PAIN HAS A WARMTH ALL ITS OWN. IT'S A FIRE INSIDE HIM.
IT ILLUMINATES HIS PLANS FOR THE FUTURE.
KLONK

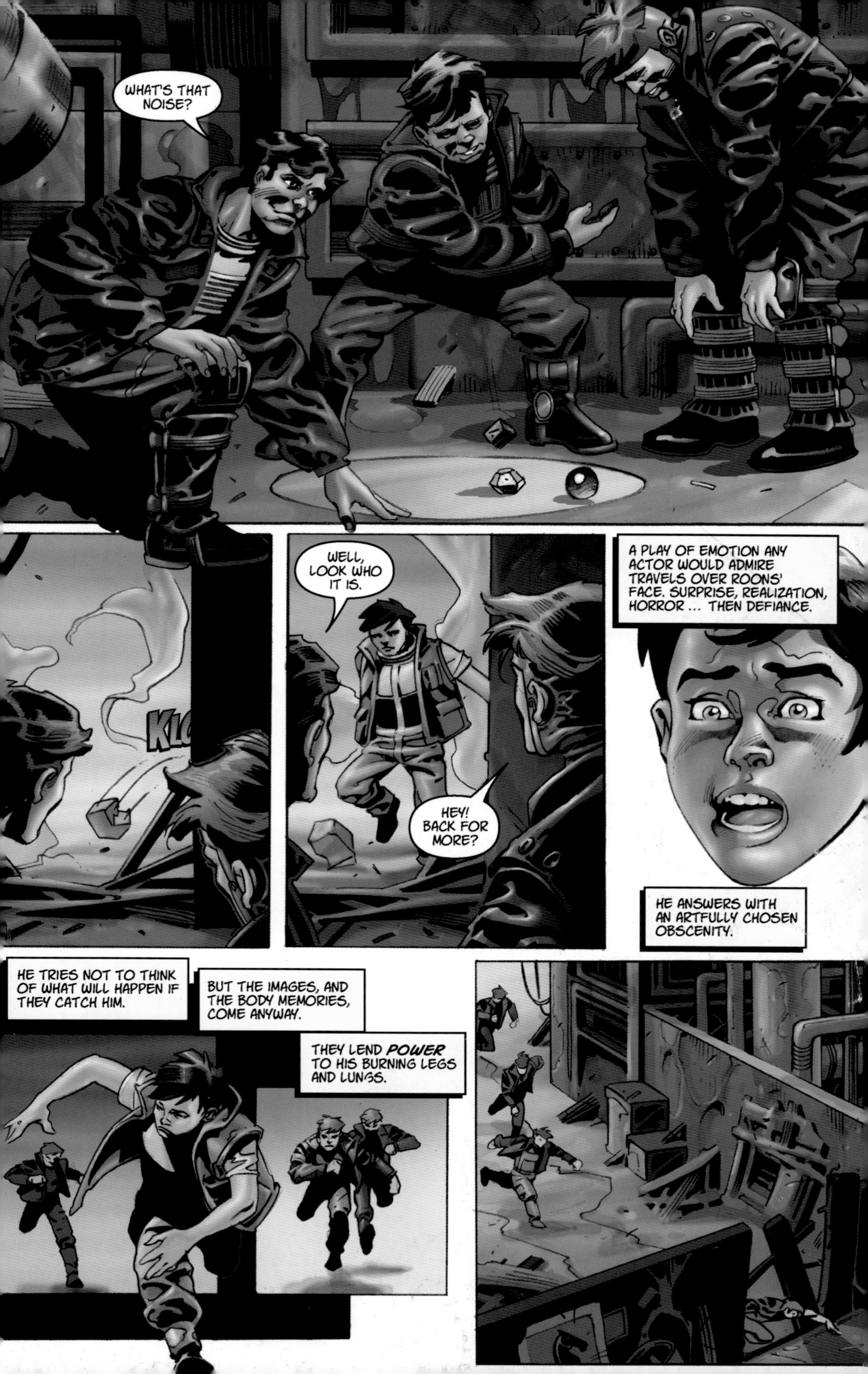
WHAT'S THAT NOISE?
KLO
WELL, LOOK WHO IT IS.
HEY! BACK FOR MORE?
A PLAY OF EMOTION ANY ACTOR WOULD ADMIRE TRAVELS OVER ROONS' FACE. SURPRISE, REALIZATION, HORROR ... THEN DEFIANCE.
HE ANSWERS WITH AN ARTFULLY CHOSEN OBSCENITY.
HE TRIES NOT TO THINK OF WHAT WILL HAPPEN IF THEY CATCH HIM.
BUT THE IMAGES, AND THE BODY MEMORIES, COME ANYWAY.
THEY LEND *POWER* TO HIS BURNING LEGS AND LUNGS.

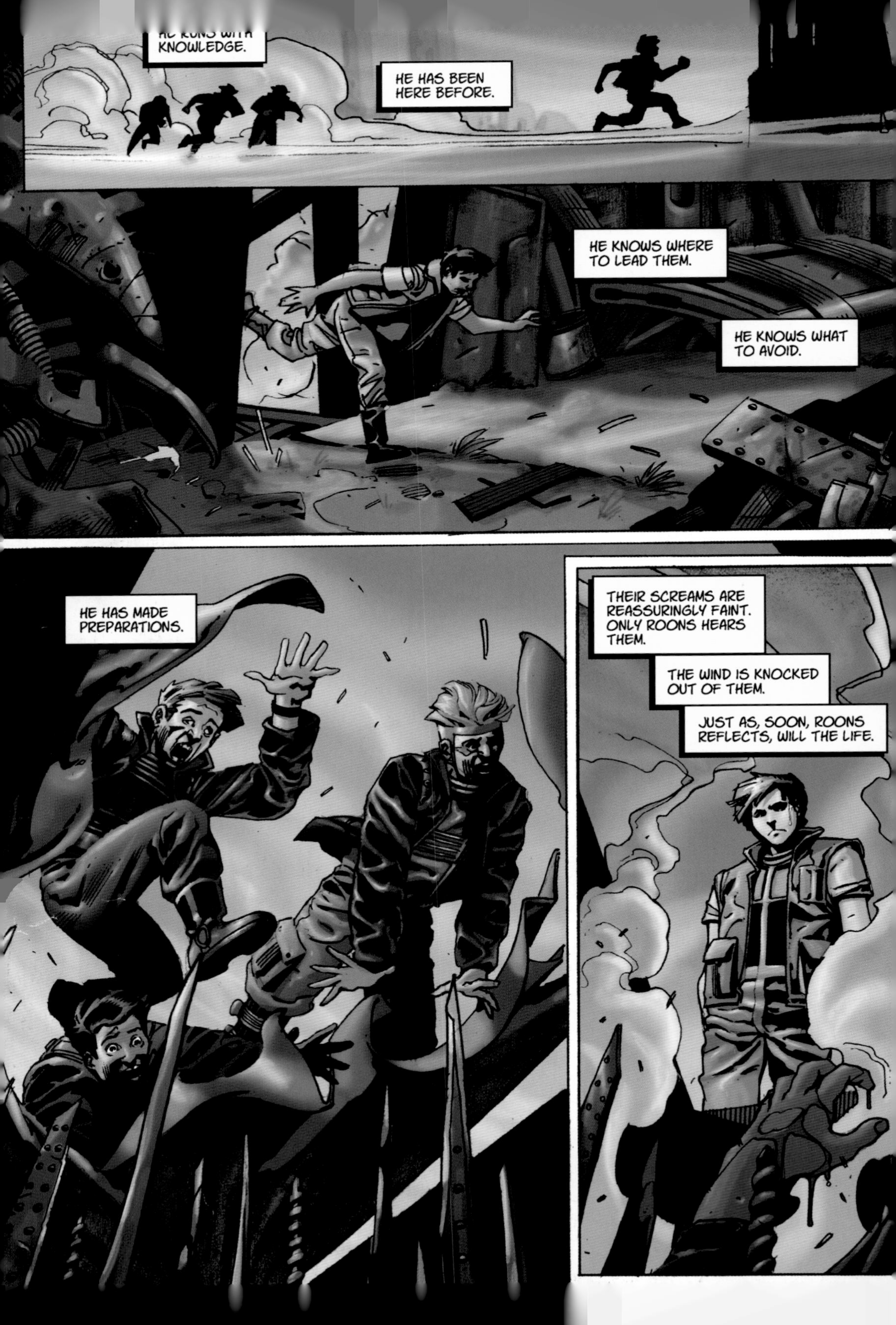
KNOWLEDGE.
HE HAS BEEN HERE BEFORE.
HE KNOWS WHERE TO LEAD THEM.
HE KNOWS WHAT TO AVOID.
HE HAS MADE PREPARATIONS.
THEIR SCREAMS ARE REASSURINGLY FAINT. ONLY ROONS HEARS THEM.
THE WIND IS KNOCKED OUT OF THEM.
JUST AS, SOON, ROONS REFLECTS, WILL THE LIFE.

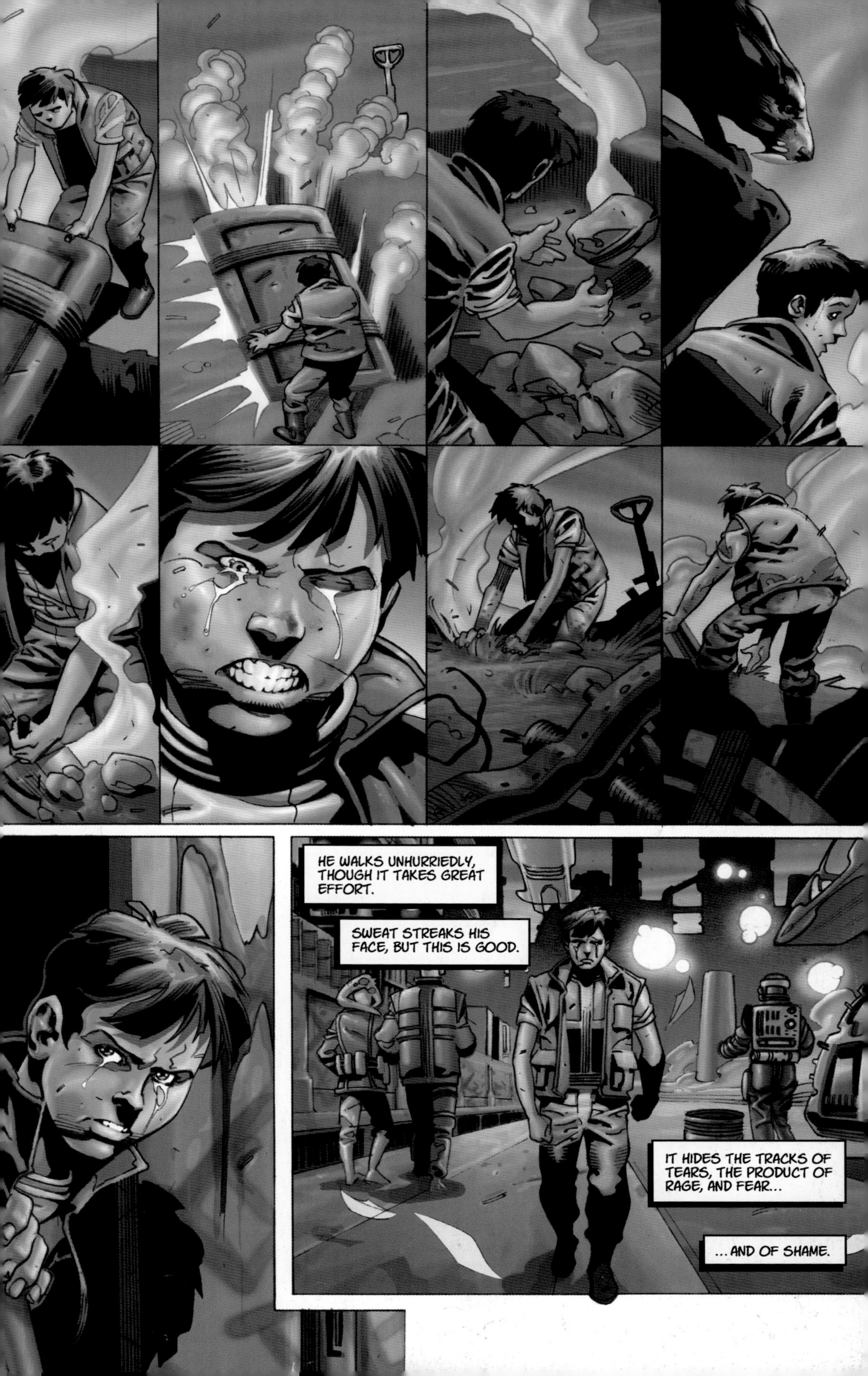
HE WALKS UNHURRIEDLY, THOUGH IT TAKES GREAT EFFORT.
SWEAT STREAKS HIS FACE, BUT THIS IS GOOD.
IT HIDES THE TRACKS OF TEARS, THE PRODUCT OF RAGE, AND FEAR...
...AND OF SHAME.

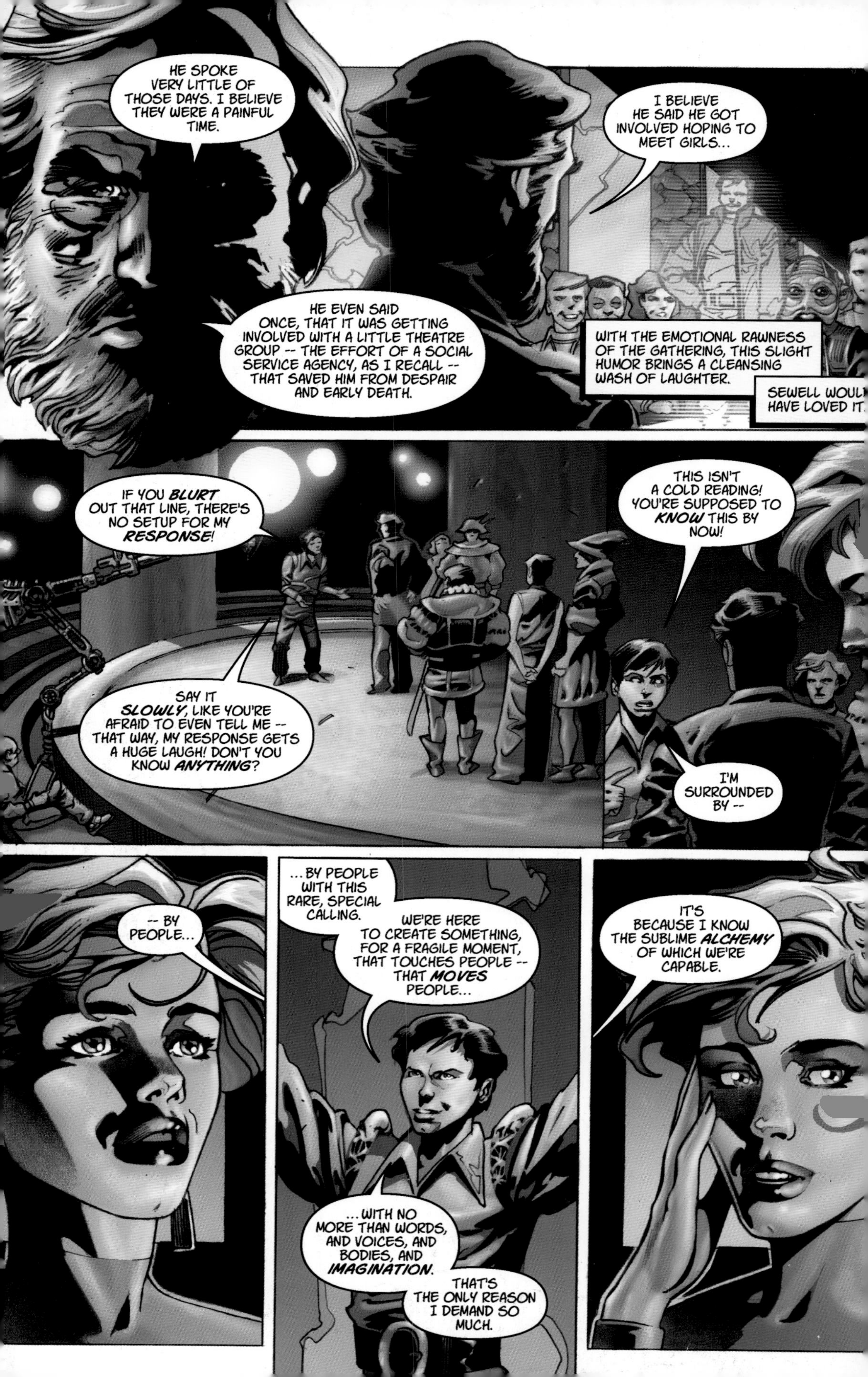
HE SPOKE VERY LITTLE OF THOSE DAYS. I BELIEVE THEY WERE A PAINFUL TIME.
I BELIEVE HE SAID HE GOT INVOLVED HOPING TO MEET GIRLS...
HE EVEN SAID ONCE, THAT IT WAS GETTING INVOLVED WITH A LITTLE THEATRE GROUP -- THE EFFORT OF A SOCIAL SERVICE AGENCY, AS I RECALL -- THAT SAVED HIM FROM DESPAIR AND EARLY DEATH.
WITH THE EMOTIONAL RAWNESS OF THE GATHERING, THIS SLIGHT HUMOR BRINGS A CLEANSING WASH OF LAUGHTER.
SEWELL WOUL HAVE LOVED IT.
IF YOU BLURT OUT THAT LINE, THERE'S NO SETUP FOR MY RESPONSE!
SAY IT SLOWLY, LIKE YOU'RE AFRAID TO EVEN TELL ME -- THAT WAY, MY RESPONSE GETS A HUGE LAUGH! DON'T YOU KNOW ANYTHING?
THIS ISN'T A COLD READING! YOU'RE SUPPOSED TO KNOW THIS BY NOW!
I'M SURROUNDED BY --
-- BY PEOPLE...
...BY PEOPLE WITH THIS RARE, SPECIAL CALLING.
WE'RE HERE TO CREATE SOMETHING, FOR A FRAGILE MOMENT, THAT TOUCHES PEOPLE -- THAT MOVES PEOPLE...
...WITH NO MORE THAN WORDS, AND VOICES, AND BODIES, AND IMAGINATION.
THAT'S THE ONLY REASON I DEMAND SO MUCH.
IT'S BECAUSE I KNOW THE SUBLIME ALCHEMY OF WHICH WE'RE CAPABLE.

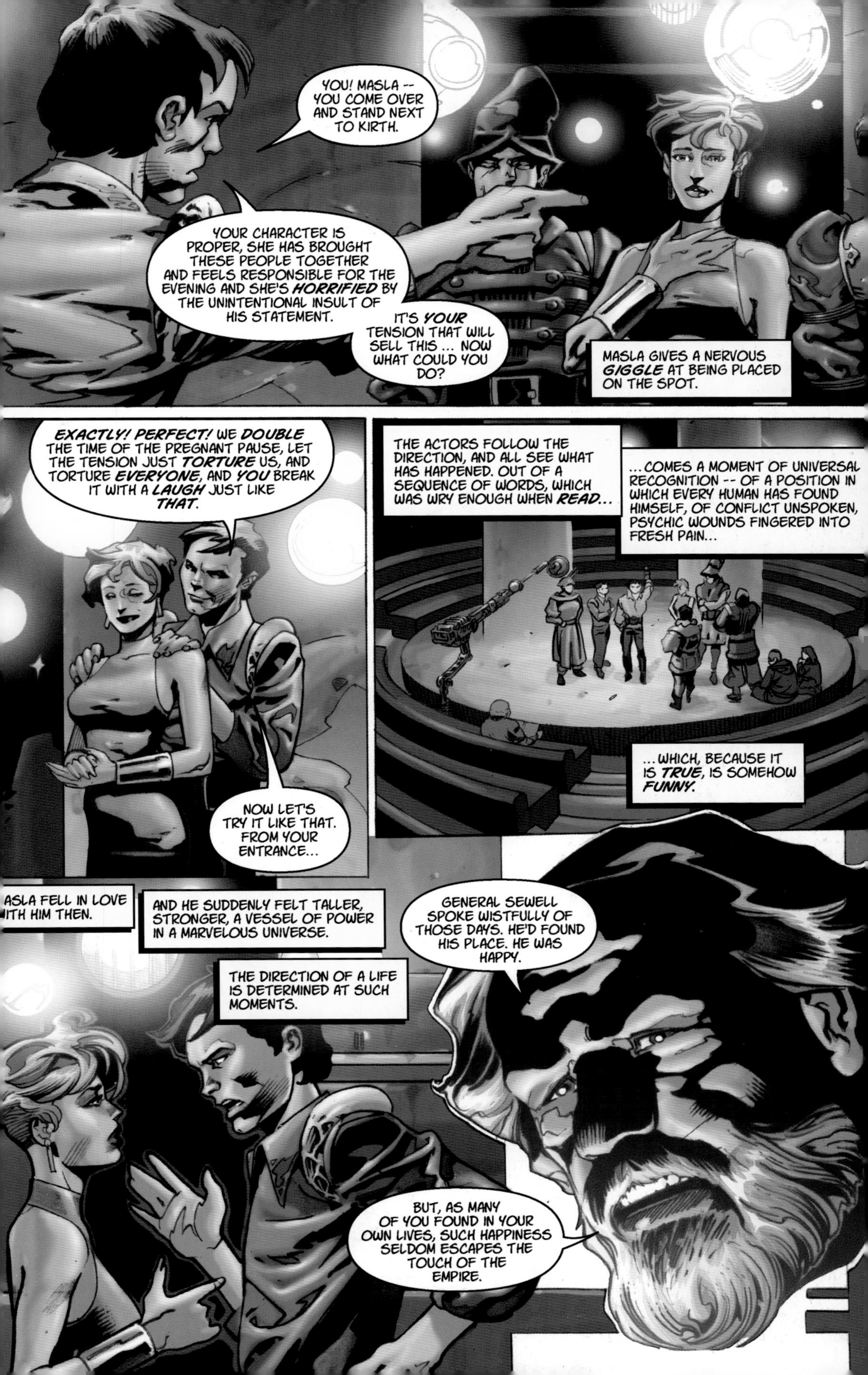

YOU! MASLA -- YOU COME OVER AND STAND NEXT TO KIRTH.
YOUR CHARACTER IS PROPER, SHE HAS BROUGHT THESE PEOPLE TOGETHER AND FEELS RESPONSIBLE FOR THE EVENING AND SHE'S HORRIFIED BY THE UNINTENTIONAL INSULT OF HIS STATEMENT.
IT'S YOUR TENSION THAT WILL SELL THIS ... NOW WHAT COULD YOU DO?
MASLA GIVES A NERVOUS GIGGLE AT BEING PLACED ON THE SPOT.
EXACTLY! PERFECT! WE DOUBLE THE TIME OF THE PREGNANT PAUSE, LET THE TENSION JUST TORTURE US, AND TORTURE EVERYONE, AND YOU BREAK IT WITH A LAUGH JUST LIKE THAT.
NOW LET'S TRY IT LIKE THAT. FROM YOUR ENTRANCE...
THE ACTORS FOLLOW THE DIRECTION, AND ALL SEE WHAT HAS HAPPENED. OUT OF A SEQUENCE OF WORDS, WHICH WAS WRY ENOUGH WHEN READ...
...COMES A MOMENT OF UNIVERSAL RECOGNITION -- OF A POSITION IN WHICH EVERY HUMAN HAS FOUND HIMSELF, OF CONFLICT UNSPOKEN, PSYCHIC WOUNDS FINGERED INTO FRESH PAIN...
...WHICH, BECAUSE IT IS TRUE, IS SOMEHOW FUNNY.
ASLA FELL IN LOVE ITH HIM THEN.
AND HE SUDDENLY FELT TALLER, STRONGER, A VESSEL OF POWER IN A MARVELOUS UNIVERSE.
THE DIRECTION OF A LIFE IS DETERMINED AT SUCH MOMENTS.
GENERAL SEWELL SPOKE WISTFULLY OF THOSE DAYS. HE'D FOUND HIS PLACE. HE WAS HAPPY.
BUT, AS MANY OF YOU FOUND IN YOUR OWN LIVES, SUCH HAPPINESS SELDOM ESCAPES THE TOUCH OF THE EMPIRE.

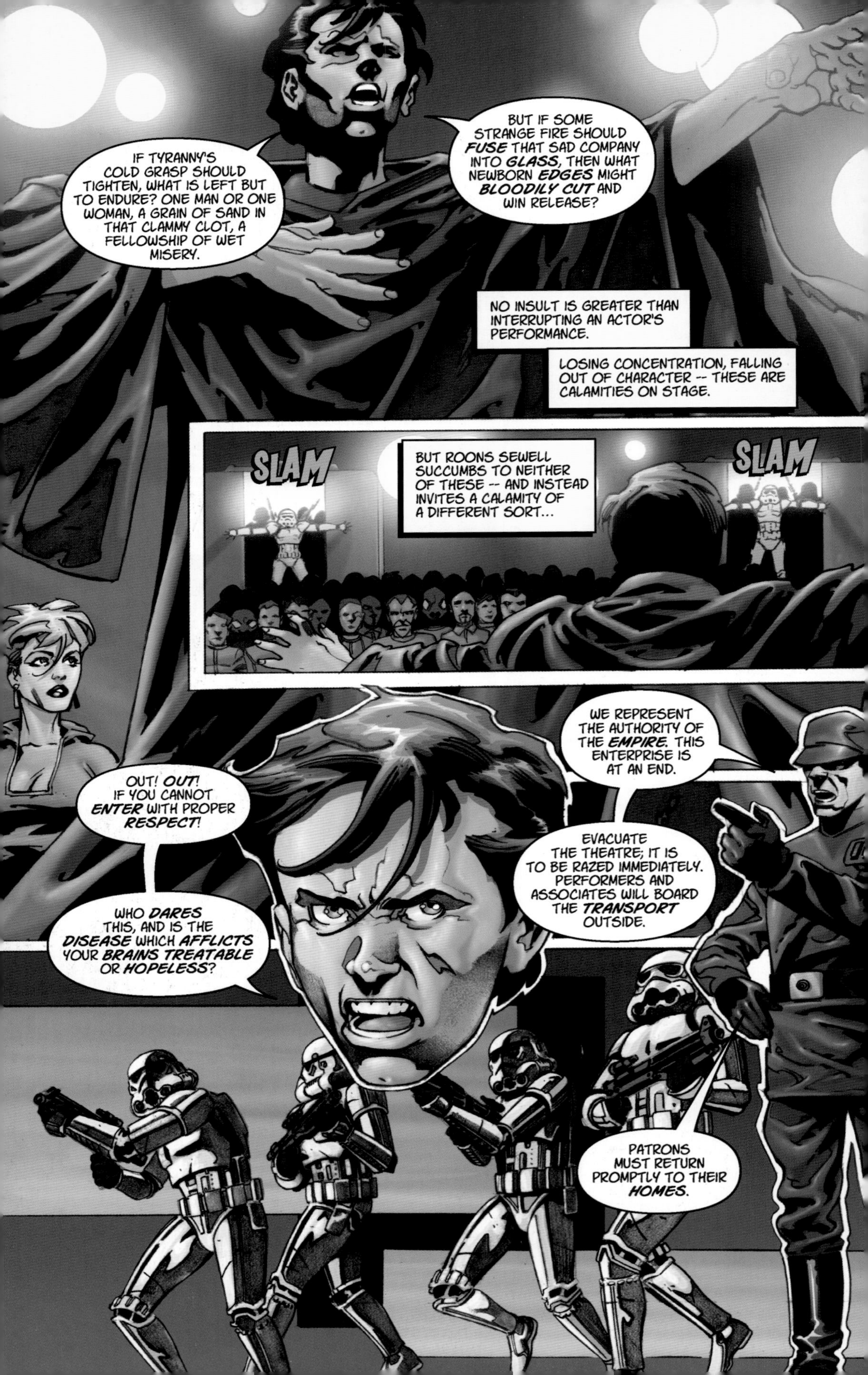
IF TYRANNY'S COLD GRASP SHOULD TIGHTEN, WHAT IS LEFT BUT TO ENDURE? ONE MAN OR ONE WOMAN, A GRAIN OF SAND IN THAT CLAMMY CLOT, A FELLOWSHIP OF WET MISERY.
BUT IF SOME STRANGE FIRE SHOULD FUSE THAT SAD COMPANY INTO GLASS, THEN WHAT NEWBORN EDGES MIGHT BLOODILY CUT AND WIN RELEASE?
NO INSULT IS GREATER THAN INTERRUPTING AN ACTOR'S PERFORMANCE.
LOSING CONCENTRATION, FALLING OUT OF CHARACTER -- THESE ARE CALAMITIES ON STAGE.
SLAM
BUT ROONS SEWELL SUCCUMBS TO NEITHER OF THESE -- AND INSTEAD INVITES A CALAMITY OF A DIFFERENT SORT...
SLAM
OUT! OUT! IF YOU CANNOT ENTER WITH PROPER RESPECT!
WHO DARES THIS, AND IS THE DISEASE WHICH AFFLICTS YOUR BRAINS TREATABLE OR HOPELESS?
WE REPRESENT THE AUTHORITY OF THE EMPIRE. THIS ENTERPRISE IS AT AN END.
EVACUATE THE THEATRE; IT IS TO BE RAZED IMMEDIATELY. PERFORMERS AND ASSOCIATES WILL BOARD THE TRANSPORT OUTSIDE.
PATRONS MUST RETURN PROMPTLY TO THEIR HOMES.

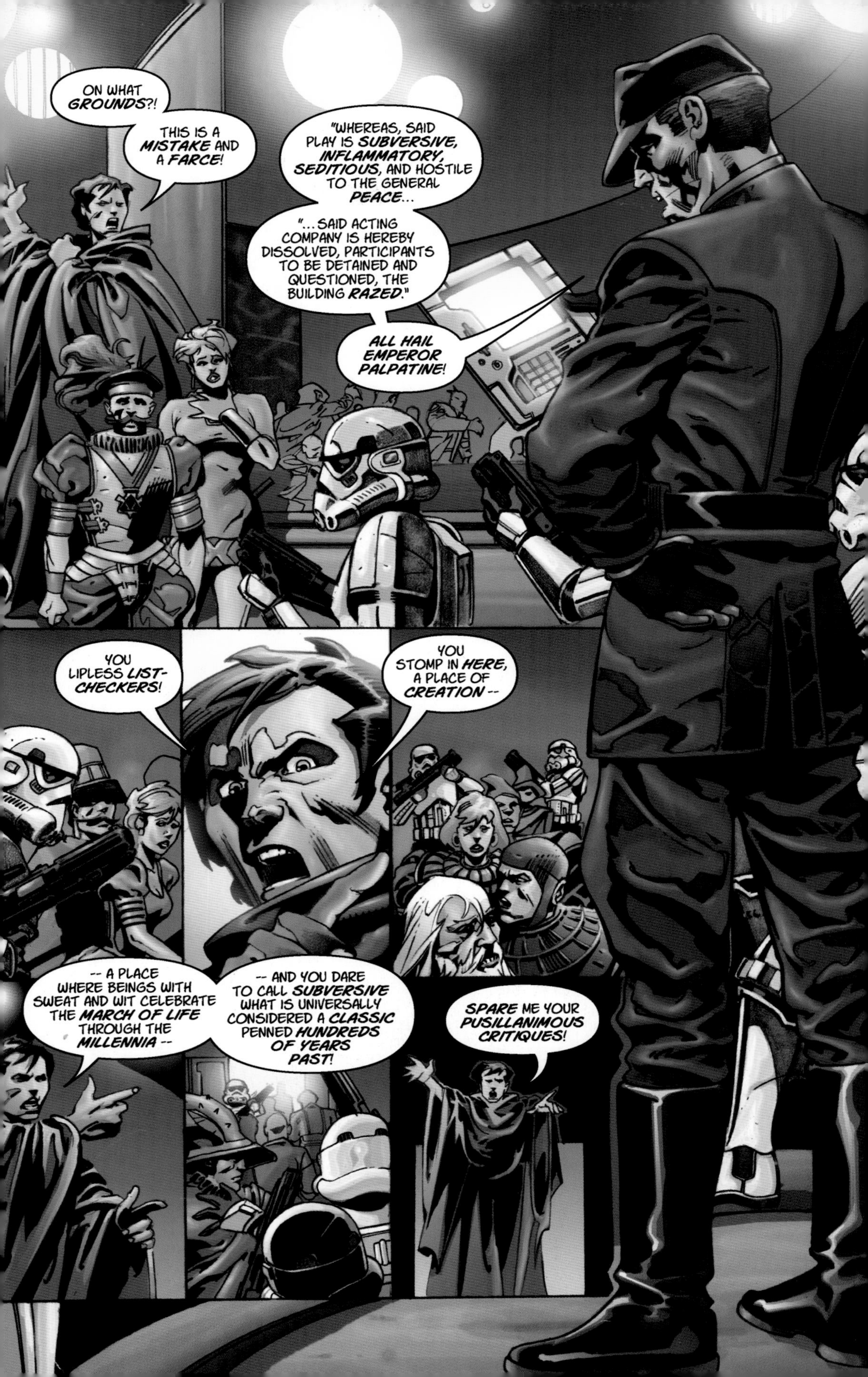

ON WHAT GROUNDS?!
THIS IS A MISTAKE AND A FARCE!
"WHEREAS, SAID PLAY IS SUBVERSIVE, INFLAMMATORY, SEDITIOUS, AND HOSTILE TO THE GENERAL PEACE...
"...SAID ACTING COMPANY IS HEREBY DISSOLVED, PARTICIPANTS TO BE DETAINED AND QUESTIONED, THE BUILDING RAZED."
ALL HAIL EMPEROR PALPATINE!
YOU LIPLESS LIST-CHECKERS!
YOU STOMP IN HERE, A PLACE OF CREATION --
-- A PLACE WHERE BEINGS WITH SWEAT AND WIT CELEBRATE THE MARCH OF LIFE THROUGH THE MILLENNIA --
-- AND YOU DARE TO CALL SUBVERSIVE WHAT IS UNIVERSALLY CONSIDERED A CLASSIC PENNED HUNDREDS OF YEARS PAST!
SPARE ME YOUR PUSILLANIMOUS CRITIQUES!

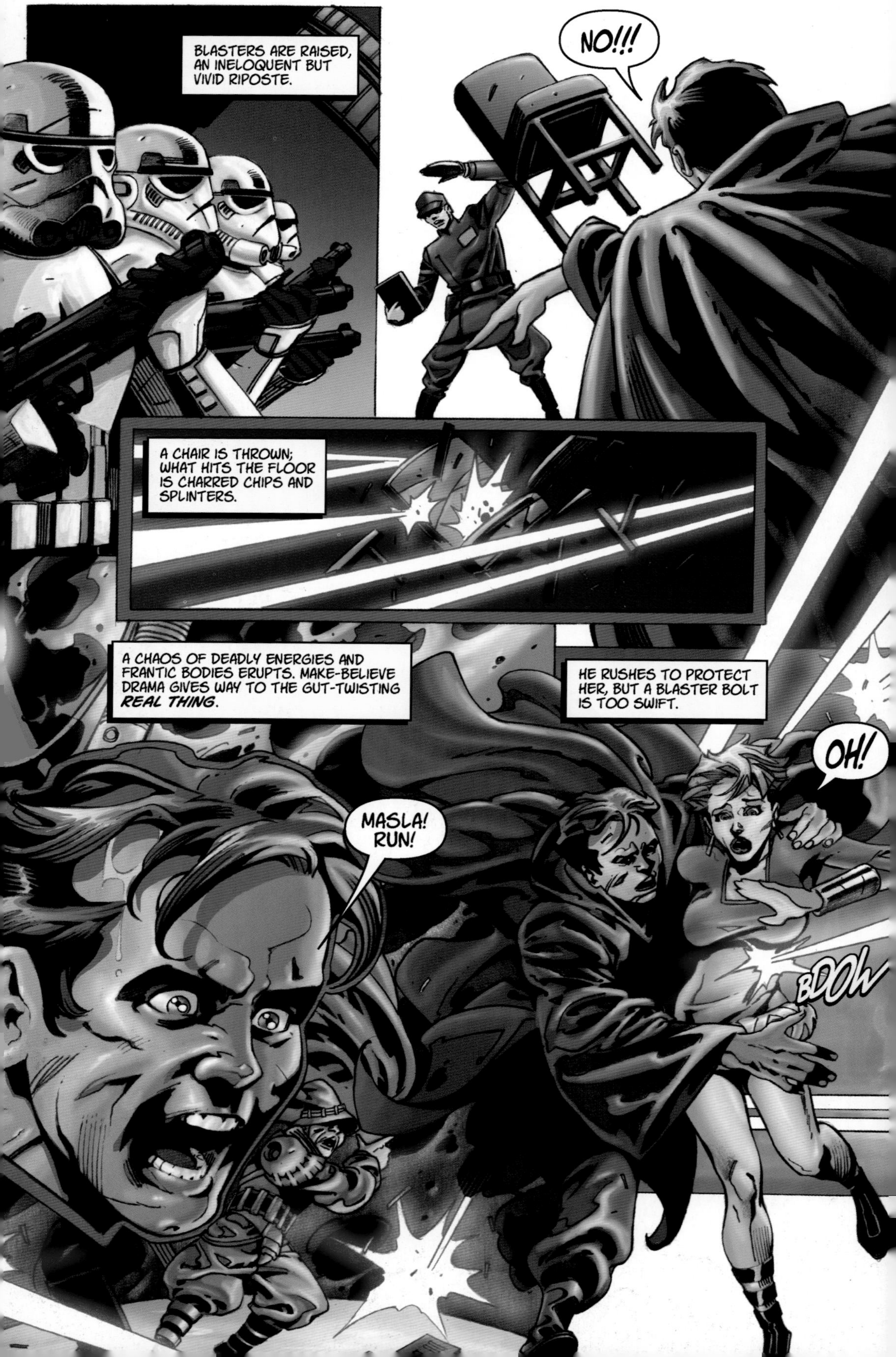
BLASTERS ARE RAISED, AN INELOQUENT BUT VIVID RIPOSTE.
NO!!!
A CHAIR IS THROWN; WHAT HITS THE FLOOR IS CHARRED CHIPS AND SPLINTERS.
A CHAOS OF DEADLY ENERGIES AND FRANTIC BODIES ERUPTS. MAKE-BELIEVE DRAMA GIVES WAY TO THE GUT-TWISTING REAL THING.
MASLA! RUN!
HE RUSHES TO PROTECT HER, BUT A BLASTER BOLT IS TOO SWIFT.
OH!
BDOW

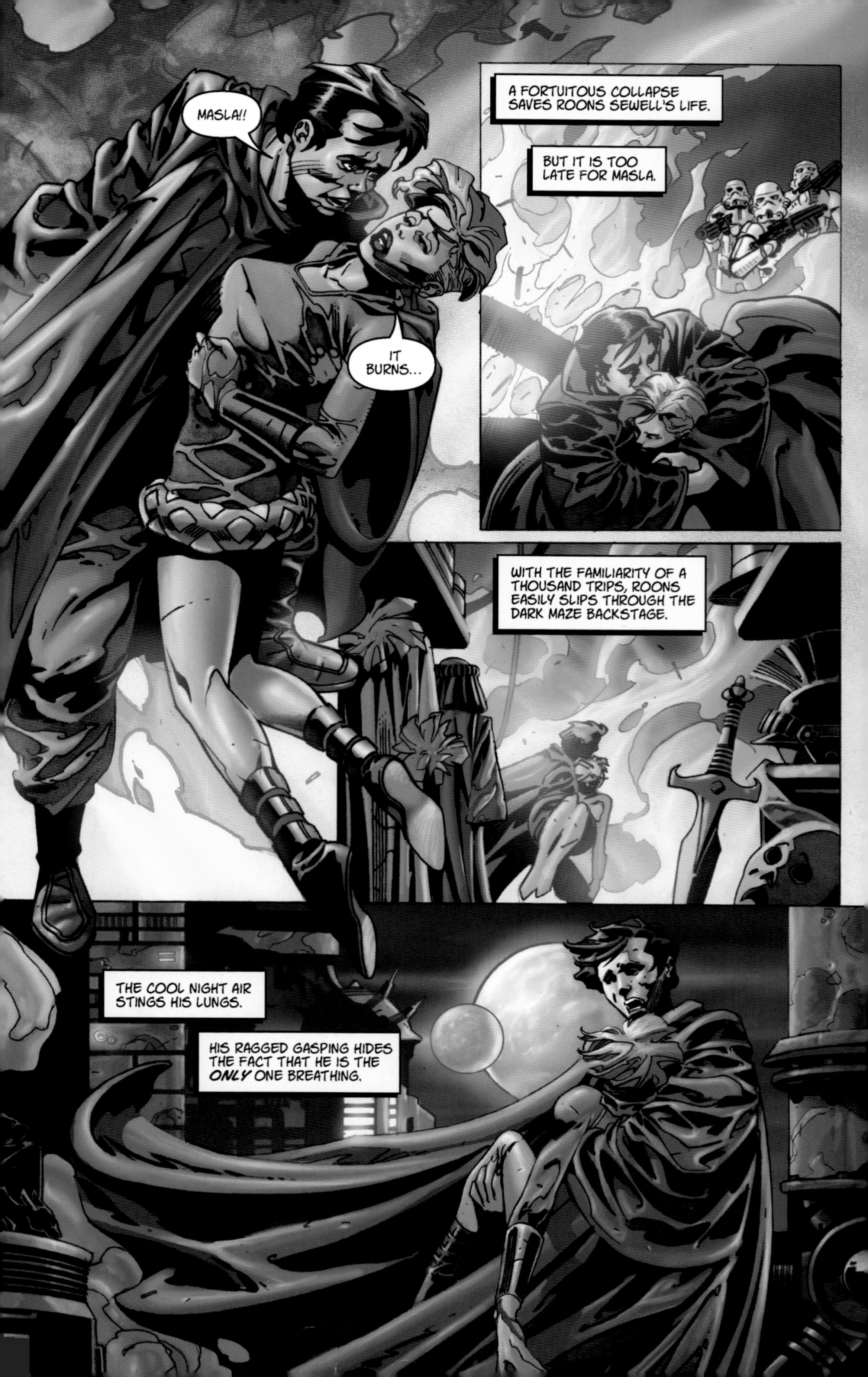
MASLA!!
IT BURNS...
A FORTUITOUS COLLAPSE SAVES ROONS SEWELL'S LIFE.
BUT IT IS TOO LATE FOR MASLA.
WITH THE FAMILIARITY OF A THOUSAND TRIPS, ROONS EASILY SLIPS THROUGH THE DARK MAZE BACKSTAGE.
THE COOL NIGHT AIR STINGS HIS LUNGS.
HIS RAGGED GASPING HIDES THE FACT THAT HE IS THE *ONLY* ONE BREATHING.

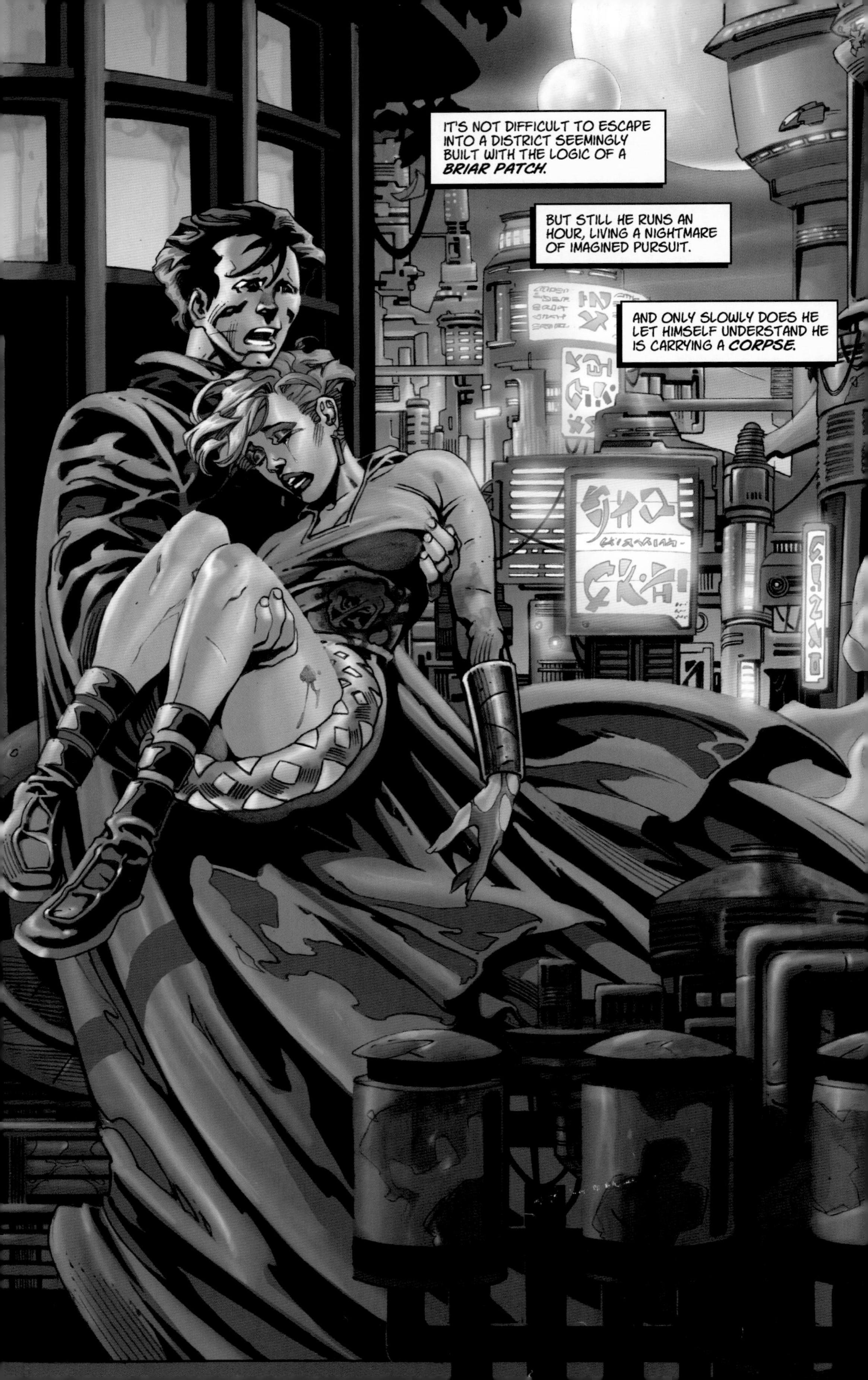
IT'S NOT DIFFICULT TO ESCAPE INTO A DISTRICT SEEMINGLY BUILT WITH THE LOGIC OF A ***BRIAR PATCH***.
BUT STILL HE RUNS AN HOUR, LIVING A NIGHTMARE OF IMAGINED PURSUIT.
AND ONLY SLOWLY DOES HE LET HIMSELF UNDERSTAND HE IS CARRYING A ***CORPSE***.

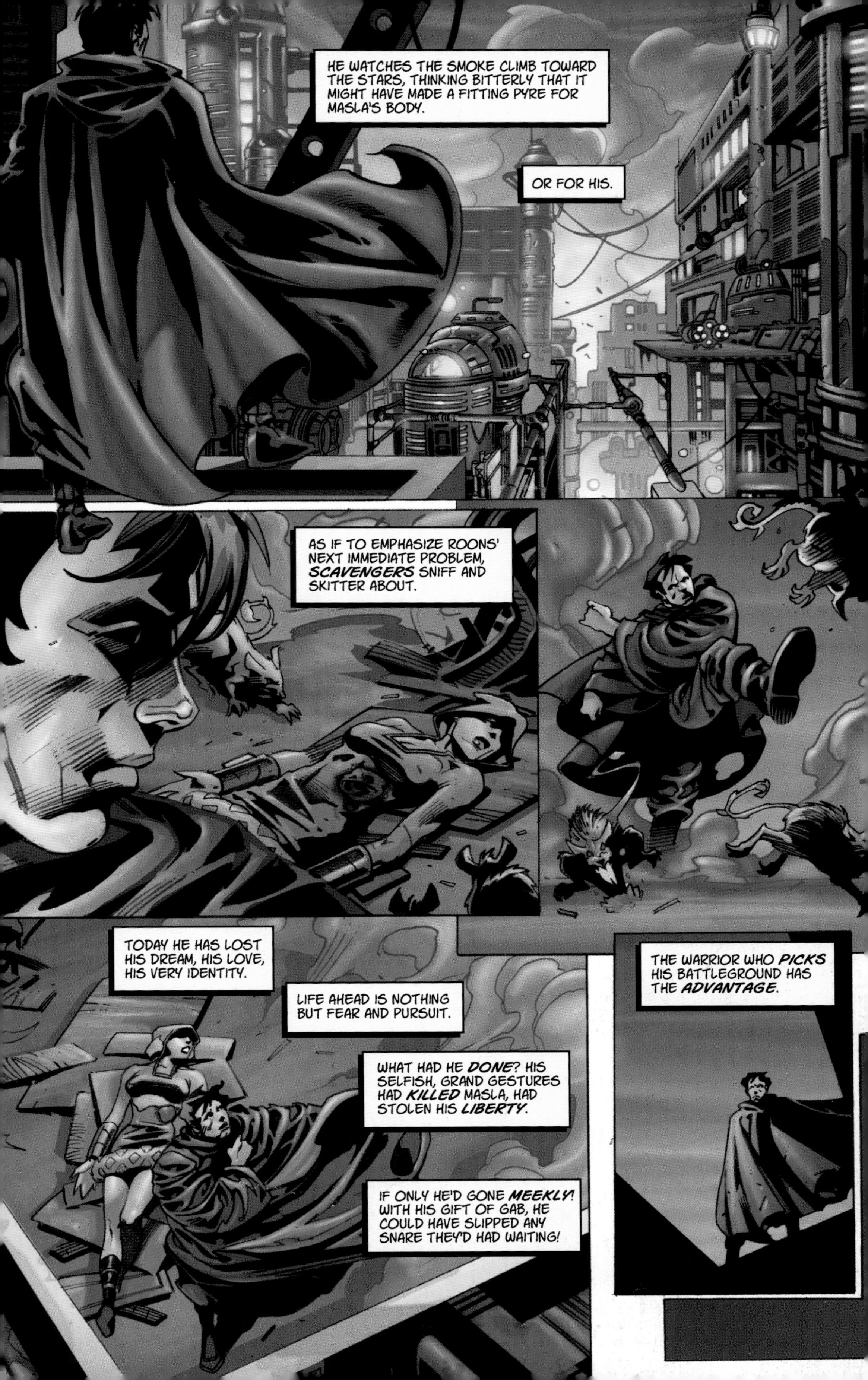
HE WATCHES THE SMOKE CLIMB TOWARD THE STARS, THINKING BITTERLY THAT IT MIGHT HAVE MADE A FITTING PYRE FOR MASLA'S BODY.
OR FOR HIS.
AS IF TO EMPHASIZE ROONS' NEXT IMMEDIATE PROBLEM, SCAVENGERS SNIFF AND SKITTER ABOUT.
TODAY HE HAS LOST HIS DREAM, HIS LOVE, HIS VERY IDENTITY.
LIFE AHEAD IS NOTHING BUT FEAR AND PURSUIT.
WHAT HAD HE DONE? HIS SELFISH, GRAND GESTURES HAD KILLED MASLA, HAD STOLEN HIS LIBERTY.
IF ONLY HE'D GONE MEEKLY! WITH HIS GIFT OF GAB, HE COULD HAVE SLIPPED ANY SNARE THEY'D HAD WAITING!
THE WARRIOR WHO PICKS HIS BATTLEGROUND HAS THE ADVANTAGE.

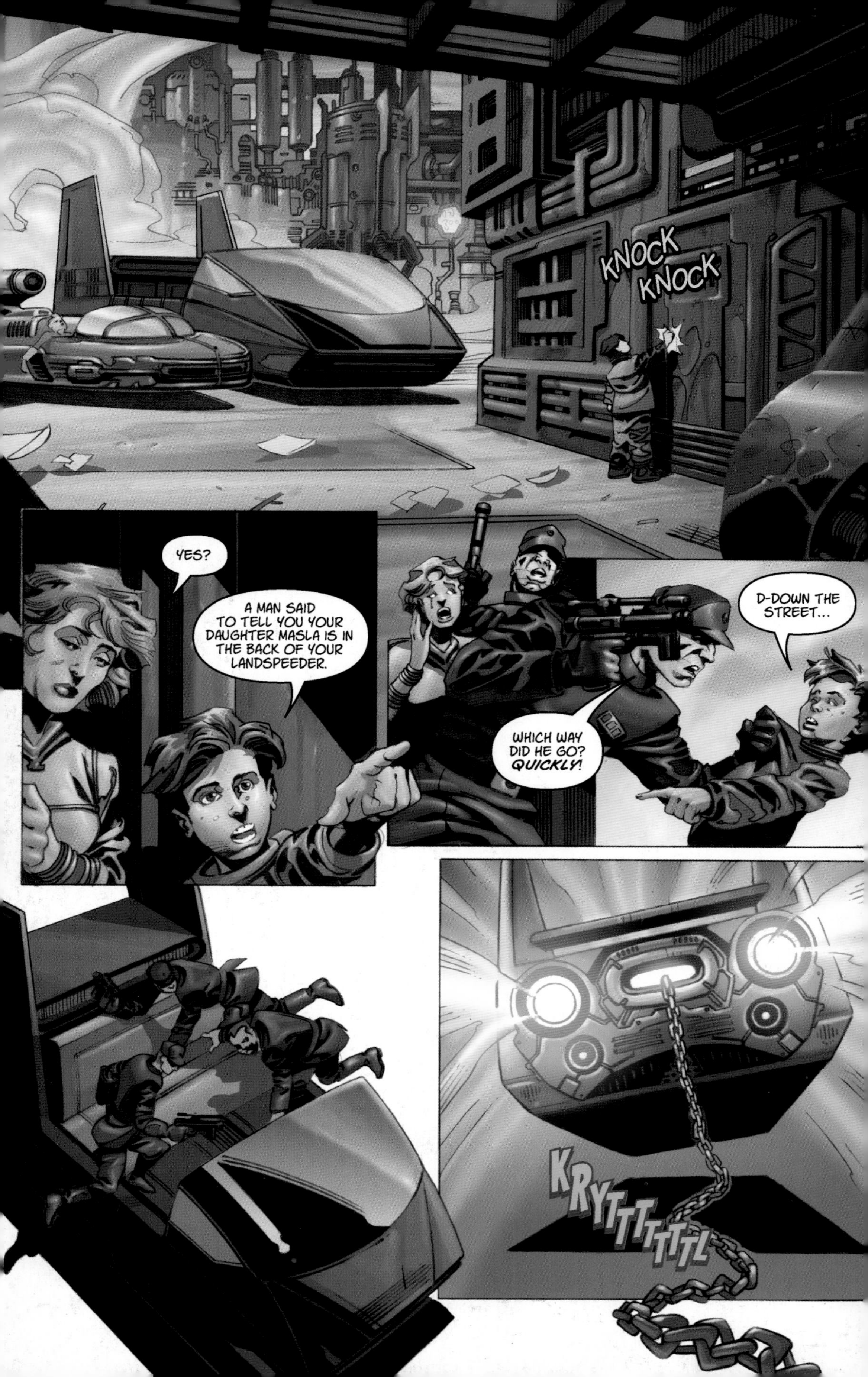
KNOCK
KNOCK
YES?
A MAN SAID TO TELL YOU YOUR DAUGHTER MASLA IS IN THE BACK OF YOUR LANDSPEEDER.
WHICH WAY DID HE GO? QUICKLY!
D-DOWN THE STREET...
KRYTTTTTTTL

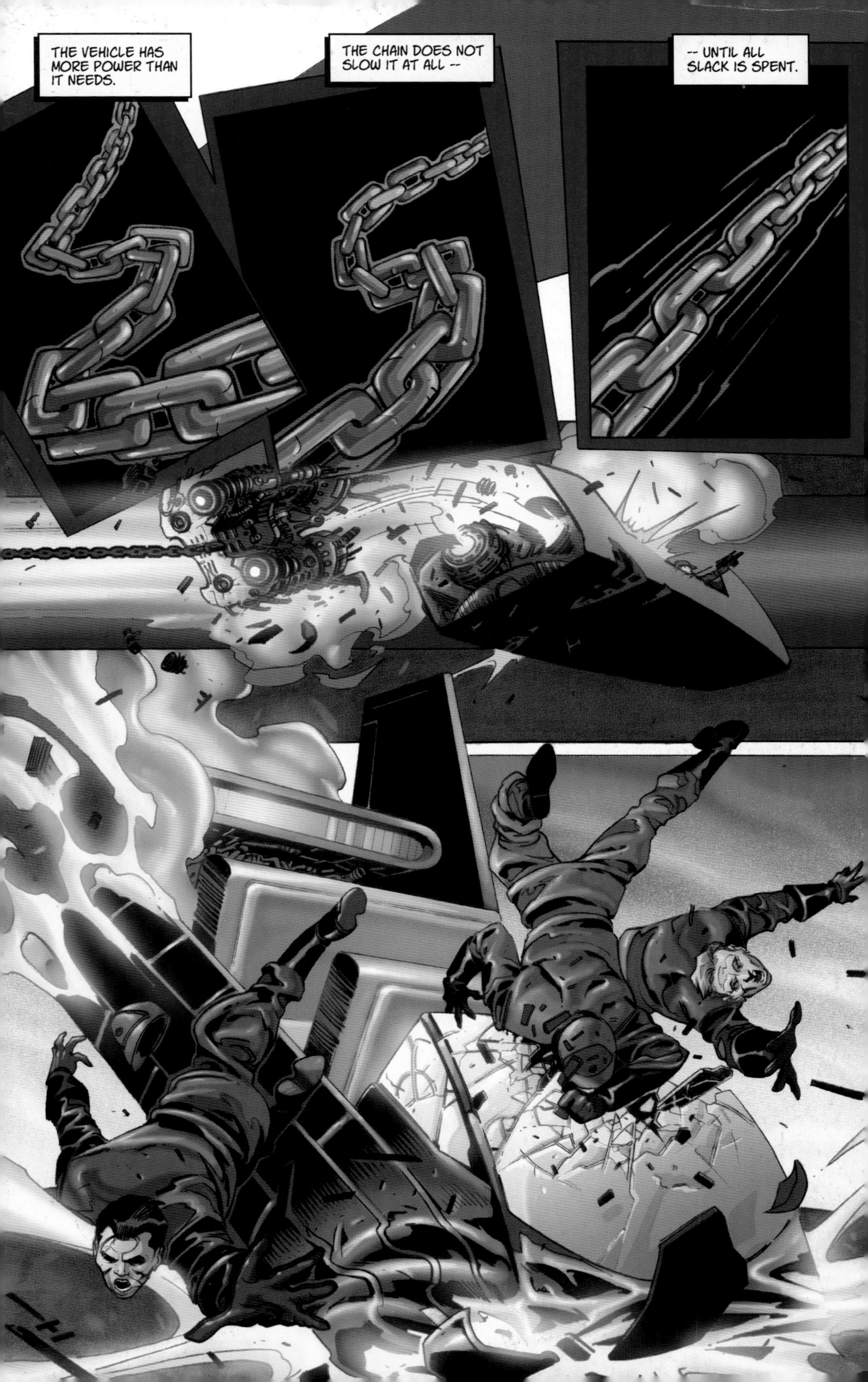
THE VEHICLE HAS MORE POWER THAN IT NEEDS.
THE CHAIN DOES NOT SLOW IT AT ALL --
-- UNTIL ALL SLACK IS SPENT.

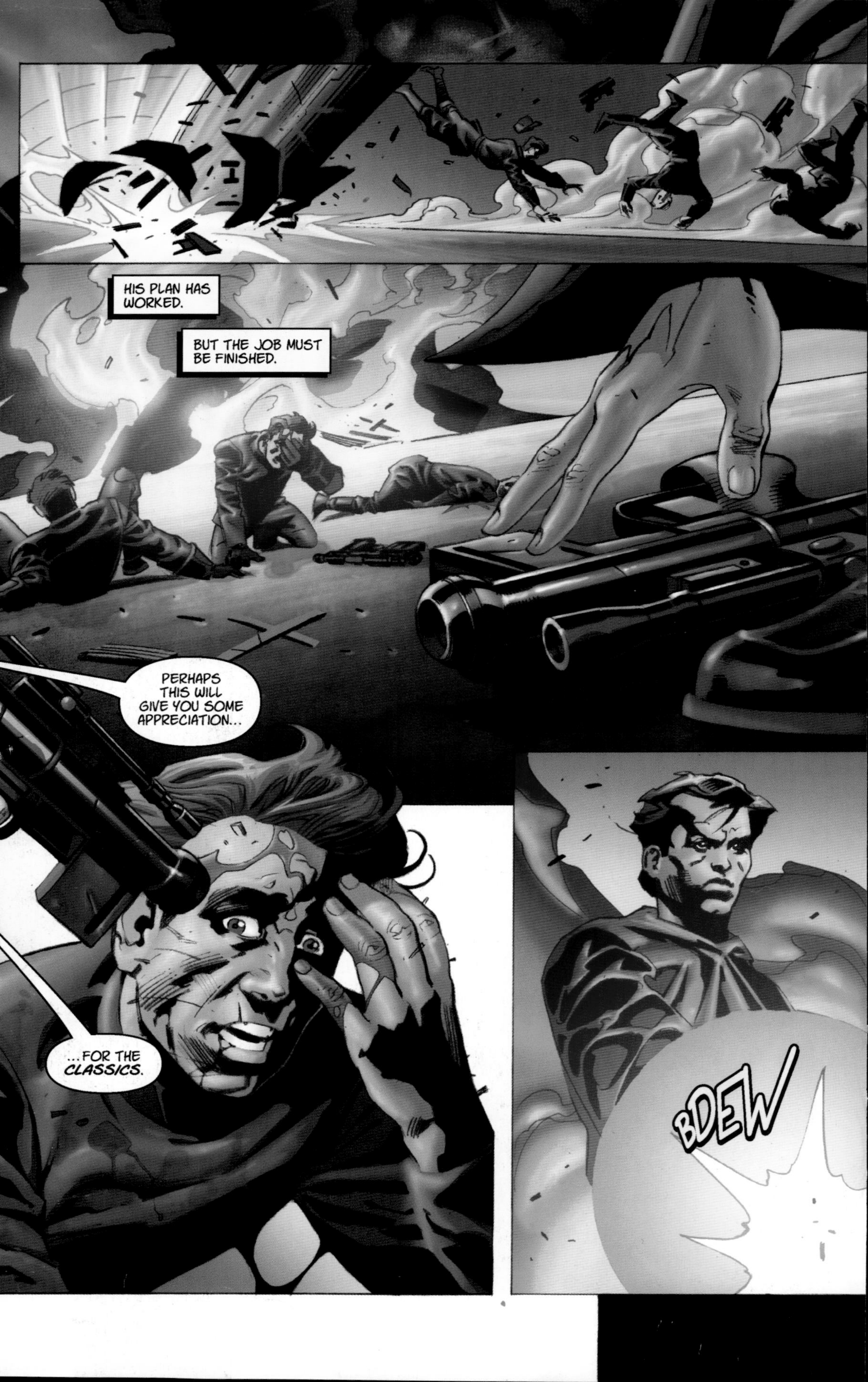
HIS PLAN HAS WORKED.
BUT THE JOB MUST BE FINISHED.
PERHAPS THIS WILL GIVE YOU SOME APPRECIATION...
...FOR THE *CLASSICS*.
BDEW

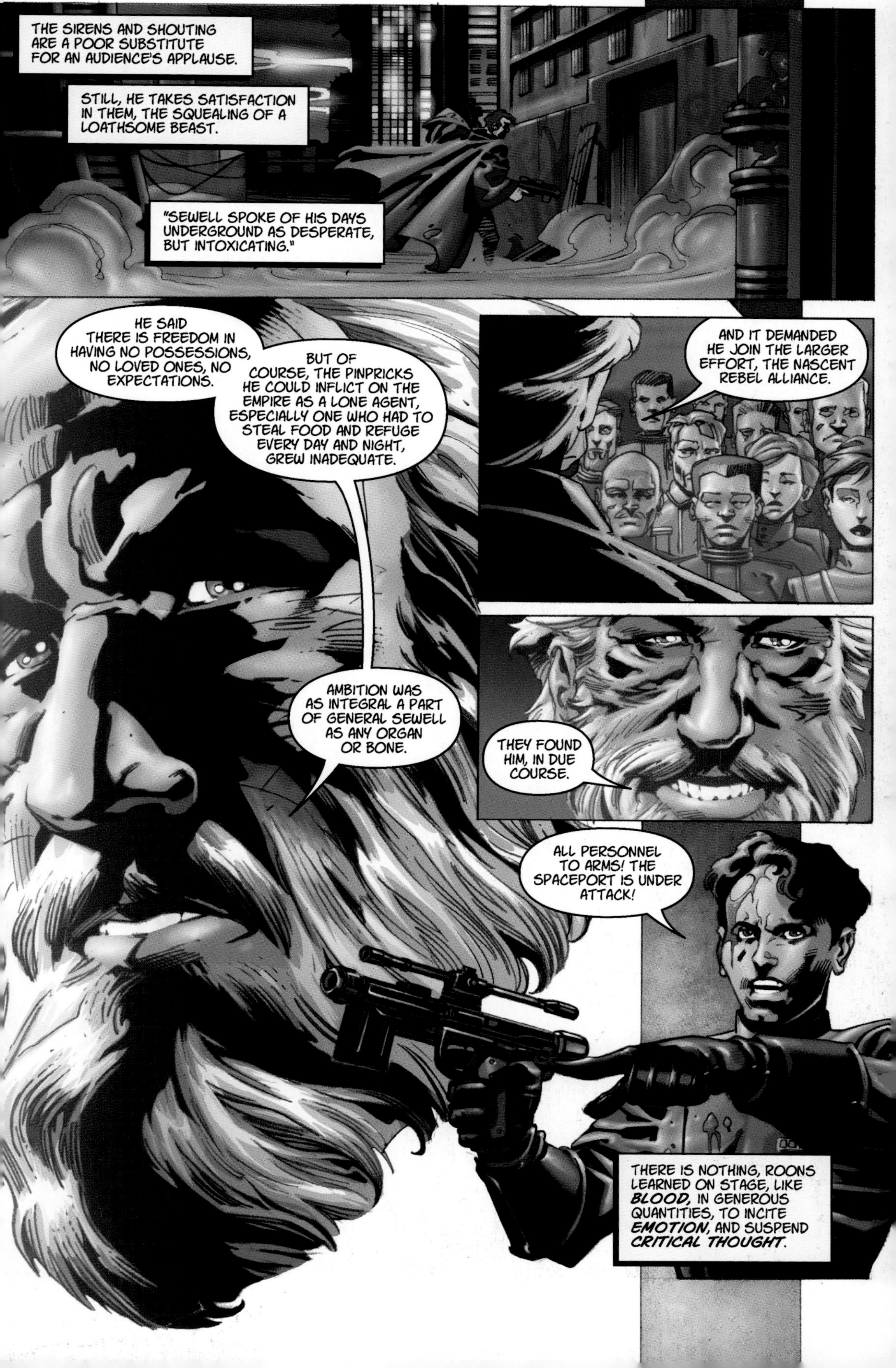
THE SIRENS AND SHOUTING ARE A POOR SUBSTITUTE FOR AN AUDIENCE'S APPLAUSE.
STILL, HE TAKES SATISFACTION IN THEM, THE SQUEALING OF A LOATHSOME BEAST.
"SEWELL SPOKE OF HIS DAYS UNDERGROUND AS DESPERATE, BUT INTOXICATING."
HE SAID THERE IS FREEDOM IN HAVING NO POSSESSIONS, NO LOVED ONES, NO EXPECTATIONS.
BUT OF COURSE, THE PINPRICKS HE COULD INFLICT ON THE EMPIRE AS A LONE AGENT, ESPECIALLY ONE WHO HAD TO STEAL FOOD AND REFUGE EVERY DAY AND NIGHT, GREW INADEQUATE.
AMBITION WAS AS INTEGRAL A PART OF GENERAL SEWELL AS ANY ORGAN OR BONE.
AND IT DEMANDED HE JOIN THE LARGER EFFORT, THE NASCENT REBEL ALLIANCE.
THEY FOUND HIM, IN DUE COURSE.
ALL PERSONNEL TO ARMS! THE SPACEPORT IS UNDER ATTACK!
THERE IS NOTHING, ROONS LEARNED ON STAGE, LIKE ***BLOOD,*** IN GENEROUS QUANTITIES, TO INCITE ***EMOTION,*** AND SUSPEND ***CRITICAL THOUGHT***.

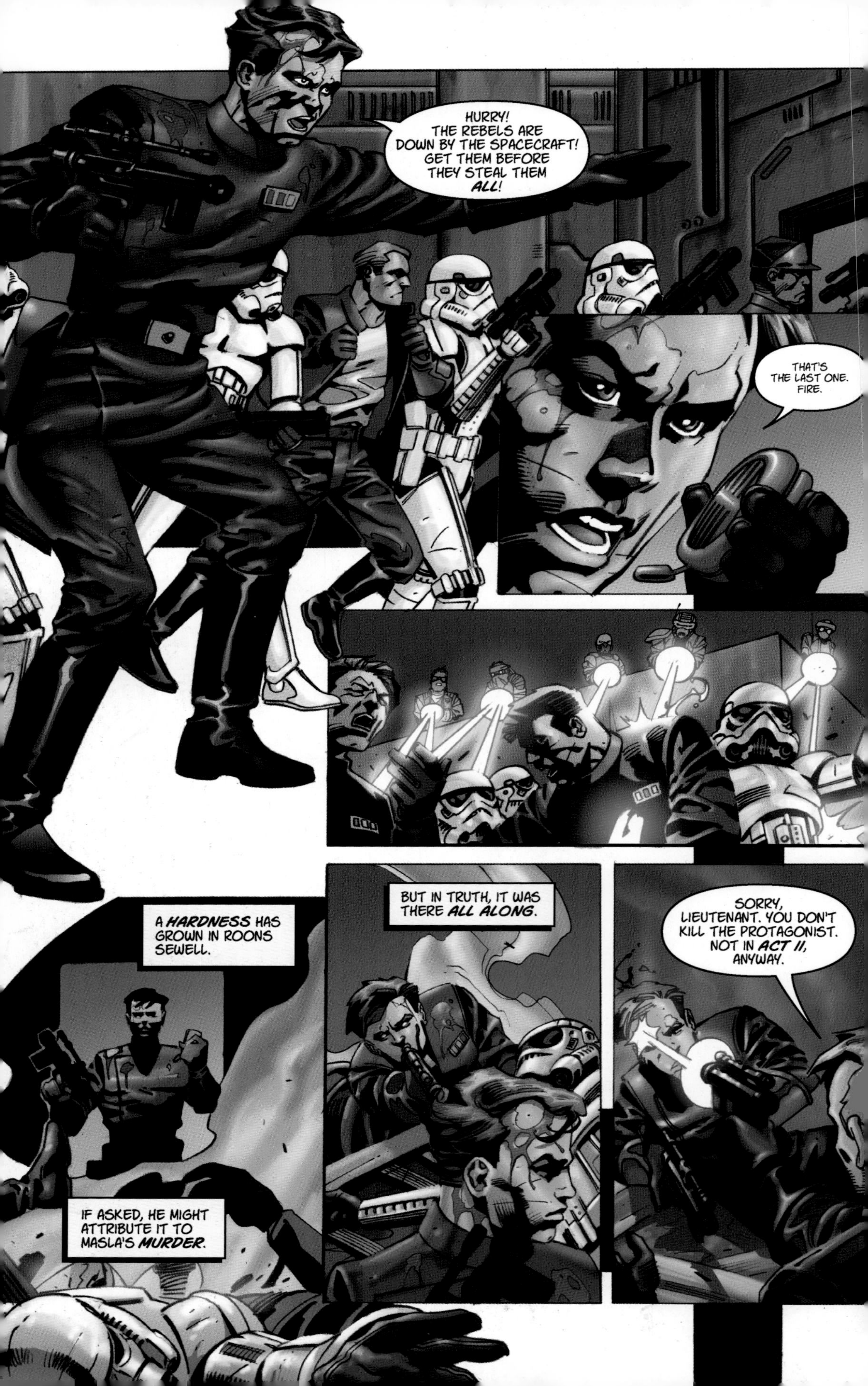
HURRY! THE REBELS ARE DOWN BY THE SPACECRAFT! GET THEM BEFORE THEY STEAL THEM ALL!
THAT'S THE LAST ONE. FIRE.
A HARDNESS HAS GROWN IN ROONS SEWELL.
IF ASKED, HE MIGHT ATTRIBUTE IT TO MASLA'S MURDER.
BUT IN TRUTH, IT WAS THERE ALL ALONG.
SORRY, LIEUTENANT. YOU DON'T KILL THE PROTAGONIST. NOT IN ACT II, ANYWAY.

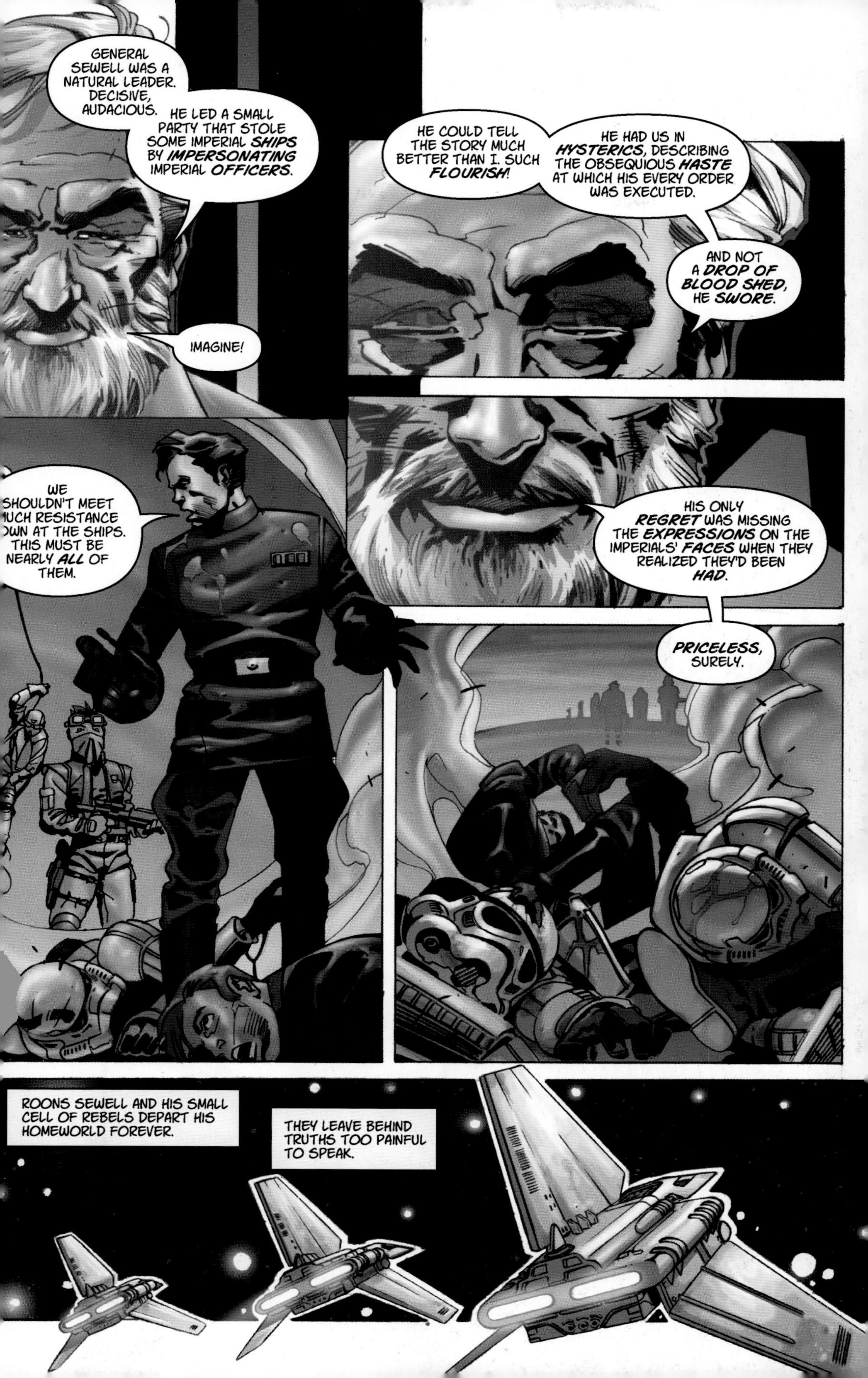
GENERAL SEWELL WAS A NATURAL LEADER. DECISIVE, AUDACIOUS.
HE LED A SMALL PARTY THAT STOLE SOME IMPERIAL SHIPS BY IMPERSONATING IMPERIAL OFFICERS.
IMAGINE!
HE COULD TELL THE STORY MUCH BETTER THAN I. SUCH FLOURISH!
HE HAD US IN HYSTERICS, DESCRIBING THE OBSEQUIOUS HASTE AT WHICH HIS EVERY ORDER WAS EXECUTED.
AND NOT A DROP OF BLOOD SHED, HE SWORE.
WE SHOULDN'T MEET MUCH RESISTANCE DOWN AT THE SHIPS. THIS MUST BE NEARLY ALL OF THEM.
HIS ONLY REGRET WAS MISSING THE EXPRESSIONS ON THE IMPERIALS' FACES WHEN THEY REALIZED THEY'D BEEN HAD.
PRICELESS, SURELY.
ROONS SEWELL AND HIS SMALL CELL OF REBELS DEPART HIS HOMEWORLD FOREVER.
THEY LEAVE BEHIND TRUTHS TOO PAINFUL TO SPEAK.

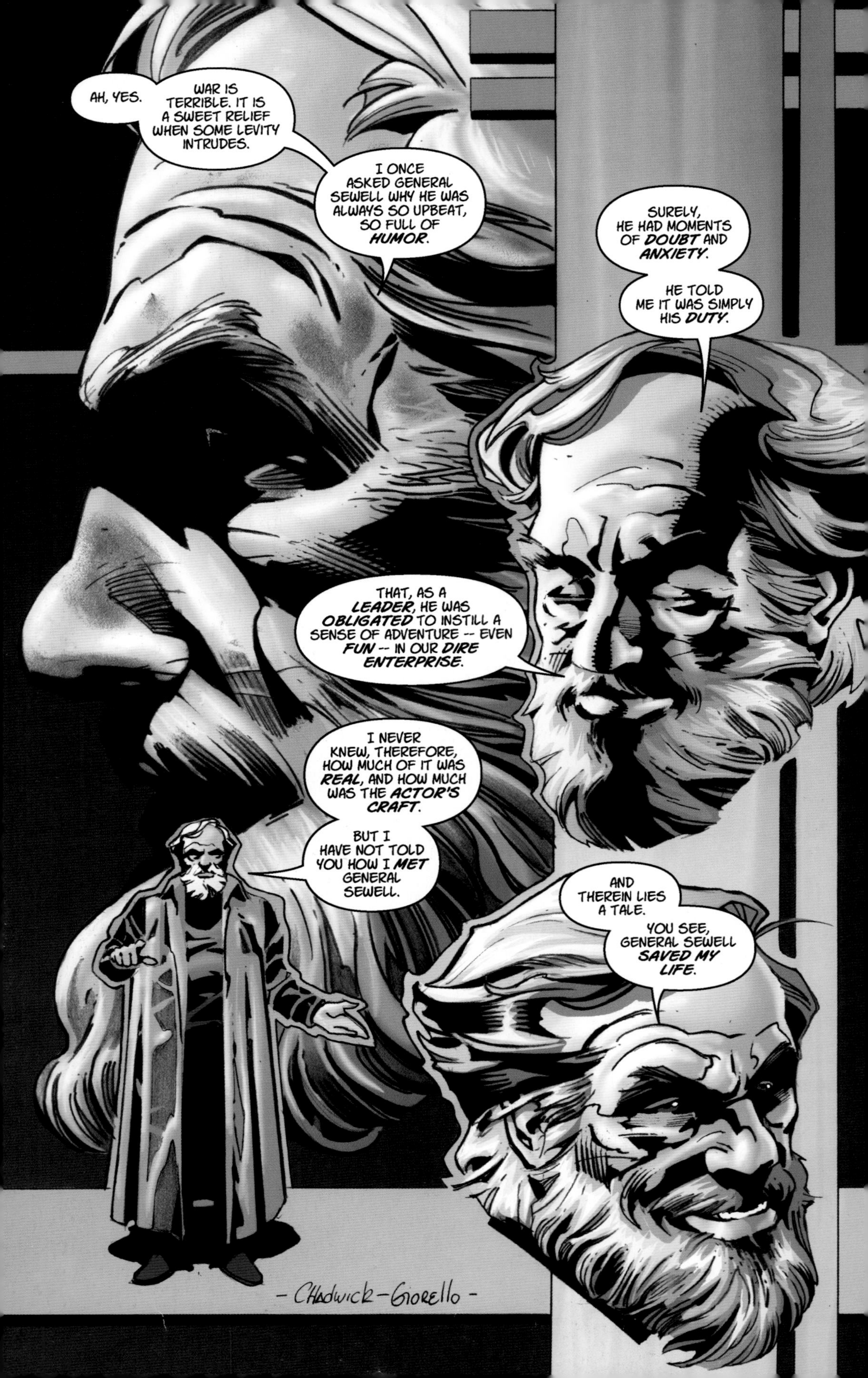
AH, YES.
WAR IS TERRIBLE. IT IS A SWEET RELIEF WHEN SOME LEVITY INTRUDES.
I ONCE ASKED GENERAL SEWELL WHY HE WAS ALWAYS SO UPBEAT, SO FULL OF ***HUMOR***.
SURELY, HE HAD MOMENTS OF ***DOUBT*** AND ***ANXIETY***.
HE TOLD ME IT WAS SIMPLY HIS ***DUTY***.
THAT, AS A ***LEADER***, HE WAS ***OBLIGATED*** TO INSTILL A SENSE OF ADVENTURE -- EVEN ***FUN*** -- IN OUR ***DIRE ENTERPRISE***.
I NEVER KNEW, THEREFORE, HOW MUCH OF IT WAS ***REAL***, AND HOW MUCH WAS THE ***ACTOR'S CRAFT***.
BUT I HAVE NOT TOLD YOU HOW I ***MET*** GENERAL SEWELL.
AND THEREIN LIES A TALE.
YOU SEE, GENERAL SEWELL ***SAVED MY LIFE***.
-CHADWICK-GIORELLO-

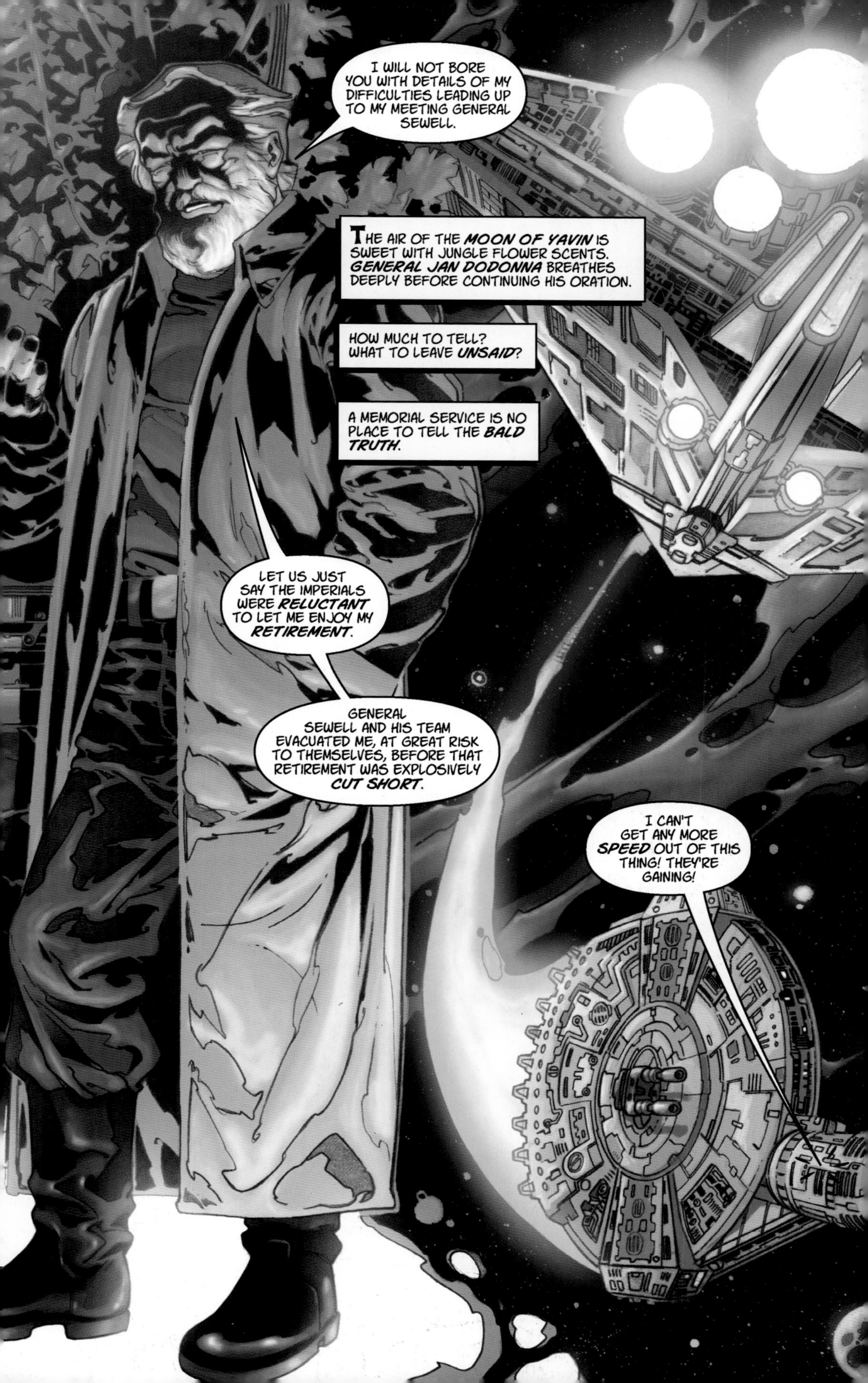
I WILL NOT BORE YOU WITH DETAILS OF MY DIFFICULTIES LEADING UP TO MY MEETING GENERAL SEWELL.
THE AIR OF THE MOON OF YAVIN IS SWEET WITH JUNGLE FLOWER SCENTS. GENERAL JAN DODONNA BREATHES DEEPLY BEFORE CONTINUING HIS ORATION.
HOW MUCH TO TELL? WHAT TO LEAVE UNSAID?
A MEMORIAL SERVICE IS NO PLACE TO TELL THE BALD TRUTH.
LET US JUST SAY THE IMPERIALS WERE RELUCTANT TO LET ME ENJOY MY RETIREMENT.
GENERAL SEWELL AND HIS TEAM EVACUATED ME, AT GREAT RISK TO THEMSELVES, BEFORE THAT RETIREMENT WAS EXPLOSIVELY CUT SHORT.
I CAN'T GET ANY MORE SPEED OUT OF THIS THING! THEY'RE GAINING!

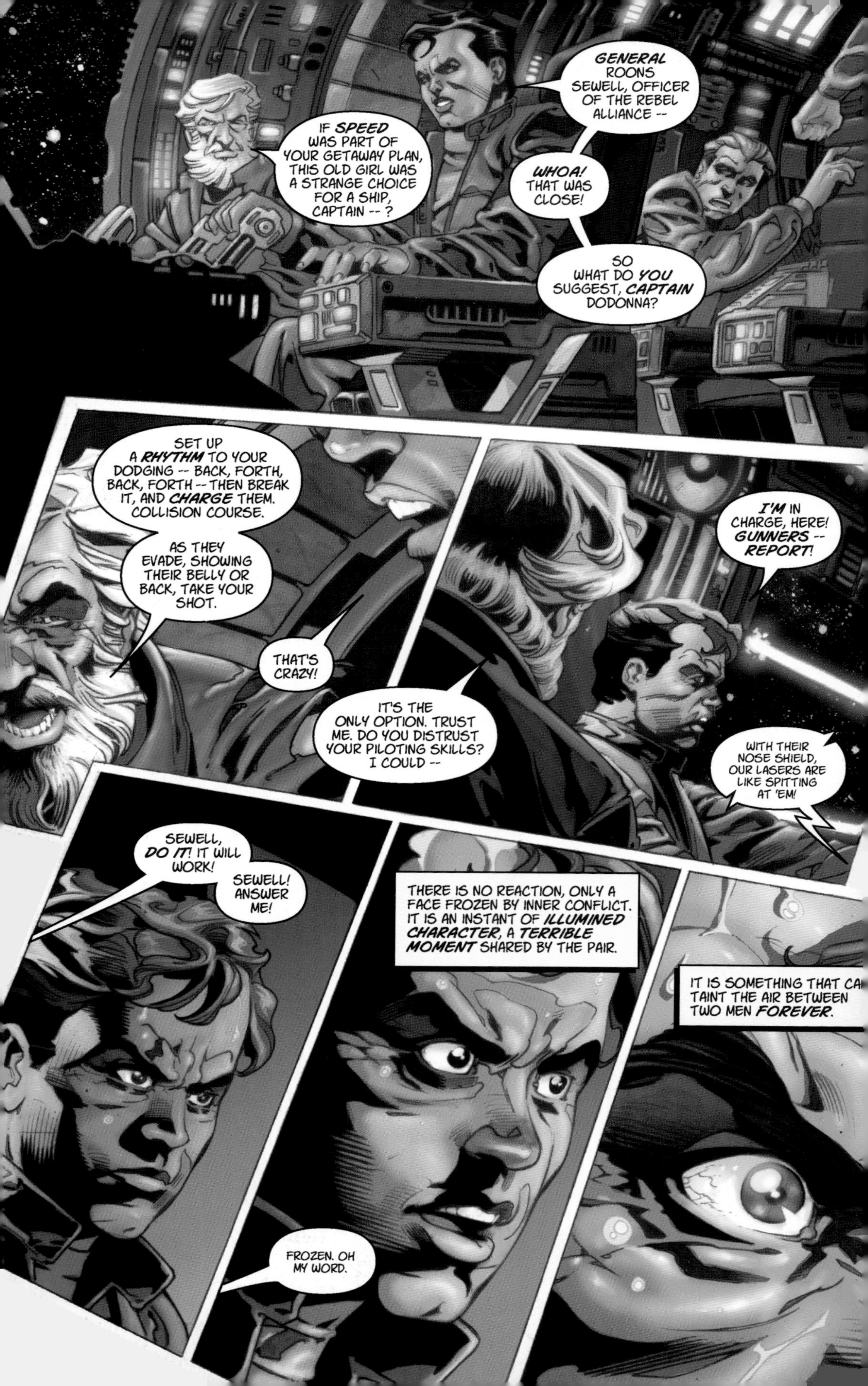
IF SPEED WAS PART OF YOUR GETAWAY PLAN, THIS OLD GIRL WAS A STRANGE CHOICE FOR A SHIP, CAPTAIN -- ?
GENERAL ROONS SEWELL, OFFICER OF THE REBEL ALLIANCE --
WHOA! THAT WAS CLOSE!
SO WHAT DO YOU SUGGEST, CAPTAIN DODONNA?
SET UP A RHYTHM TO YOUR DODGING -- BACK, FORTH, BACK, FORTH -- THEN BREAK IT, AND CHARGE THEM. COLLISION COURSE.
AS THEY EVADE, SHOWING THEIR BELLY OR BACK, TAKE YOUR SHOT.
THAT'S CRAZY!
IT'S THE ONLY OPTION. TRUST ME. DO YOU DISTRUST YOUR PILOTING SKILLS? I COULD --
I'M IN CHARGE, HERE! GUNNERS -- REPORT!
WITH THEIR NOSE SHIELD, OUR LASERS ARE LIKE SPITTING AT 'EM!
SEWELL, DO IT! IT WILL WORK!
SEWELL! ANSWER ME!
FROZEN. OH MY WORD.
THERE IS NO REACTION, ONLY A FACE FROZEN BY INNER CONFLICT. IT IS AN INSTANT OF ILLUMINED CHARACTER, A TERRIBLE MOMENT SHARED BY THE PAIR.
IT IS SOMETHING THAT CA TAINT THE AIR BETWEEN TWO MEN FOREVER.

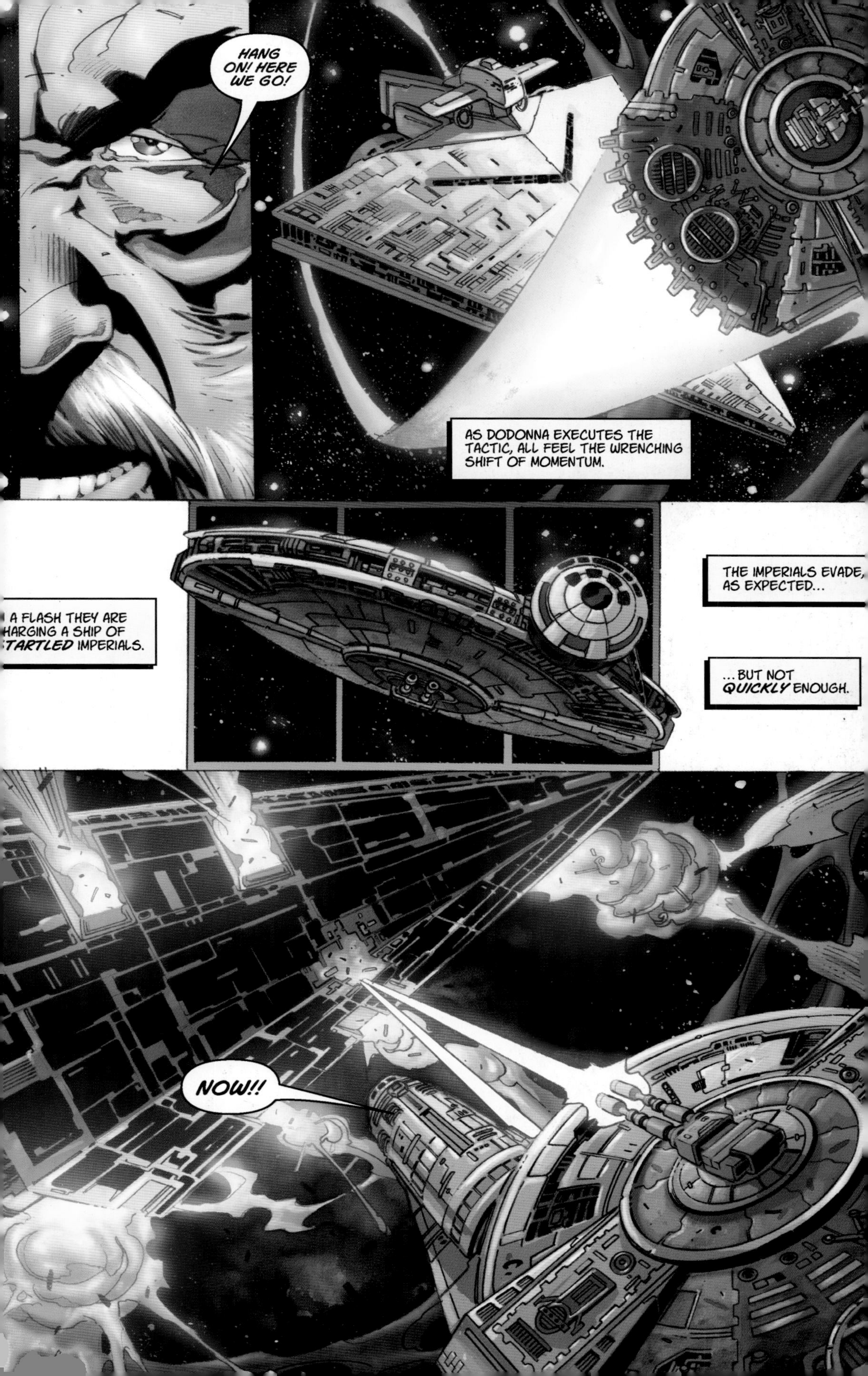
HANG ON! HERE WE GO!
AS DODONNA EXECUTES THE TACTIC, ALL FEEL THE WRENCHING SHIFT OF MOMENTUM.
A FLASH THEY ARE HARGING A SHIP OF TARTLED IMPERIALS.
THE IMPERIALS EVADE, AS EXPECTED...
...BUT NOT QUICKLY ENOUGH.
NOW!!

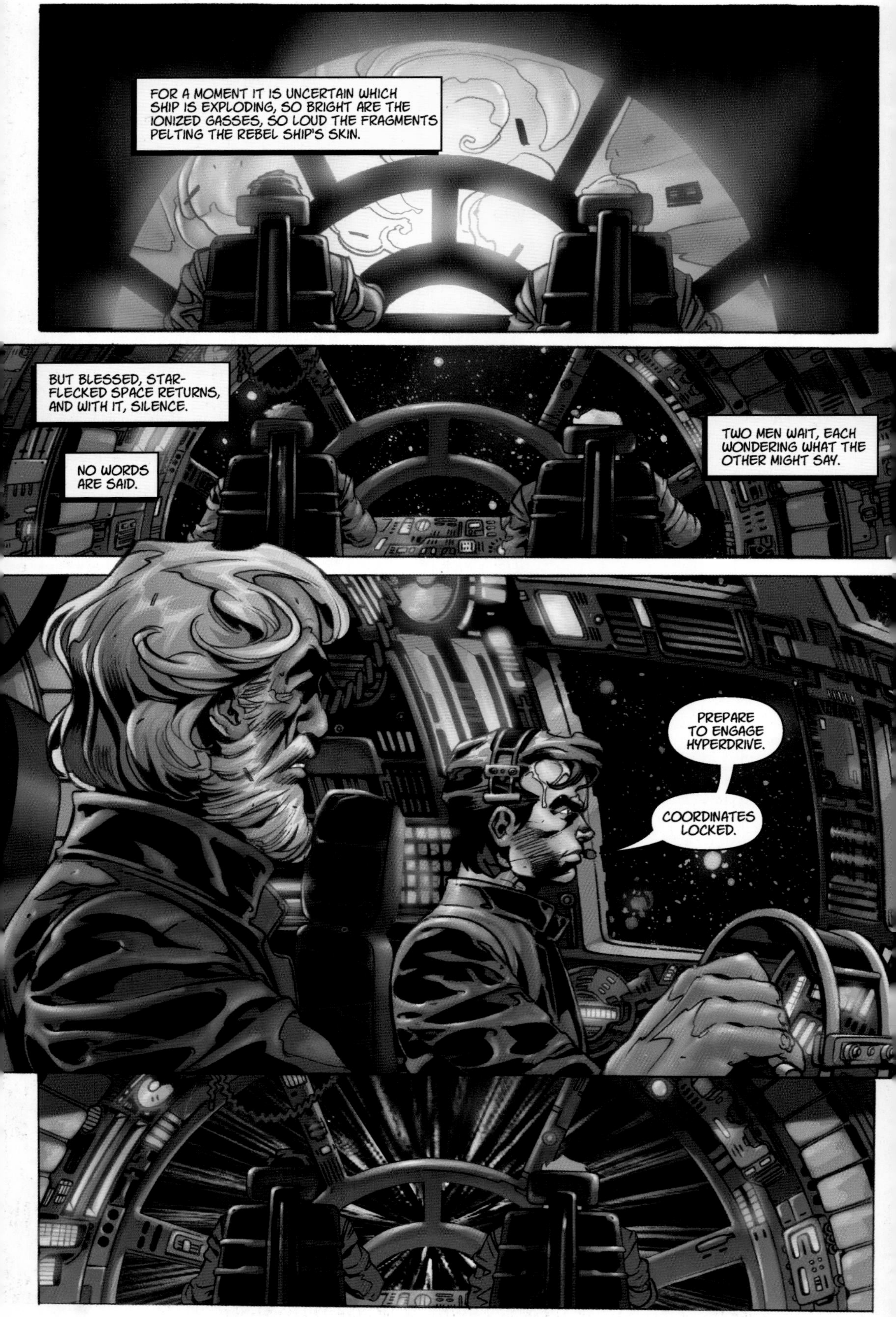
FOR A MOMENT IT IS UNCERTAIN WHICH SHIP IS EXPLODING, SO BRIGHT ARE THE IONIZED GASSES, SO LOUD THE FRAGMENTS PELTING THE REBEL SHIP'S SKIN.
BUT BLESSED, STAR-FLECKED SPACE RETURNS, AND WITH IT, SILENCE.
NO WORDS ARE SAID.
TWO MEN WAIT, EACH WONDERING WHAT THE OTHER MIGHT SAY.
PREPARE TO ENGAGE HYPERDRIVE.
COORDINATES LOCKED.

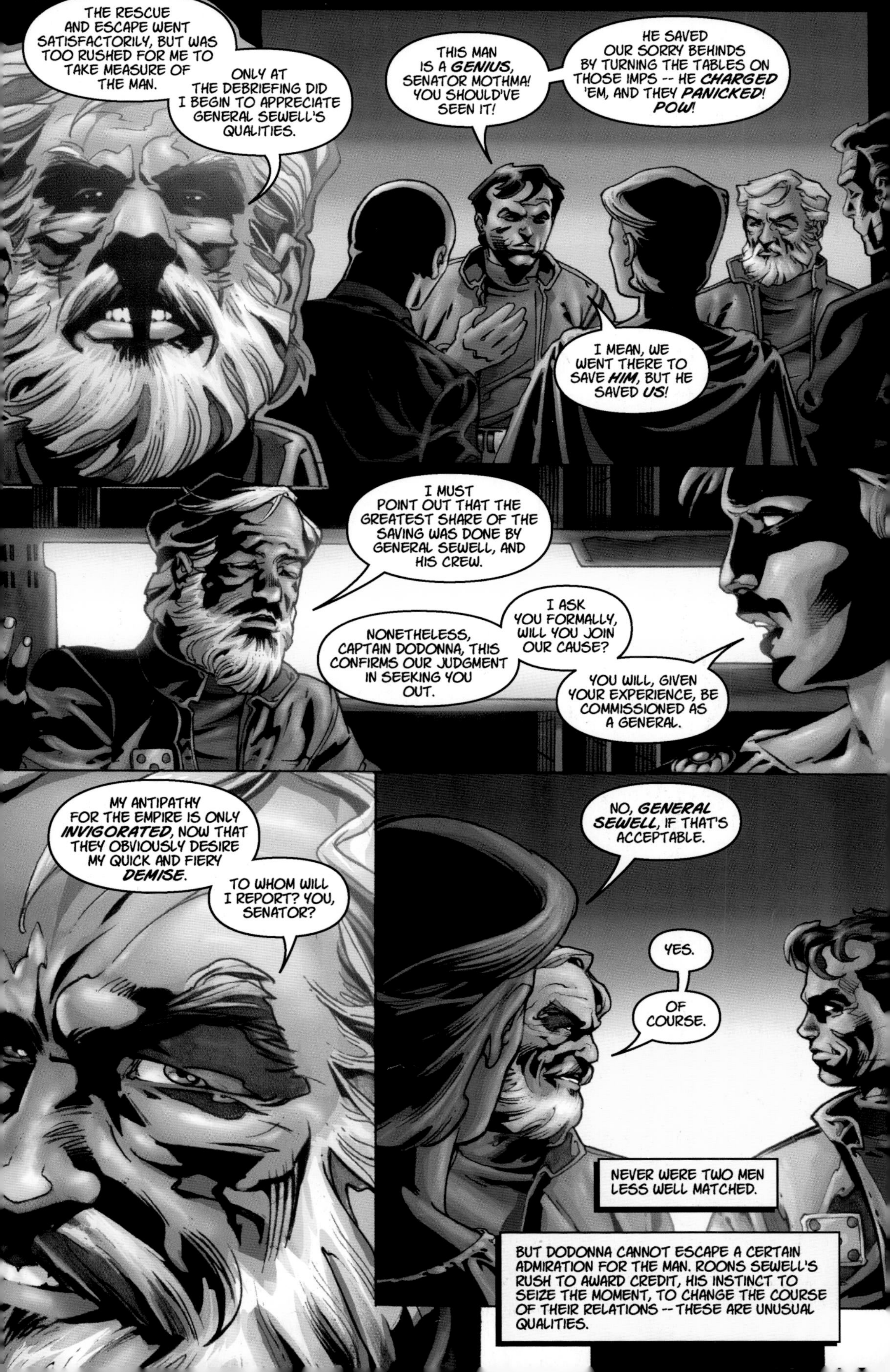
THE RESCUE AND ESCAPE WENT SATISFACTORILY, BUT WAS TOO RUSHED FOR ME TO TAKE MEASURE OF THE MAN.
ONLY AT THE DEBRIEFING DID I BEGIN TO APPRECIATE GENERAL SEWELL'S QUALITIES.
THIS MAN IS A GENIUS, SENATOR MOTHMA! YOU SHOULD'VE SEEN IT!
HE SAVED OUR SORRY BEHINDS BY TURNING THE TABLES ON THOSE IMPS -- HE CHARGED 'EM, AND THEY PANICKED! POW!
I MEAN, WE WENT THERE TO SAVE HIM, BUT HE SAVED US!
I MUST POINT OUT THAT THE GREATEST SHARE OF THE SAVING WAS DONE BY GENERAL SEWELL, AND HIS CREW.
NONETHELESS, CAPTAIN DODONNA, THIS CONFIRMS OUR JUDGMENT IN SEEKING YOU OUT.
I ASK YOU FORMALLY, WILL YOU JOIN OUR CAUSE?
YOU WILL, GIVEN YOUR EXPERIENCE, BE COMMISSIONED AS A GENERAL.
MY ANTIPATHY FOR THE EMPIRE IS ONLY INVIGORATED, NOW THAT THEY OBVIOUSLY DESIRE MY QUICK AND FIERY DEMISE.
TO WHOM WILL I REPORT? YOU, SENATOR?
NO, GENERAL SEWELL, IF THAT'S ACCEPTABLE.
YES.
OF COURSE.
NEVER WERE TWO MEN LESS WELL MATCHED.
BUT DODONNA CANNOT ESCAPE A CERTAIN ADMIRATION FOR THE MAN. ROONS SEWELL'S RUSH TO AWARD CREDIT, HIS INSTINCT TO SEIZE THE MOMENT, TO CHANGE THE COURSE OF THEIR RELATIONS -- THESE ARE UNUSUAL QUALITIES.

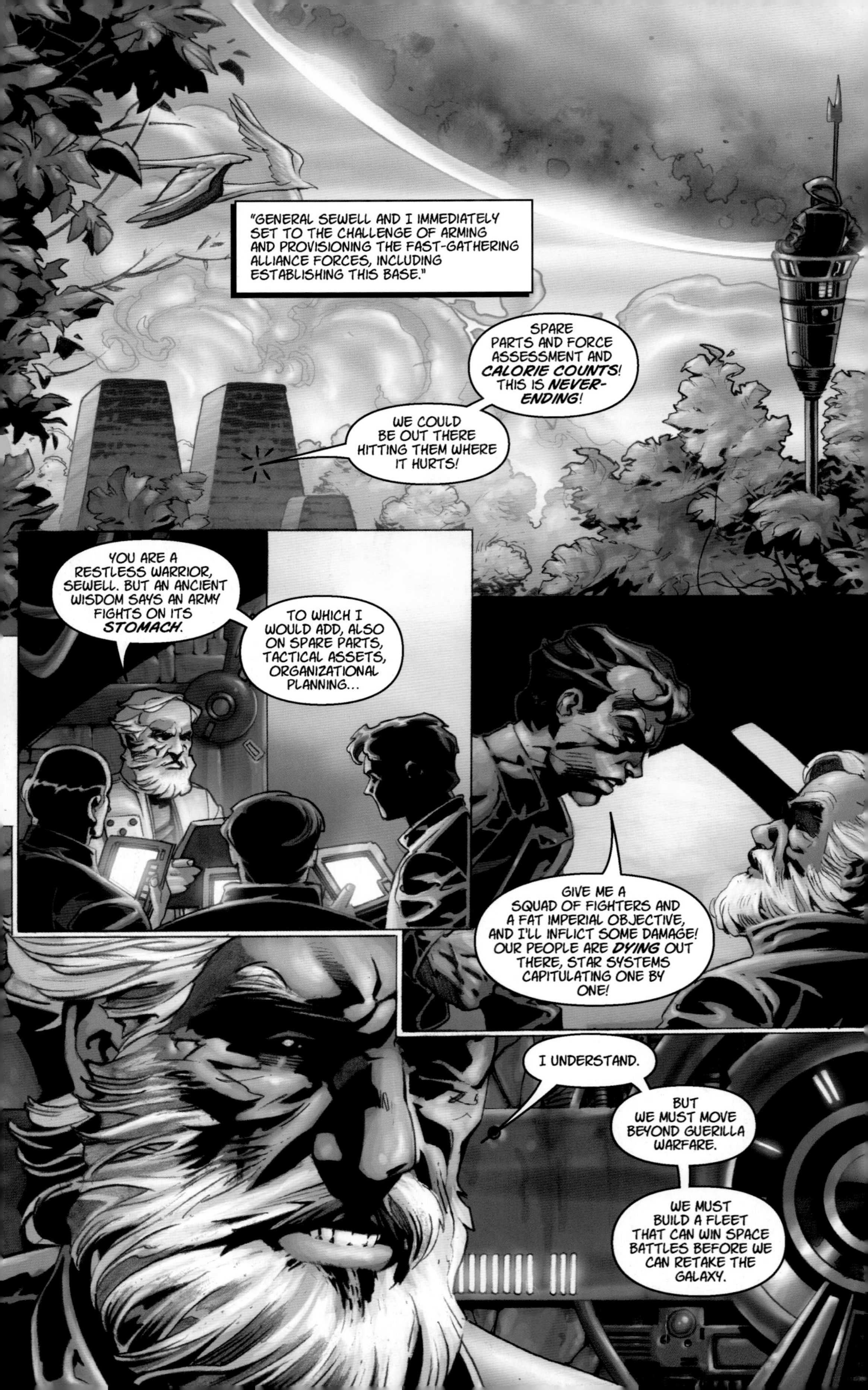
"GENERAL SEWELL AND I IMMEDIATELY SET TO THE CHALLENGE OF ARMING AND PROVISIONING THE FAST-GATHERING ALLIANCE FORCES, INCLUDING ESTABLISHING THIS BASE."
SPARE PARTS AND FORCE ASSESSMENT AND CALORIE COUNTS! THIS IS NEVER-ENDING!
WE COULD BE OUT THERE HITTING THEM WHERE IT HURTS!
YOU ARE A RESTLESS WARRIOR, SEWELL. BUT AN ANCIENT WISDOM SAYS AN ARMY FIGHTS ON ITS STOMACH.
TO WHICH I WOULD ADD, ALSO ON SPARE PARTS, TACTICAL ASSETS, ORGANIZATIONAL PLANNING...
GIVE ME A SQUAD OF FIGHTERS AND A FAT IMPERIAL OBJECTIVE, AND I'LL INFLICT SOME DAMAGE! OUR PEOPLE ARE DYING OUT THERE, STAR SYSTEMS CAPITULATING ONE BY ONE!
I UNDERSTAND.
BUT WE MUST MOVE BEYOND GUERILLA WARFARE.
WE MUST BUILD A FLEET THAT CAN WIN SPACE BATTLES BEFORE WE CAN RETAKE THE GALAXY.

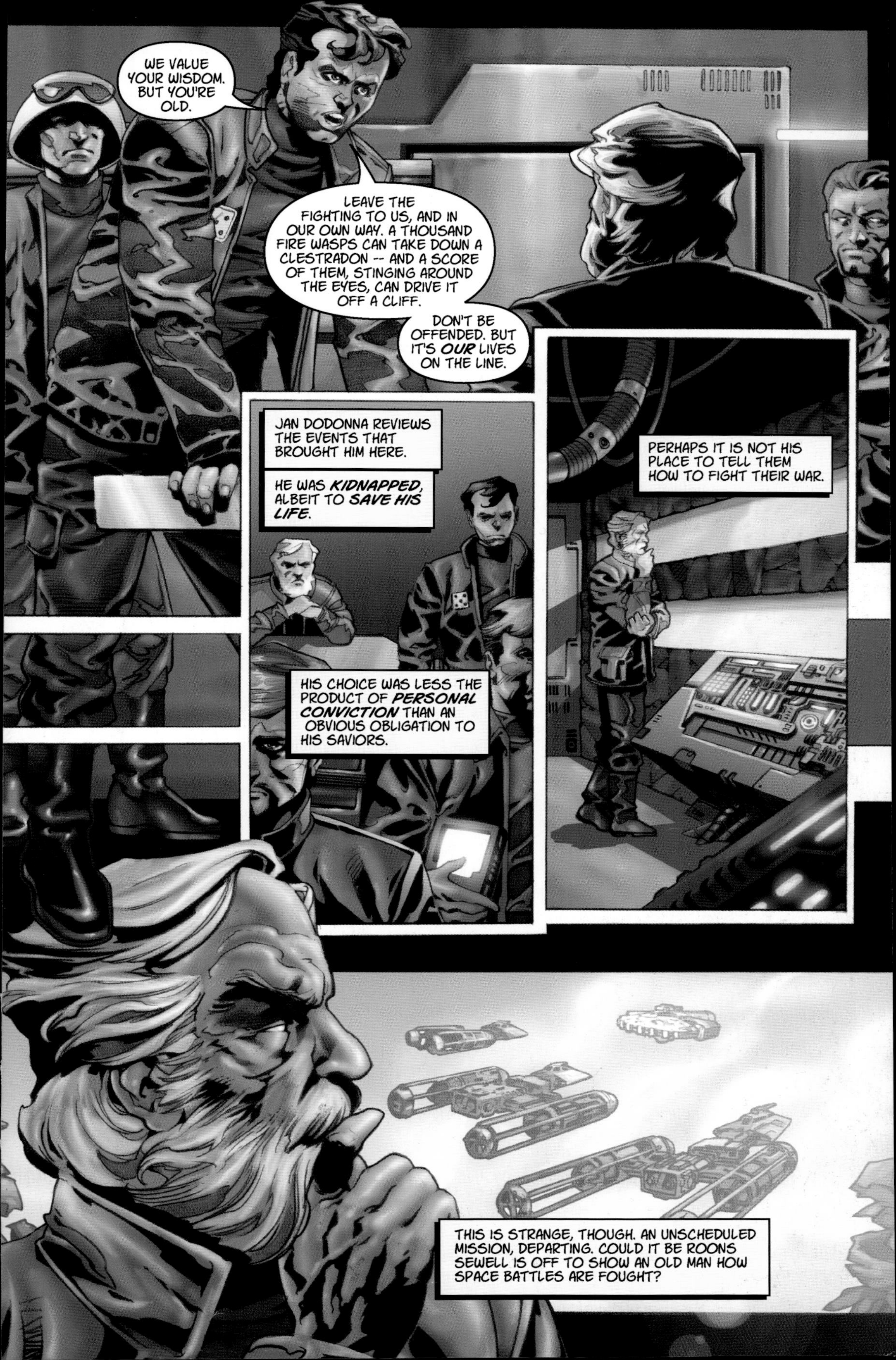
WE VALUE YOUR WISDOM. BUT YOU'RE OLD.
LEAVE THE FIGHTING TO US, AND IN OUR OWN WAY. A THOUSAND FIRE WASPS CAN TAKE DOWN A CLESTRADON -- AND A SCORE OF THEM, STINGING AROUND THE EYES, CAN DRIVE IT OFF A CLIFF.
DON'T BE OFFENDED. BUT IT'S OUR LIVES ON THE LINE.
JAN DODONNA REVIEWS THE EVENTS THAT BROUGHT HIM HERE.
HE WAS KIDNAPPED, ALBEIT TO SAVE HIS LIFE.
HIS CHOICE WAS LESS THE PRODUCT OF PERSONAL CONVICTION THAN AN OBVIOUS OBLIGATION TO HIS SAVIORS.
PERHAPS IT IS NOT HIS PLACE TO TELL THEM HOW TO FIGHT THEIR WAR.
THIS IS STRANGE, THOUGH. AN UNSCHEDULED MISSION, DEPARTING. COULD IT BE ROONS SEWELL IS OFF TO SHOW AN OLD MAN HOW SPACE BATTLES ARE FOUGHT?

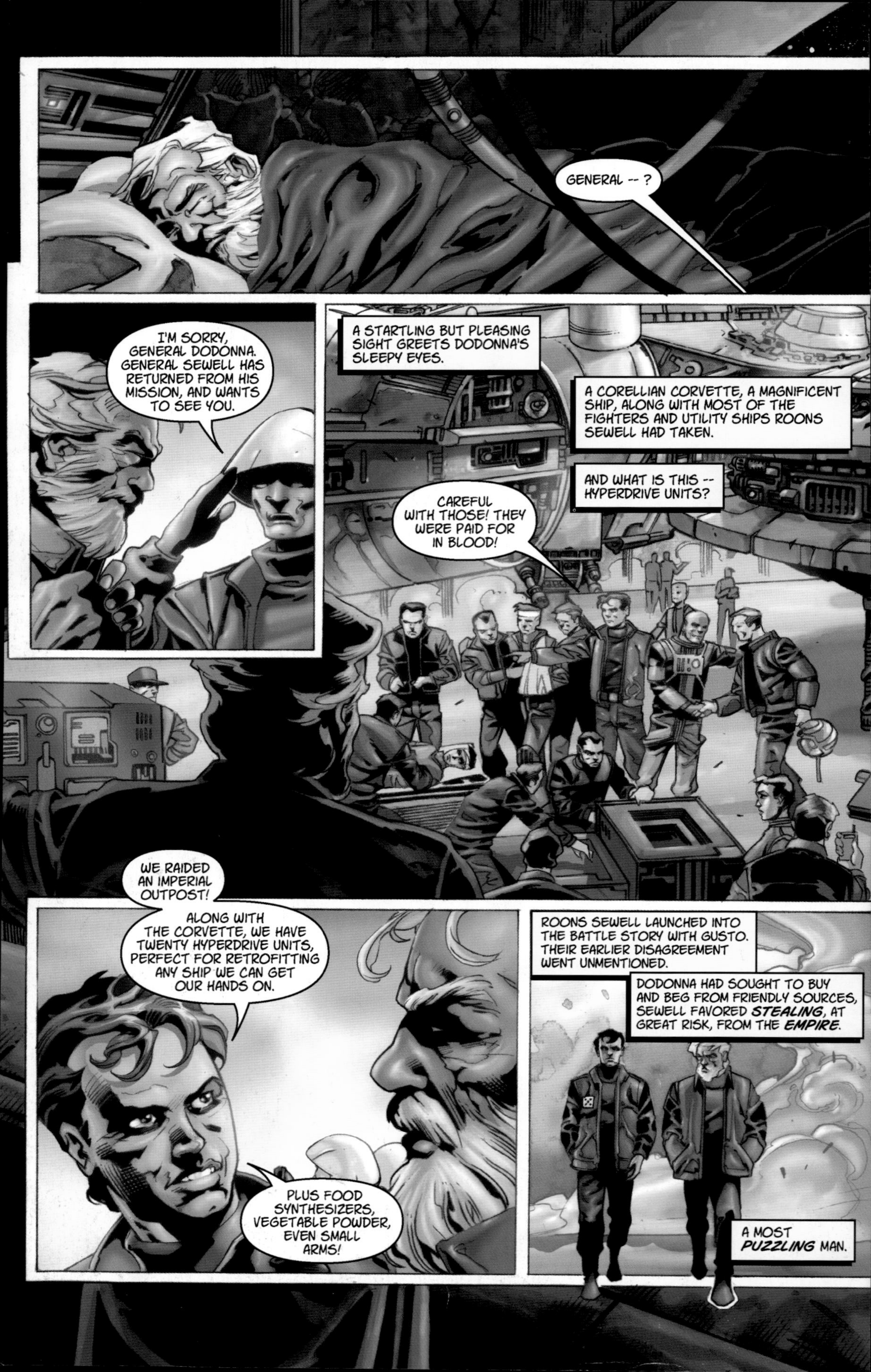
GENERAL -- ?
I'M SORRY, GENERAL DODONNA. GENERAL SEWELL HAS RETURNED FROM HIS MISSION, AND WANTS TO SEE YOU.
A STARTLING BUT PLEASING SIGHT GREETS DODONNA'S SLEEPY EYES.
A CORELLIAN CORVETTE, A MAGNIFICENT SHIP, ALONG WITH MOST OF THE FIGHTERS AND UTILITY SHIPS ROONS SEWELL HAD TAKEN.
AND WHAT IS THIS -- HYPERDRIVE UNITS?
CAREFUL WITH THOSE! THEY WERE PAID FOR IN BLOOD!
WE RAIDED AN IMPERIAL OUTPOST!
ALONG WITH THE CORVETTE, WE HAVE TWENTY HYPERDRIVE UNITS, PERFECT FOR RETROFITTING ANY SHIP WE CAN GET OUR HANDS ON.
PLUS FOOD SYNTHESIZERS, VEGETABLE POWDER, EVEN SMALL ARMS!
ROONS SEWELL LAUNCHED INTO THE BATTLE STORY WITH GUSTO. THEIR EARLIER DISAGREEMENT WENT UNMENTIONED.
DODONNA HAD SOUGHT TO BUY AND BEG FROM FRIENDLY SOURCES, SEWELL FAVORED STEALING, AT GREAT RISK, FROM THE EMPIRE.
A MOST PUZZLING MAN.

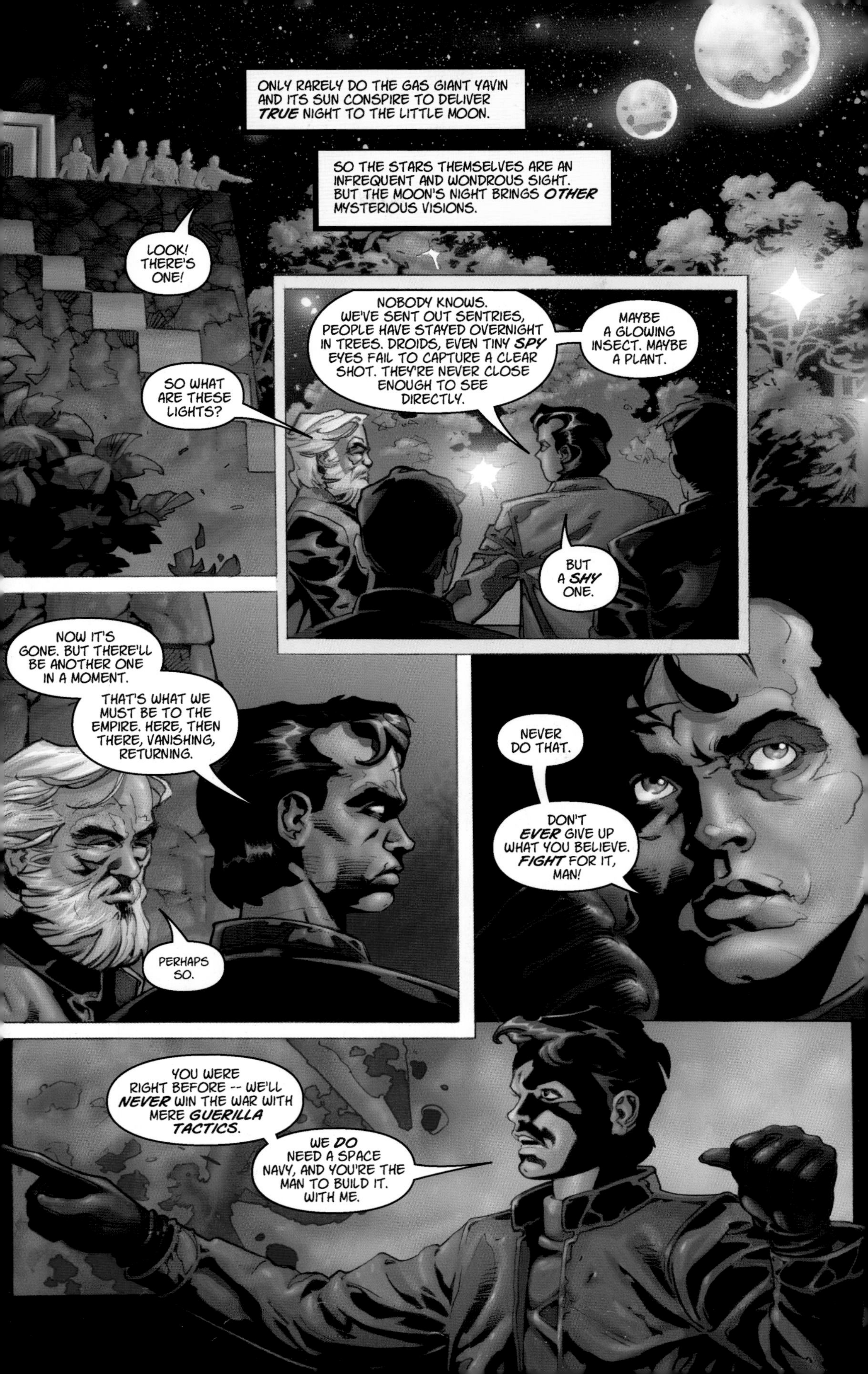

ONLY RARELY DO THE GAS GIANT YAVIN AND ITS SUN CONSPIRE TO DELIVER *TRUE* NIGHT TO THE LITTLE MOON.
SO THE STARS THEMSELVES ARE AN INFREQUENT AND WONDROUS SIGHT. BUT THE MOON'S NIGHT BRINGS *OTHER* MYSTERIOUS VISIONS.
LOOK! THERE'S ONE!
SO WHAT ARE THESE LIGHTS?
NOBODY KNOWS. WE'VE SENT OUT SENTRIES, PEOPLE HAVE STAYED OVERNIGHT IN TREES. DROIDS, EVEN TINY *SPY* EYES FAIL TO CAPTURE A CLEAR SHOT. THEY'RE NEVER CLOSE ENOUGH TO SEE DIRECTLY.
MAYBE A GLOWING INSECT. MAYBE A PLANT.
BUT A *SHY* ONE.
NOW IT'S GONE. BUT THERE'LL BE ANOTHER ONE IN A MOMENT.
THAT'S WHAT WE MUST BE TO THE EMPIRE. HERE, THEN THERE, VANISHING, RETURNING.
PERHAPS SO.
NEVER DO THAT.
DON'T *EVER* GIVE UP WHAT YOU BELIEVE. *FIGHT* FOR IT, MAN!
YOU WERE RIGHT BEFORE -- WE'LL *NEVER* WIN THE WAR WITH MERE *GUERILLA TACTICS*.
WE *DO* NEED A SPACE NAVY, AND YOU'RE THE MAN TO BUILD IT. WITH ME.

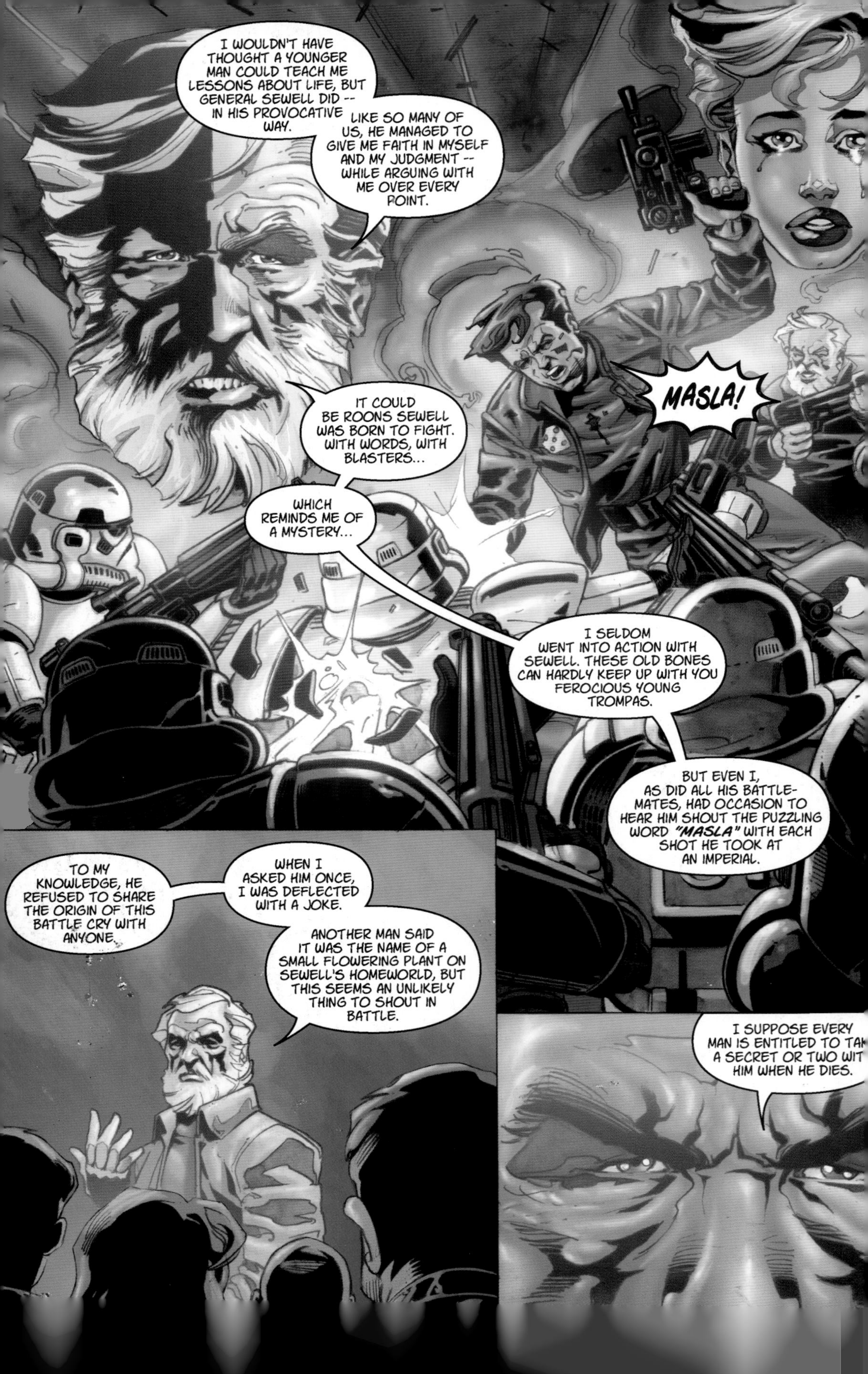
I WOULDN'T HAVE THOUGHT A YOUNGER MAN COULD TEACH ME LESSONS ABOUT LIFE, BUT GENERAL SEWELL DID -- IN HIS PROVOCATIVE WAY.
LIKE SO MANY OF US, HE MANAGED TO GIVE ME FAITH IN MYSELF AND MY JUDGMENT -- WHILE ARGUING WITH ME OVER EVERY POINT.
IT COULD BE ROONS SEWELL WAS BORN TO FIGHT. WITH WORDS, WITH BLASTERS...
MASLA!
WHICH REMINDS ME OF A MYSTERY...
I SELDOM WENT INTO ACTION WITH SEWELL. THESE OLD BONES CAN HARDLY KEEP UP WITH YOU FEROCIOUS YOUNG TROMPAS.
BUT EVEN I, AS DID ALL HIS BATTLE-MATES, HAD OCCASION TO HEAR HIM SHOUT THE PUZZLING WORD "MASLA" WITH EACH SHOT HE TOOK AT AN IMPERIAL.
TO MY KNOWLEDGE, HE REFUSED TO SHARE THE ORIGIN OF THIS BATTLE CRY WITH ANYONE.
WHEN I ASKED HIM ONCE, I WAS DEFLECTED WITH A JOKE.
ANOTHER MAN SAID IT WAS THE NAME OF A SMALL FLOWERING PLANT ON SEWELL'S HOMEWORLD, BUT THIS SEEMS AN UNLIKELY THING TO SHOUT IN BATTLE.
I SUPPOSE EVERY MAN IS ENTITLED TO TAK A SECRET OR TWO WIT HIM WHEN HE DIES.

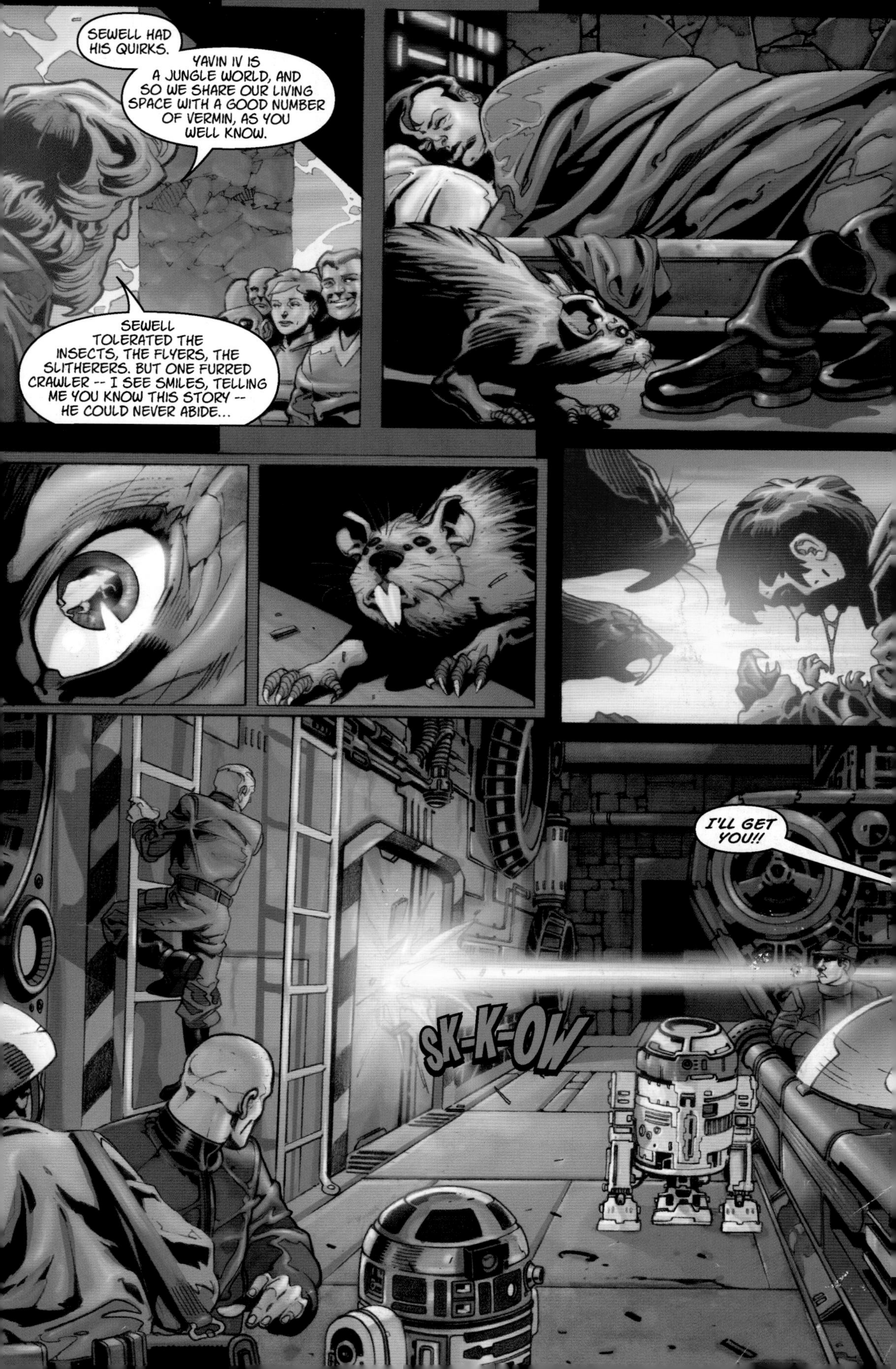
SEWELL HAD HIS QUIRKS.
YAVIN IV IS A JUNGLE WORLD, AND SO WE SHARE OUR LIVING SPACE WITH A GOOD NUMBER OF VERMIN, AS YOU WELL KNOW.
SEWELL TOLERATED THE INSECTS, THE FLYERS, THE SLITHERERS. BUT ONE FURRED CRAWLER -- I SEE SMILES, TELLING ME YOU KNOW THIS STORY -- HE COULD NEVER ABIDE...
I'LL GET YOU!!
SK-K-OW

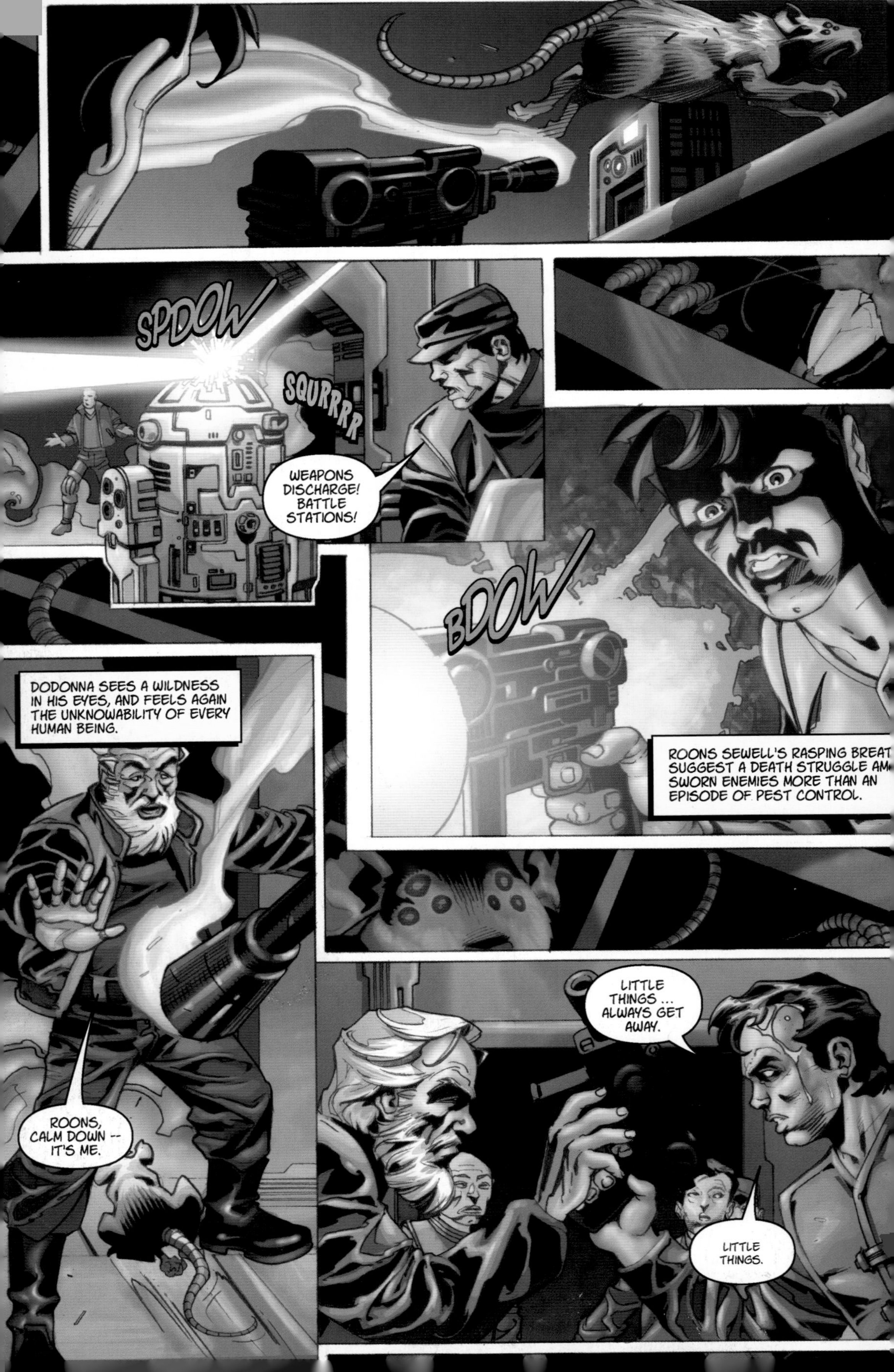
SPDOW
SQURRRR
WEAPONS DISCHARGE! BATTLE STATIONS!
BDOW
ROONS SEWELL'S RASPING BREAT SUGGEST A DEATH STRUGGLE AM SWORN ENEMIES MORE THAN AN EPISODE OF PEST CONTROL.
DODONNA SEES A WILDNESS IN HIS EYES, AND FEELS AGAIN THE UNKNOWABILITY OF EVERY HUMAN BEING.
ROONS, CALM DOWN -- IT'S ME.
LITTLE THINGS ... ALWAYS GET AWAY.
LITTLE THINGS.

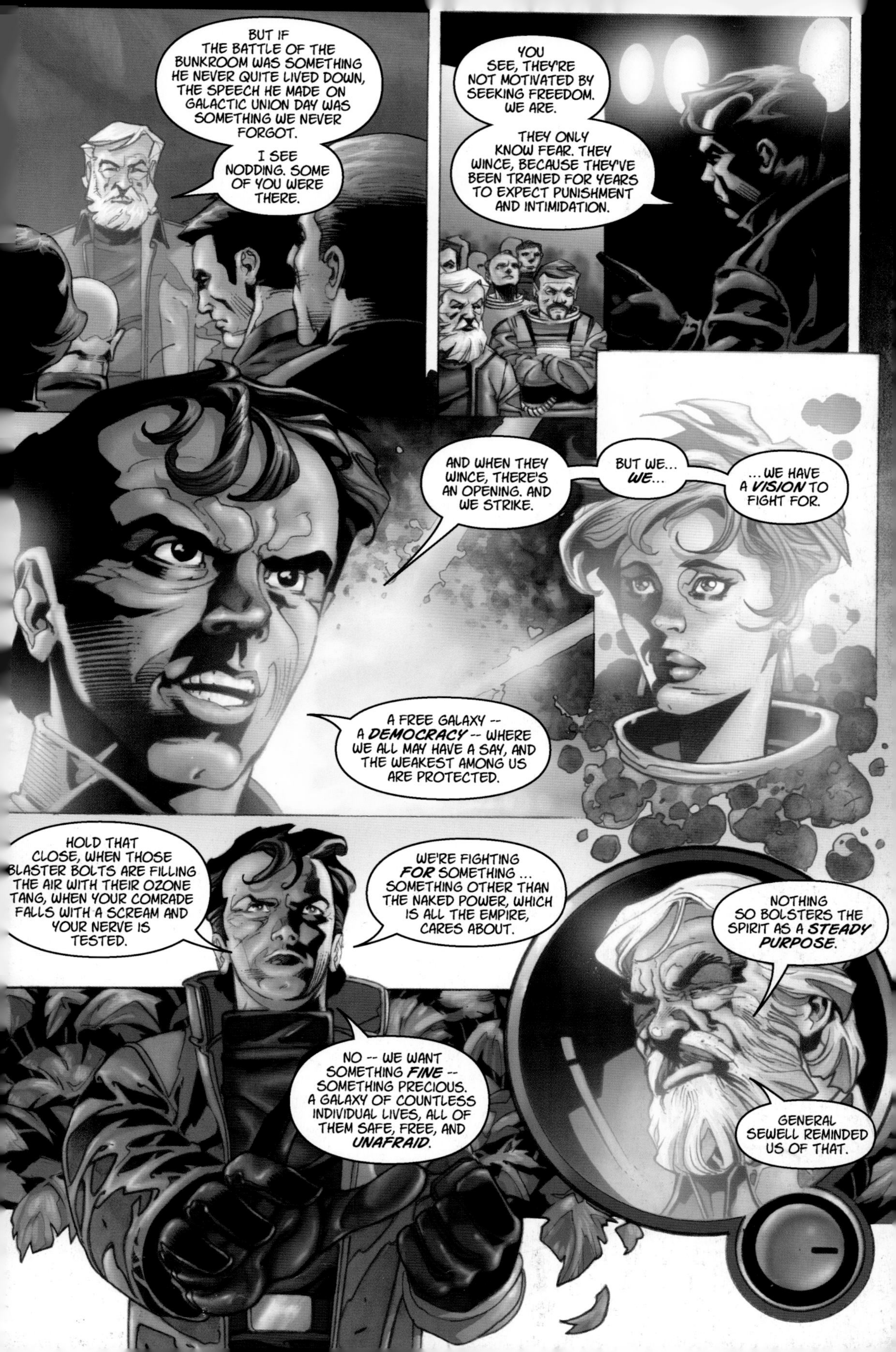
BUT IF THE BATTLE OF THE BUNKROOM WAS SOMETHING HE NEVER QUITE LIVED DOWN, THE SPEECH HE MADE ON GALACTIC UNION DAY WAS SOMETHING WE NEVER FORGOT.
I SEE NODDING. SOME OF YOU WERE THERE.
YOU SEE, THEY'RE NOT MOTIVATED BY SEEKING FREEDOM. WE ARE.
THEY ONLY KNOW FEAR. THEY WINCE, BECAUSE THEY'VE BEEN TRAINED FOR YEARS TO EXPECT PUNISHMENT AND INTIMIDATION.
AND WHEN THEY WINCE, THERE'S AN OPENING. AND WE STRIKE.
BUT WE... *WE*...
...WE HAVE A *VISION* TO FIGHT FOR.
A FREE GALAXY -- A *DEMOCRACY* -- WHERE WE ALL MAY HAVE A SAY, AND THE WEAKEST AMONG US ARE PROTECTED.
HOLD THAT CLOSE, WHEN THOSE BLASTER BOLTS ARE FILLING THE AIR WITH THEIR OZONE TANG, WHEN YOUR COMRADE FALLS WITH A SCREAM AND YOUR NERVE IS TESTED.
WE'RE FIGHTING *FOR* SOMETHING ... SOMETHING OTHER THAN THE NAKED POWER, WHICH IS ALL THE EMPIRE, CARES ABOUT.
NO -- WE WANT SOMETHING *FINE* -- SOMETHING PRECIOUS. A GALAXY OF COUNTLESS INDIVIDUAL LIVES, ALL OF THEM SAFE, FREE, AND *UNAFRAID*.
NOTHING SO BOLSTERS THE SPIRIT AS A *STEADY PURPOSE*.
GENERAL SEWELL REMINDED US OF THAT.

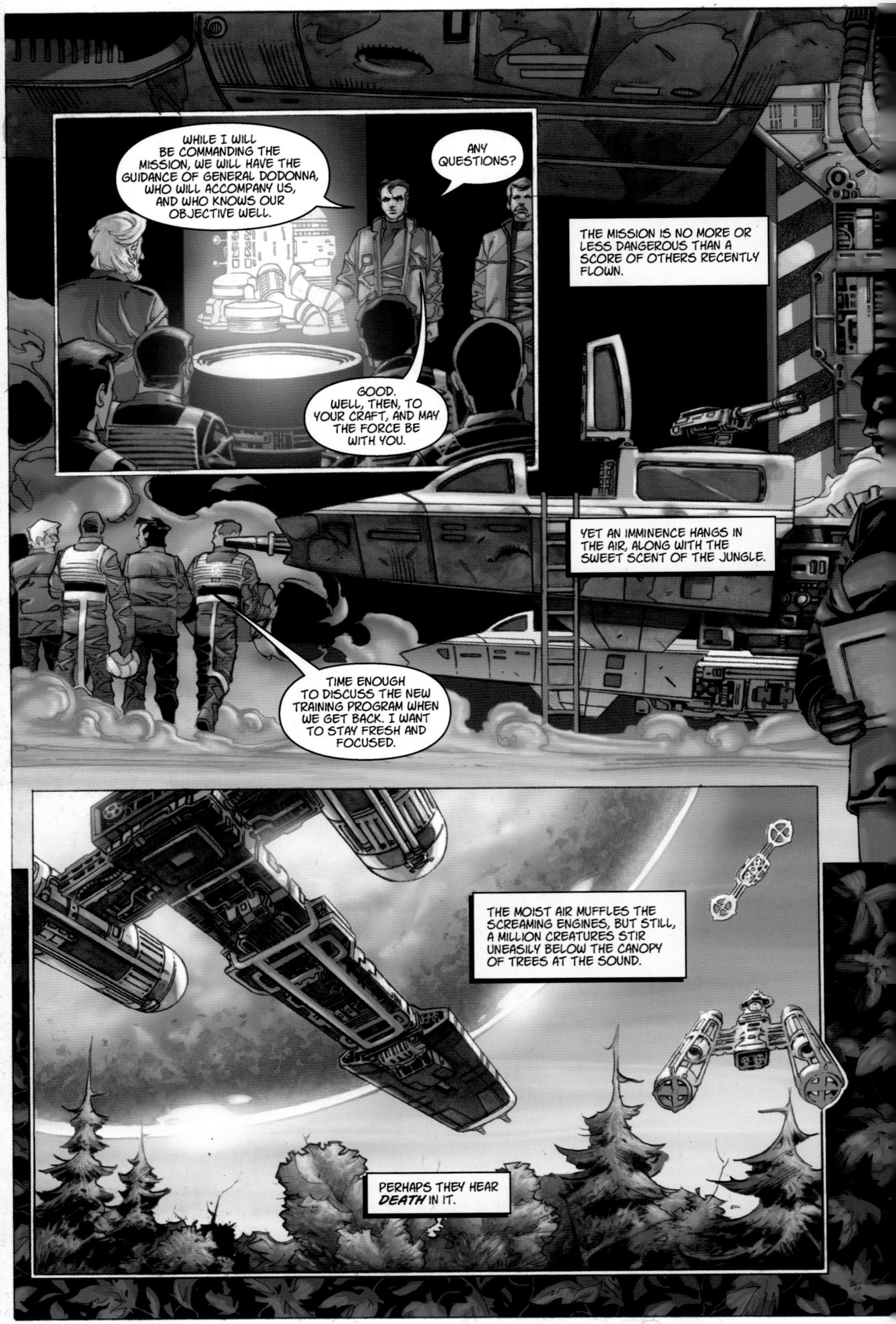
WHILE I WILL BE COMMANDING THE MISSION, WE WILL HAVE THE GUIDANCE OF GENERAL DODONNA, WHO WILL ACCOMPANY US, AND WHO KNOWS OUR OBJECTIVE WELL.
ANY QUESTIONS?
GOOD. WELL, THEN, TO YOUR CRAFT, AND MAY THE FORCE BE WITH YOU.
THE MISSION IS NO MORE OR LESS DANGEROUS THAN A SCORE OF OTHERS RECENTLY FLOWN.
YET AN IMMINENCE HANGS IN THE AIR, ALONG WITH THE SWEET SCENT OF THE JUNGLE.
TIME ENOUGH TO DISCUSS THE NEW TRAINING PROGRAM WHEN WE GET BACK. I WANT TO STAY FRESH AND FOCUSED.
THE MOIST AIR MUFFLES THE SCREAMING ENGINES, BUT STILL, A MILLION CREATURES STIR UNEASILY BELOW THE CANOPY OF TREES AT THE SOUND.
PERHAPS THEY HEAR DEATH IN IT.

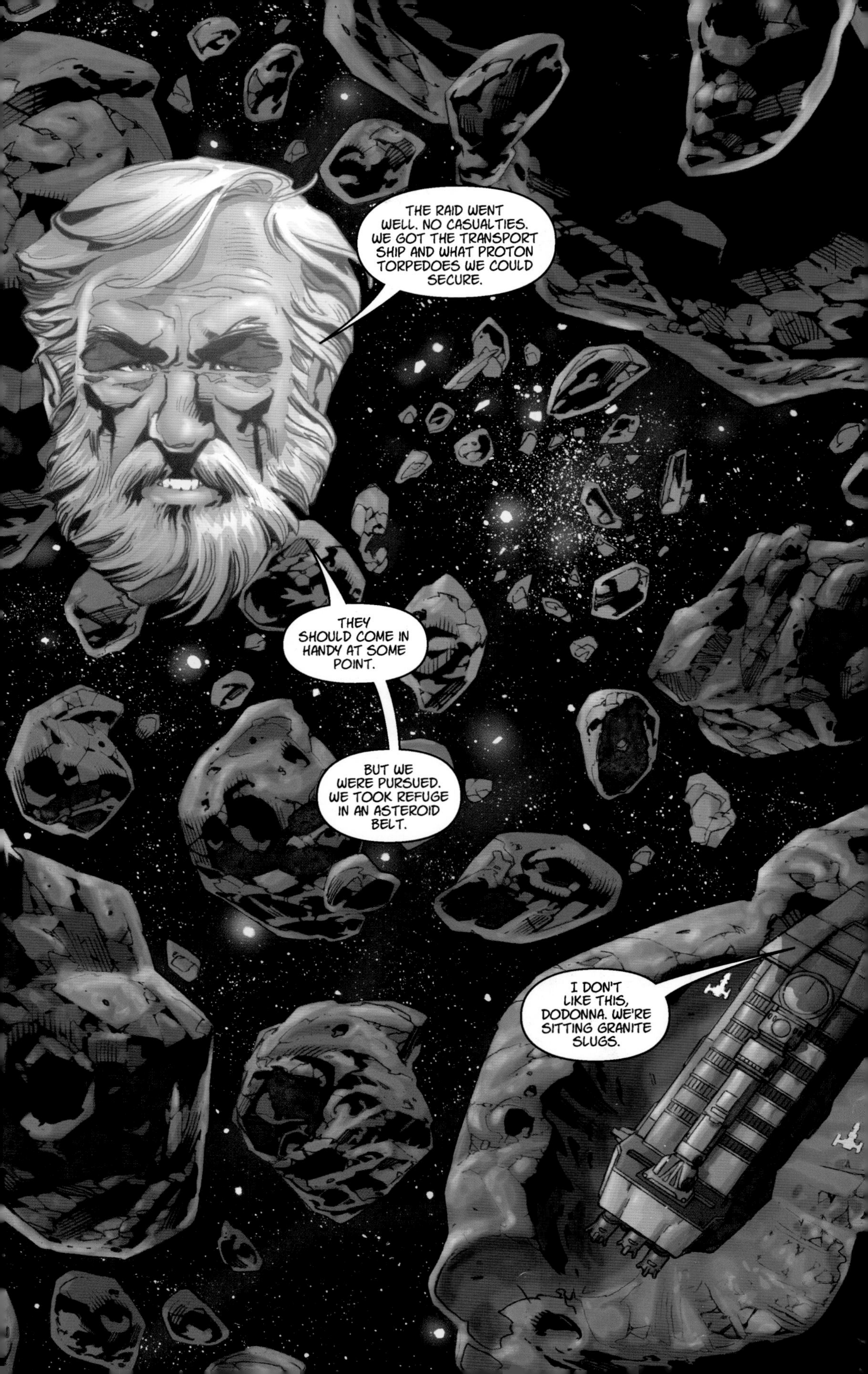
THE RAID WENT WELL. NO CASUALTIES. WE GOT THE TRANSPORT SHIP AND WHAT PROTON TORPEDOES WE COULD SECURE.
THEY SHOULD COME IN HANDY AT SOME POINT.
BUT WE WERE PURSUED. WE TOOK REFUGE IN AN ASTEROID BELT.
I DON'T LIKE THIS, DODONNA. WE'RE SITTING GRANITE SLUGS.

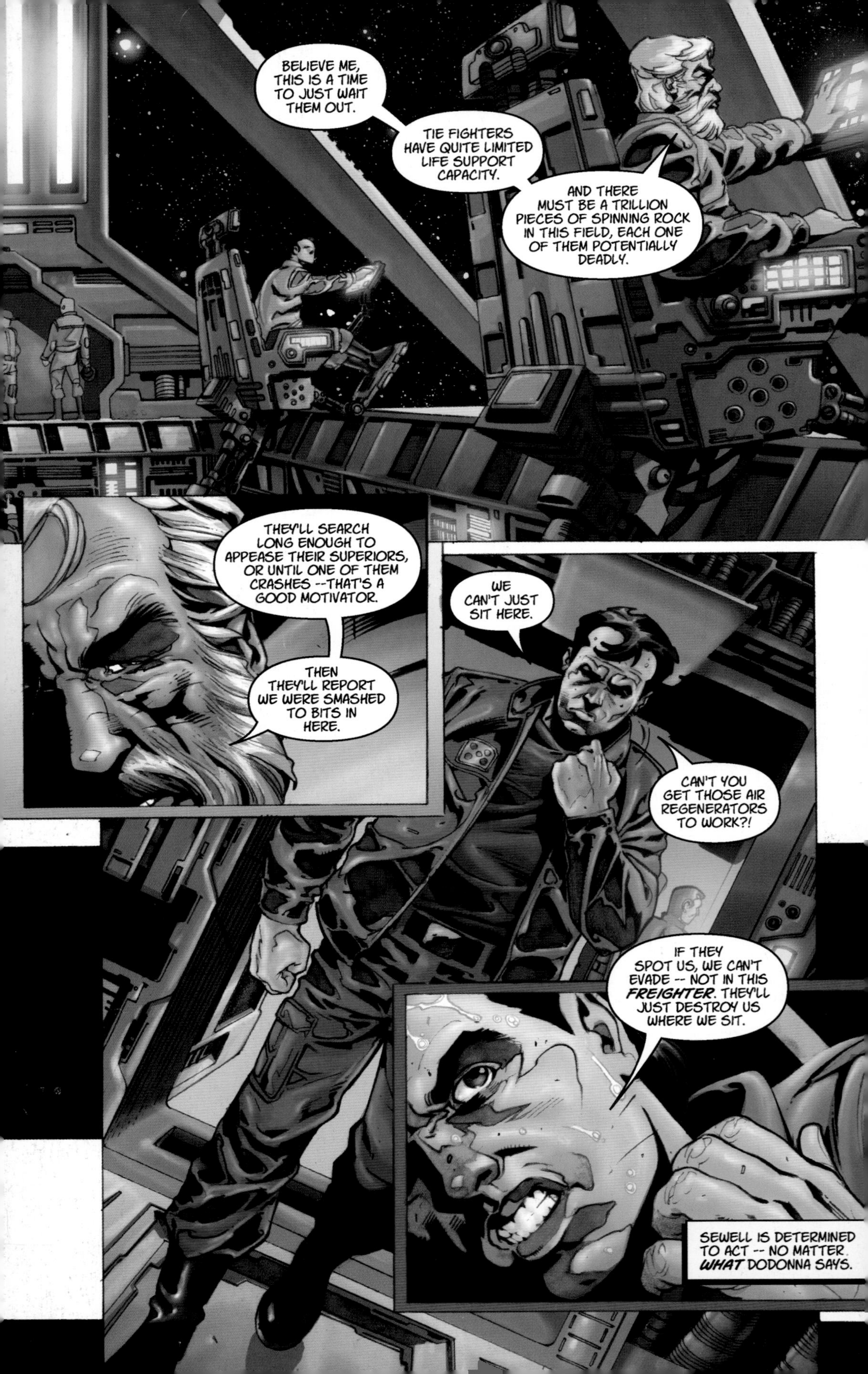
BELIEVE ME, THIS IS A TIME TO JUST WAIT THEM OUT.
TIE FIGHTERS HAVE QUITE LIMITED LIFE SUPPORT CAPACITY.
AND THERE MUST BE A TRILLION PIECES OF SPINNING ROCK IN THIS FIELD, EACH ONE OF THEM POTENTIALLY DEADLY.
THEY'LL SEARCH LONG ENOUGH TO APPEASE THEIR SUPERIORS, OR UNTIL ONE OF THEM CRASHES --THAT'S A GOOD MOTIVATOR.
THEN THEY'LL REPORT WE WERE SMASHED TO BITS IN HERE.
WE CAN'T JUST SIT HERE.
CAN'T YOU GET THOSE AIR REGENERATORS TO WORK?!
IF THEY SPOT US, WE CAN'T EVADE -- NOT IN THIS *FREIGHTER*. THEY'LL JUST DESTROY US WHERE WE SIT.
SEWELL IS DETERMINED TO ACT -- NO MATTER *WHAT* DODONNA SAYS.

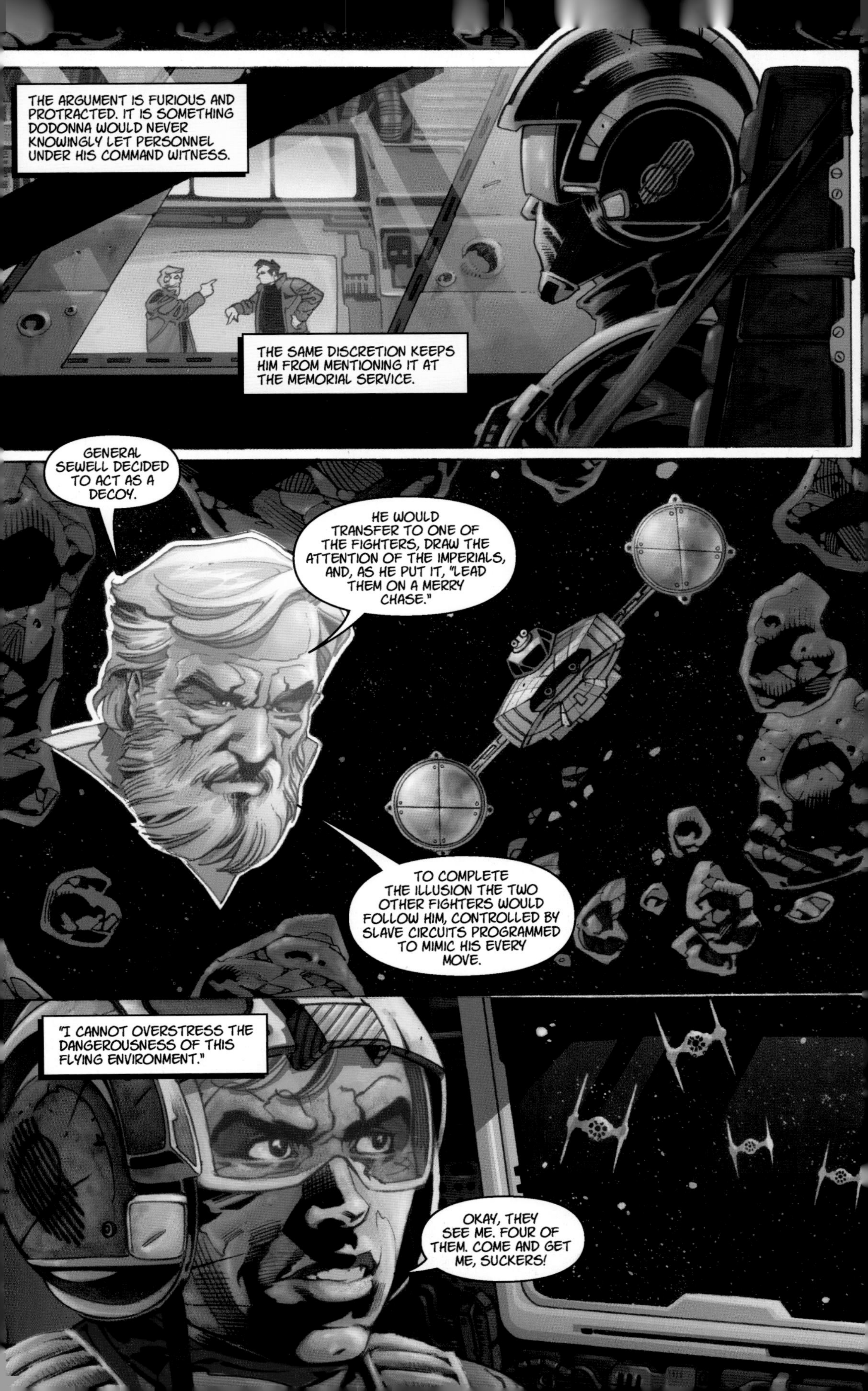
THE ARGUMENT IS FURIOUS AND PROTRACTED. IT IS SOMETHING DODONNA WOULD NEVER KNOWINGLY LET PERSONNEL UNDER HIS COMMAND WITNESS.
THE SAME DISCRETION KEEPS HIM FROM MENTIONING IT AT THE MEMORIAL SERVICE.
GENERAL SEWELL DECIDED TO ACT AS A DECOY.
HE WOULD TRANSFER TO ONE OF THE FIGHTERS, DRAW THE ATTENTION OF THE IMPERIALS, AND, AS HE PUT IT, "LEAD THEM ON A MERRY CHASE."
TO COMPLETE THE ILLUSION THE TWO OTHER FIGHTERS WOULD FOLLOW HIM, CONTROLLED BY SLAVE CIRCUITS PROGRAMMED TO MIMIC HIS EVERY MOVE.
"I CANNOT OVERSTRESS THE DANGEROUSNESS OF THIS FLYING ENVIRONMENT."
OKAY, THEY SEE ME. FOUR OF THEM. COME AND GET ME, SUCKERS!

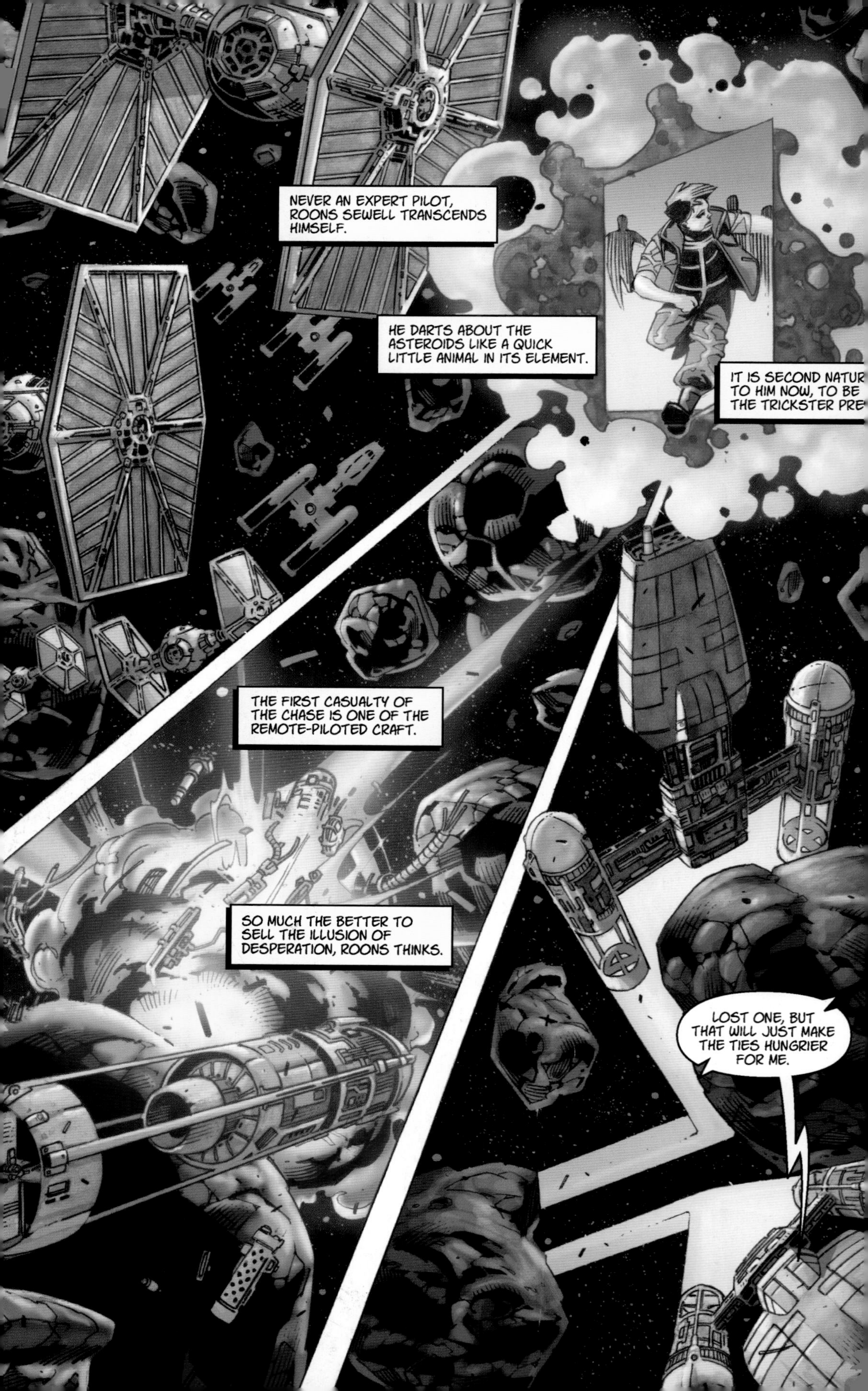
NEVER AN EXPERT PILOT, ROONS SEWELL TRANSCENDS HIMSELF.
HE DARTS ABOUT THE ASTEROIDS LIKE A QUICK LITTLE ANIMAL IN ITS ELEMENT.
IT IS SECOND NATUR TO HIM NOW, TO BE THE TRICKSTER PRE
THE FIRST CASUALTY OF THE CHASE IS ONE OF THE REMOTE-PILOTED CRAFT.
SO MUCH THE BETTER TO SELL THE ILLUSION OF DESPERATION, ROONS THINKS.
LOST ONE, BUT THAT WILL JUST MAKE THE TIES HUNGRIER FOR ME.

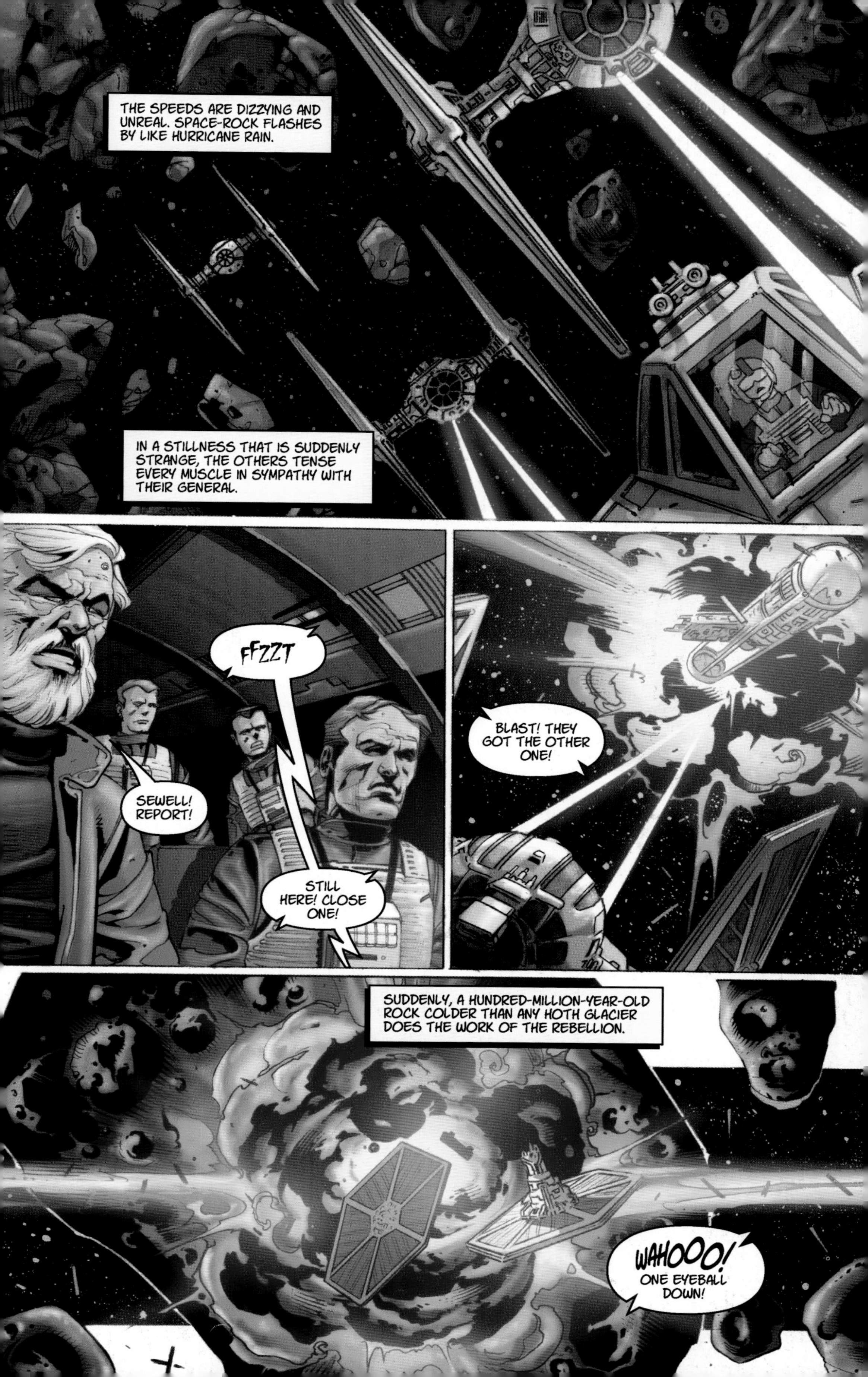
THE SPEEDS ARE DIZZYING AND UNREAL. SPACE-ROCK FLASHES BY LIKE HURRICANE RAIN.
IN A STILLNESS THAT IS SUDDENLY STRANGE, THE OTHERS TENSE EVERY MUSCLE IN SYMPATHY WITH THEIR GENERAL.
FFZZT
SEWELL! REPORT!
STILL HERE! CLOSE ONE!
BLAST! THEY GOT THE OTHER ONE!
SUDDENLY, A HUNDRED-MILLION-YEAR-OLD ROCK COLDER THAN ANY HOTH GLACIER DOES THE WORK OF THE REBELLION.
WAHOOO! ONE EYEBALL DOWN!

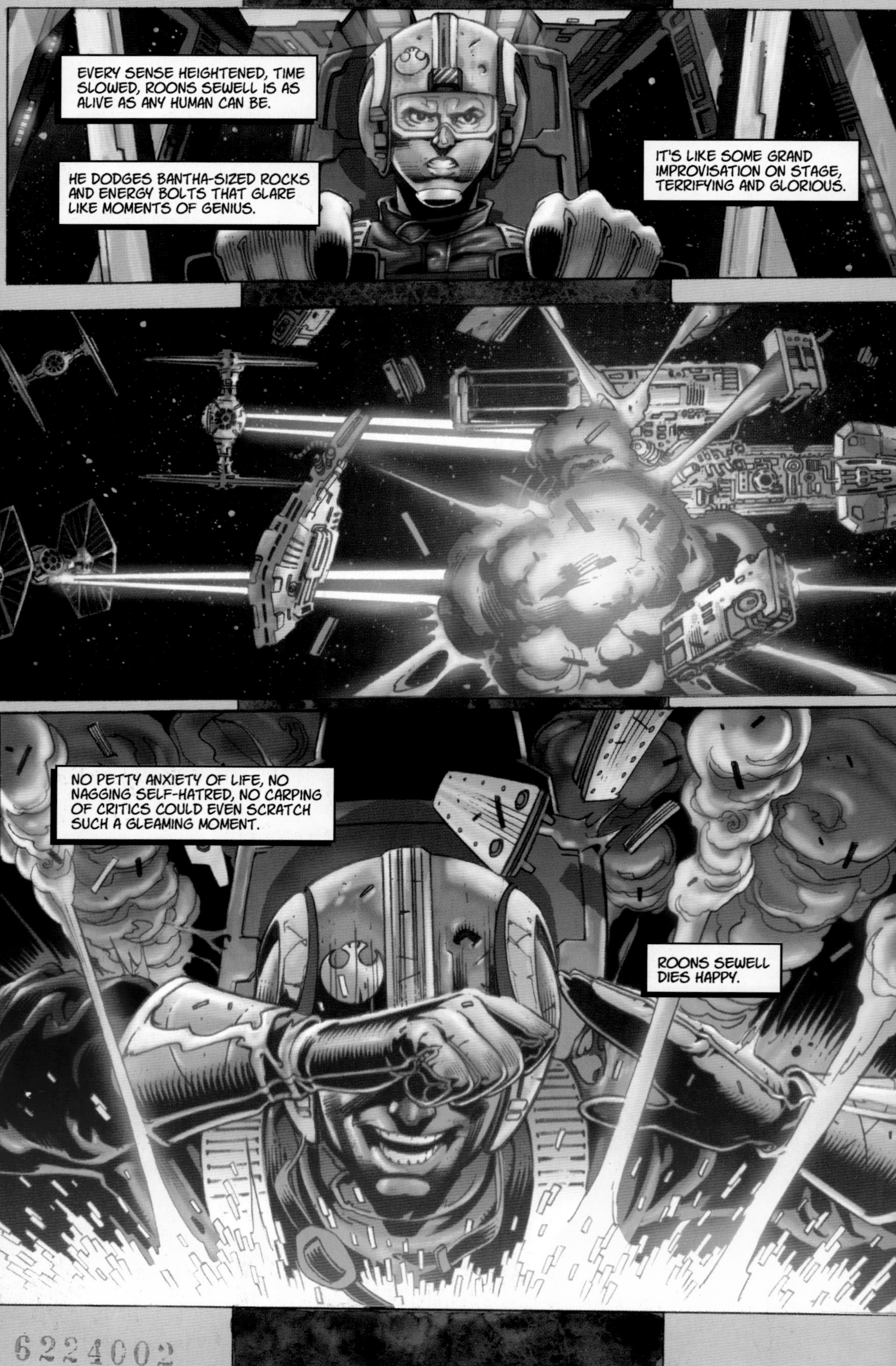
EVERY SENSE HEIGHTENED, TIME SLOWED, ROONS SEWELL IS AS ALIVE AS ANY HUMAN CAN BE.
HE DODGES BANTHA-SIZED ROCKS AND ENERGY BOLTS THAT GLARE LIKE MOMENTS OF GENIUS.
IT'S LIKE SOME GRAND IMPROVISATION ON STAGE, TERRIFYING AND GLORIOUS.
NO PETTY ANXIETY OF LIFE, NO NAGGING SELF-HATRED, NO CARPING OF CRITICS COULD EVEN SCRATCH SUCH A GLEAMING MOMENT.
ROONS SEWELL DIES HAPPY.

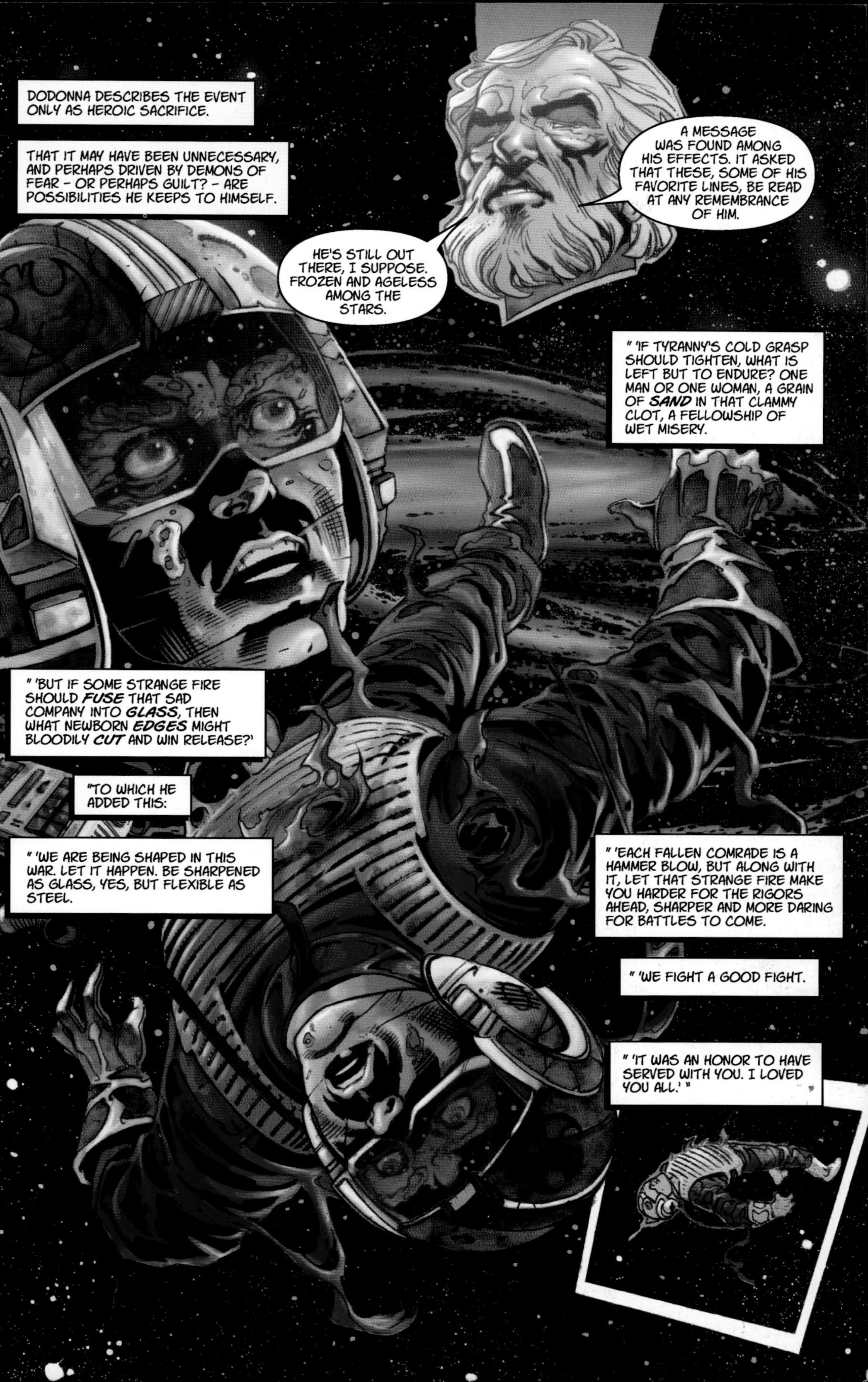
DODONNA DESCRIBES THE EVENT ONLY AS HEROIC SACRIFICE.
THAT IT MAY HAVE BEEN UNNECESSARY, AND PERHAPS DRIVEN BY DEMONS OF FEAR – OR PERHAPS GUILT? – ARE POSSIBILITIES HE KEEPS TO HIMSELF.
A MESSAGE WAS FOUND AMONG HIS EFFECTS. IT ASKED THAT THESE, SOME OF HIS FAVORITE LINES, BE READ AT ANY REMEMBRANCE OF HIM.
HE'S STILL OUT THERE, I SUPPOSE. FROZEN AND AGELESS AMONG THE STARS.
" 'IF TYRANNY'S COLD GRASP SHOULD TIGHTEN, WHAT IS LEFT BUT TO ENDURE? ONE MAN OR ONE WOMAN, A GRAIN OF SAND IN THAT CLAMMY CLOT, A FELLOWSHIP OF WET MISERY.
" 'BUT IF SOME STRANGE FIRE SHOULD FUSE THAT SAD COMPANY INTO GLASS, THEN WHAT NEWBORN EDGES MIGHT BLOODILY CUT AND WIN RELEASE?'
"TO WHICH HE ADDED THIS:
" 'WE ARE BEING SHAPED IN THIS WAR. LET IT HAPPEN. BE SHARPENED AS GLASS, YES, BUT FLEXIBLE AS STEEL.
" 'EACH FALLEN COMRADE IS A HAMMER BLOW, BUT ALONG WITH IT, LET THAT STRANGE FIRE MAKE YOU HARDER FOR THE RIGORS AHEAD, SHARPER AND MORE DARING FOR BATTLES TO COME.
" 'WE FIGHT A GOOD FIGHT.
" 'IT WAS AN HONOR TO HAVE SERVED WITH YOU. I LOVED YOU ALL.' "

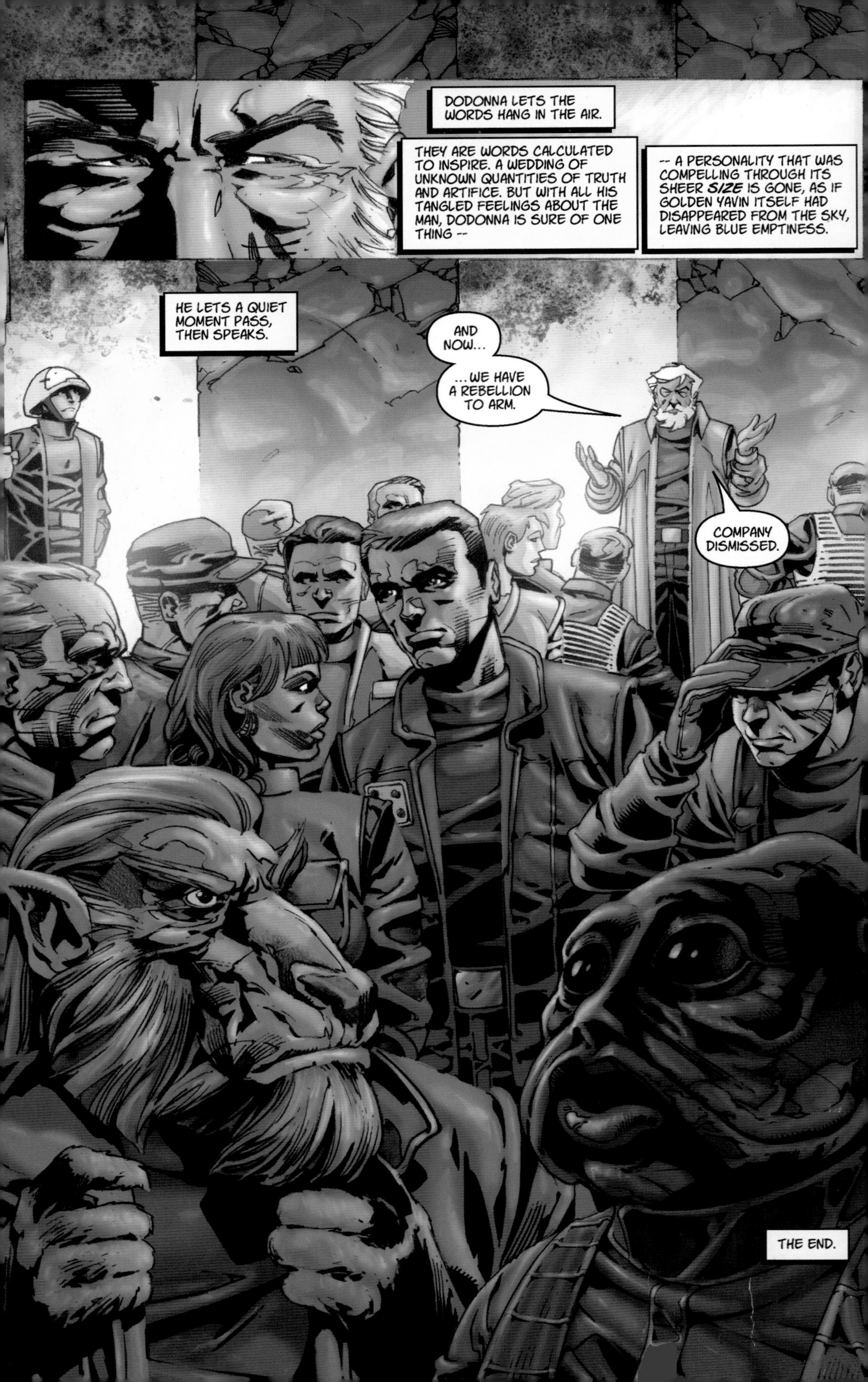
DODONNA LETS THE WORDS HANG IN THE AIR.
THEY ARE WORDS CALCULATED TO INSPIRE. A WEDDING OF UNKNOWN QUANTITIES OF TRUTH AND ARTIFICE. BUT WITH ALL HIS TANGLED FEELINGS ABOUT THE MAN, DODONNA IS SURE OF ONE THING --
-- A PERSONALITY THAT WAS COMPELLING THROUGH ITS SHEER SIZE IS GONE, AS IF GOLDEN YAVIN ITSELF HAD DISAPPEARED FROM THE SKY, LEAVING BLUE EMPTINESS.
HE LETS A QUIET MOMENT PASS, THEN SPEAKS.
AND NOW...
...WE HAVE A REBELLION TO ARM.
COMPANY DISMISSED.
THE END.

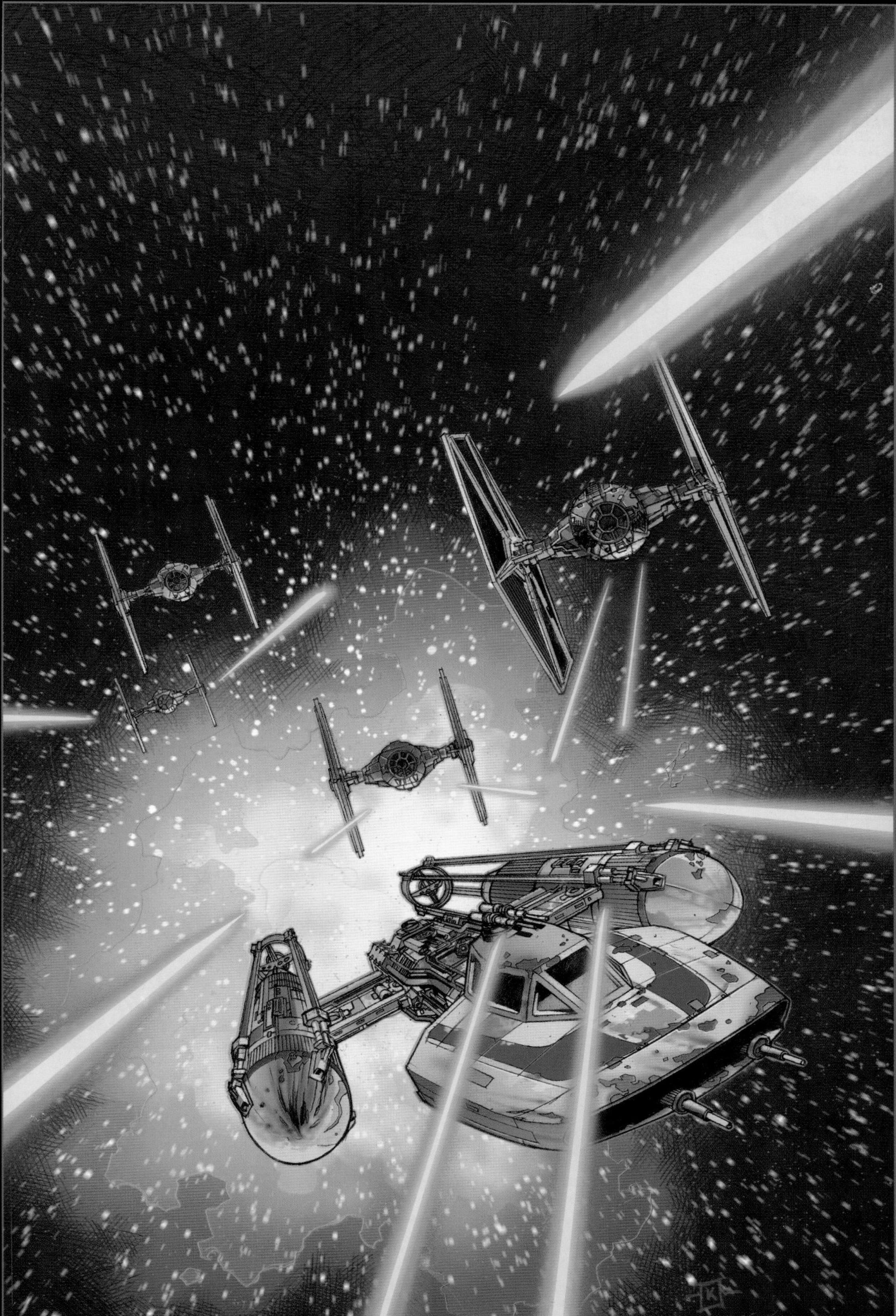

STAR WARS TIMELINE

GRAPHIC NOVELS AND TRADE PAPERBACKS FROM DARK HORSE COMICS

For more information go to www.darkhorse.com

TALES OF THE SITH ERA 25,000-1000 YEARS BEFORE STAR WARS: A NEW HOPE

TALES OF THE JEDI
THE GOLDEN AGE OF THE SITH
Anderson • Carrasco, Jr. • Gossett
ISBN: 1-56971-229-8 $16.95
FALL OF THE SITH EMPIRE
Anderson • Heike • Carrasco, Jr.
ISBN: 1-56971-320-0 $14 .95
KNIGHTS OF THE OLD REPUBLIC
Veitch • Gossett
ISBN: 1-56971-020-1 $14.95
THE FREEDON NADD UPRISING
Veitch • Akins • Rodier
ISBN: 1-56971-307-3 $5.95
DARK LORDS OF THE SITH
Veitch • Anderson • Gossett
ISBN: 1-56971-095-3 $17.95
THE SITH WAR
Anderson • Carrasco, Jr.
ISBN: 1-56971-173-9 $17.95

STAR WARS
TALES OF THE JEDI
REDEMPTION

***REDEMPTION**
Anderson • Gossett • Pepoy • McDaniel
ISBN: 1-56971-535-1 $14.95

STAR WARS
JEDI VS SITH

***JEDI VS. SITH**
Macan • Bachs • Fernandez
ISBN: 1-56971-649-8 $15.95

PREQUEL ERA 1000-0 YEARS BEFORE STAR WARS: A NEW HOPE

***JEDI COUNCIL**
ACTS OF WAR
Stradley • Fabbri • Vecchia
ISBN: 1-56971-539-4 $12.95

STAR WARS
JEDI COUNCIL
ACTS OF WAR

***DARTH MAUL**
Marz • Duursema • Magyar • Struzan
ISBN: 1-56971-542-4 $12.95

STAR WARS
DARTH MAUL
MARZ • DUURSEMA • MAGYAR • McCAIG

PRELUDE TO REBELLION
Strnad • Winn • Jones
ISBN: 1-56971-448-7 $14.95
OUTLANDER
Truman • Leonardi • Rio
ISBN: 1-56971-514-9 $14.95
***JEDI COUNCIL**
EMMISSARIES TO MALASTARE
Truman • Duursema • Others
ISBN: 1-56971-545-9 $15.95

STAR WARS
TWILIGHT

STAR WARS: TWILIGHT
Ostrander • Duursema • Magyar
ISBN: 1-56971-558-0 $12.95
EPISODE 1 —
THE PHANTOM MENACE
Gilroy • Damaggio • Williamson
ISBN: 1-56971-359-6 $12.95
EPISODE 1 —
THE PHANTOM MENACE ADVENTURES
ISBN: 1-56971-443-6 $12.95

MANGA EDITIONS
Translated into English
EPISODE 1 —
THE PHANTOM MENACE
George Lucas • Kia Asamiya
VOLUME 1
ISBN: 1-56971-483-5 $9.95
VOLUME 2
ISBN: 1-56971-484-3 $9.95

STAR WARS
JANGO FETT

***JANGO FETT**
Marz • Fowler
ISBN: 1-56971-623-4 $5.95

STAR WARS
ZAM WESELL

***ZAM WESELL**
Marz • Naifeh
ISBN: 1-56971-624-2 $5.95

STAR WARS
EPISODE II
ATTACK OF THE CLONES

EPISODE 2 —
ATTACK OF THE CLONES
Gilroy • Duursema • Kryssing • McCaig
ISBN: 1-56971-609-9 $17.95
DROIDS
THE KALARBA ADVENTURES
Thorsland • Windham • Gibson
ISBN: 1-56971-064-3 $17.95
REBELLION
Windham • Gibson
ISBN: 1-56971-224-7 $14.95

JABBA THE HUTT
THE ART OF THE DEAL
Woodring • Wetherell • Sheldon
ISBN: 1-56971-310-3 $9.95
***UNDERWORLD**
THE YAVIN VASSILIKA
Kennedy • Meglia
ISBN: 1-56971-618-8 $14.95
CLASSIC STAR WARS
HAN SOLO AT STARS' END
Goodwin • Alcala
ISBN: 1-56971-254-9 $6.95
BOBA FETT
ENEMY OF THE EMPIRE
Wagner • Gibson • Nadeau • Ezquerra
ISBN: 1-56971-407-X $12.95

TRILOGY ERA 0-5 YEARS AFTER STAR WARS: A NEW HOPE

***A NEW HOPE* SPECIAL EDITION**
Jones • Barreto • Williamson
ISBN: 1-56971-213-1 $9.95
MANGA EDITIONS
Translated into English
A NEW HOPE
George Lucas • Hisao Tamaki
VOLUME 1
ISBN: 1-56971-362-6 $9.95
VOLUME 2
ISBN: 1-56971-363-4 $9.95
VOLUME 3
ISBN: 1-56971-364-2 $9.95
VOLUME 4
ISBN: 1-56971-365-0 $9.95
VADER'S QUEST
Macan • Gibbons
ISBN: 1-56971-415-0 $11.95

CLASSIC
STAR WARS
THE EARLY ADVENTURES

CLASSIC STAR WARS
THE EARLY ADVENTURES
Manning • Hoberg
ISBN: 1-56971-178-X $19.95
SPLINTER OF THE MIND'S EYE
Austin • Sprouse
ISBN: 1-56971-223-9 $14.95
CLASSIC STAR WARS
IN DEADLY PURSUIT
Goodwin • Williamson
ISBN: 1-56971-109-7 $16.95
THE EMPIRE STRIKES BACK SPECIAL EDITION
Goodwin • Williamson
ISBN: 1-56971-234-4 $9.95
MANGA EDITIONS
Translated into English
THE EMPIRE STRIKES BACK
George Lucas • Toshiki Kudo
VOLUME 1
ISBN: 1-56971-390-1 $9.95

LUME 2
3N: 1-56971-391-X $9.95
LUME 3
3N: 1-56971-392-8 $9.95
LUME 4
3N: 1-56971-393-6 $9.95
ASSIC STAR WARS
E REBEL STORM
odwin • Williamson
3N: 1-56971-106-2 $16.95
ASSIC STAR WARS
CAPE TO HOTH
odwin • Williamson
3N: 1-56971-093-7 $16.95
ADOWS OF THE EMPIRE
ADOWS OF THE EMPIRE
gner • Plunkett • Russell
3N: 1-56971-183-6 $17.95
TURN OF THE JEDI
ECIAL EDITION
odwin • Williamson
3N: 1-56971-235-2 $9.95
ANGA EDITIONS
nslated into English
TURN OF THE JEDI
orge Lucas • Shin-ichi Hiromoto

LUME 1
N: 1-56971-394-4 $9.95
LUME 2
N: 1-56971-395-2 $9.95
LUME 3
N: 1-56971-396-0 $9.95
LUME 4
N: 1-56971-397-9 $9.95

LASSIC SPIN-OFF ERA
5-25 YEARS
AFTER STAR WARS:
A NEW HOPE

RA JADE
THE EMPEROR'S HAND
n • Stackpole • Ezquerra
N: 1-56971-401-0 $15.95

SHADOWS OF THE EMPIRE
EVOLUTION
Perry • Randall • Simmons
ISBN: 1-56971-441-X $14.95
X-WING ROGUE SQUADRON
THE PHANTOM AFFAIR
Stackpole • Macan • Biukovic
ISBN: 1-56971-251-4 $12.95

BATTLEGROUND: TATOOINE
Stackpole • Strnad • Nadeau • Ensign
ISBN: 1-56971-276-X $12.95
THE WARRIOR PRINCESS
Stackpole • Tolson • Nadeau • Ensign
ISBN: 1-56971-330-8 $12.95

REQUIEM FOR A ROGUE
Stackpole • Strnad • Barr • Erskine
ISBN: 1-56971-331-6 $12.95
IN THE EMPIRE'S SERVICE
Stackpole • Nadeau • Ensign
ISBN: 1-56971-383-9 $12.95
BLOOD AND HONOR
Stackpole • Crespo • Hall • Martin
ISBN: 1-56971-387-1 $12.95
MASQUERADE
Stackpole • Johnson • Martin
ISBN: 1-56971-487-8 $12.95

MANDATORY RETIREMENT
Stackpole • Crespo • Nadeau
ISBN: 1-56971-492-4 $12.95
THE THRAWN TRILOGY
HEIR TO THE EMPIRE
Baron • Vatine • Blanchard
ISBN: 1-56971-202-6 $19.95
DARK FORCE RISING
Baron • Dodson • Nowlan
ISBN: 1-56971-269-7 $17.95
THE LAST COMMAND
Baron • Biukovic • Shanower
ISBN: 1-56971-378-2 $17.95
DARK EMPIRE
DARK EMPIRE
Veitch • Kennedy
ISBN: 1-56971-073-2 $17.95
DARK EMPIRE II
Veitch • Kennedy
ISBN: 1-56971-119-4 $17.95
EMPIRE'S END
Veitch • Baikie
ISBN: 1-56971-306-5 $5.95

BOBA FETT
DEATH, LIES,
& TREACHERY
Wagner • Kennedy
ISBN: 1-56971-311-1 $12.95
CRIMSON EMPIRE
CRIMSON EMPIRE
Richardson • Stradley • Gulacy •
Russell
ISBN: 1-56971-355-3 $17.95

COUNCIL OF BLOOD
Richardson • Stradley • Gulacy •
Emberlin
ISBN: 1-56971-410-X $17.95
JEDI ACADEMY
LEVIATHAN
Anderson • Carrasco • Heike
ISBN: 1-56971-456-8 $11.95

THE NEW JEDI ORDER ERA
25+ YEARS
AFTER STAR WARS:
A NEW HOPE

UNION
Stackpole • Teranishi • Chuckry
ISBN: 1-56971-464-9 $12.95

CHEWBACCA
Macan • Duursema • Others
ISBN: 1-56971-515-7 $12.95

INFINITIES — DOES
NOT APPLY TO TIMELINE

*TALES VOLUME 1
Marz • Plunkett • Duursema • Others
ISBN: 1-56971-619-6 $19.95
*INFINITIES — A NEW HOPE
Warner • Johnson • Snyder • Rio • Nelson
ISBN: 1-56971-648-X $12.95

BATTLE OF THE BOUNTY HUNTERS
POP-UP COMIC BOOK
Windham • Moeller
ISBN: 1-56971-129-1 $17.95
DARK FORCES
Prose novellas, heavily illustrated
SOLDIER FOR THE EMPIRE
Dietz • Williams
hardcover edition
ISBN: 1-56971-155-0 $24.95
paperback edition
ISBN: 1-56971-348-0 $14.95
REBEL AGENT
Dietz • Tucker
hardcover edition
ISBN: 1-56971-156-9 $24.95
paperback edition
ISBN: 1-56971-400-2 $14.95
JEDI KNIGHT
Dietz • Dorman
hardcover edition
ISBN: 1-56971-157-7 $24.95
paperback edition
ISBN: 1-56971-433-9 $14.95

SPANS MULTIPLE ERAS

BOUNTY HUNTERS
Truman • Schultz • Stradley • Mangels
ISBN: 1-56971-467-3 $12.95

* New

•*Prices and availability subject to change without notice*

STAR WARS
TIMELINE OF TRADE PAPERBACKS FROM DARK HORSE

TALES OF THE SITH ERA — 25,000-1000 YEARS BEFORE STAR WARS: A NEW HOPE

TALES OF THE JEDI
THE GOLDEN AGE OF THE SITH
Anderson • Carrasco, Jr. • Gossett
ISBN: 1-56971-229-8 $16.95
FALL OF THE SITH EMPIRE
Anderson • Heike • Carrasco, Jr.
ISBN: 1-56971-320-0 $14 .95
KNIGHTS OF THE OLD REPUBLIC
Veitch • Gossett
ISBN: 1-56971-020-1 $14.95
THE FREEDON NADD UPRISING
Veitch • Akins • Rodier
ISBN: 1-56971-307-3 $5.95
DARK LORDS OF THE SITH
Veitch • Anderson • Gossett
ISBN: 1-56971-095-3 $17.95
THE SITH WAR
Anderson • Carrasco, Jr.
ISBN: 1-56971-173-9 $17.95
*REDEMPTION
Anderson • Gossett • Pepoy • McDaniel
ISBN: 1-56971-535-1 $14.95
*JEDI VS. SITH
Macan • Bachs • Fernandez
ISBN: 1-56971-649-6 $15.95

PREQUEL ERA — 1000-0 YEARS BEFORE STAR WARS: A NEW HOPE

**JEDI COUNCIL
ACTS OF WAR*
Stradley • Fabbri • Vecchia
ISBN: 1-56971-539-4 $12.95
*DARTH MAUL
Marz • Duursema • Magyar • Struzan
ISBN: 1-56971-542-4 $12.95
PRELUDE TO REBELLION
Strnad • Winn • Jones
ISBN: 1-56971-448-7 $14.95
OUTLANDER
Truman • Leonardi • Rio
ISBN: 1-56971-514-9 $14.95
**JEDI COUNCIL
EMMISSARIES TO MALASTARE*
Truman • Duursema • Others
ISBN: 1-56971-545-9 $15.95
STAR WARS: TWILIGHT
Ostrander • Duursema • Magyar
ISBN: 1-56971-558-0 $12.95
*EPISODE 1 —
THE PHANTOM MENACE*
Gilroy • Damaggio • Williamson
ISBN: 1-56971-359-6 $12.95
*EPISODE 1 —
THE PHANTOM MENACE ADVENTURES*
ISBN: 1-56971-443-6 $12.95
MANGA EDITIONS
Translated into English
EPISODE 1 — THE PHANTOM MENACE
George Lucas • Kia Asamiya
VOLUME 1
ISBN: 1-56971-483-5 $9.95
VOLUME 2
ISBN: 1-56971-484-3 $9.95
*JANGO FETT
Marz • Fowler
ISBN: 1-56971-623-4 $5.95
*ZAM WESELL
Marz • Naifeh
ISBN: 1-56971-624-2 $5.95
*EPISODE 2 —
ATTACK OF THE CLONES*
Gilroy • Duursema • Kryssing • McCaig
ISBN: 1-56971-609-9 $17.95
DROIDS
THE KALARBA ADVENTURES
Thorsland • Windham • Gibson
ISBN: 1-56971-064-3 $17.95
REBELLION
Windham • Gibson
ISBN: 1-56971-224-7 $14.95
JABBA THE HUTT
THE ART OF THE DEAL
Woodring • Wetherell • Sheldon
ISBN: 1-56971-310-3 $9.95
**UNDERWORLD
THE YAVIN VASSILIKA*
Kennedy • Meglia
ISBN: 1-56971-618-8 $14.95
CLASSIC STAR WARS
HAN SOLO AT STARS' END
Goodwin • Alcala
ISBN: 1-56971-254-9 $6.95
BOBA FETT
ENEMY OF THE EMPIRE
Wagner • Gibson • Nadeau • Ezquerra
ISBN: 1-56971-407-X $12.95

TRILOGY ERA — 0-5 YEARS AFTER STAR WARS: A NEW HOPE

A NEW HOPE SPECIAL EDITION
Jones • Barreto • Williamson
ISBN: 1-56971-213-1 $9.95
MANGA EDITIONS
Translated into English
A NEW HOPE
George Lucas • Hisao Tamaki
VOLUME 1
ISBN: 1-56971-362-6 $9.95
VOLUME 2
ISBN: 1-56971-363-4 $9.95
VOLUME 3
ISBN: 1-56971-364-2 $9.95
VOLUME 4
ISBN: 1-56971-365-0 $9.95
VADER'S QUEST
Macan • Gibbons
ISBN: 1-56971-415-0 $11.95
CLASSIC STAR WARS
THE EARLY ADVENTURES
Manning • Hoberg
ISBN: 1-56971-178-X $19.95
SPLINTER OF THE MIND'S EYE
Austin • Sprouse
ISBN: 1-56971-223-9 $14.95
CLASSIC STAR WARS
IN DEADLY PURSUIT
Goodwin • Williamson
ISBN: 1-56971-109-7 $16.95
*THE EMPIRE STRIKES BACK
SPECIAL EDITION*
Goodwin • Williamson
ISBN: 1-56971-234-4 $9.95
MANGA EDITIONS
Translated into English
THE EMPIRE STRIKES BACK
George Lucas • Toshiki Kudo
VOLUME 1
ISBN: 1-56971-390-1 $9.95
VOLUME 2
ISBN: 1-56971-391-X $9.95
VOLUME 3
ISBN: 1-56971-392-8 $9.95
VOLUME 4
ISBN: 1-56971-393-6 $9.95
CLASSIC STAR WARS
THE REBEL STORM
Goodwin • Williamson
ISBN: 1-56971-106-2 $16.95
CLASSIC STAR WARS
ESCAPE TO HOTH
Goodwin • Williamson
ISBN: 1-56971-093-7 $16.95
SHADOWS OF THE EMPIRE
SHADOWS OF THE EMPIRE
Wagner • Plunkett • Russell
ISBN: 1-56971-183-6 $17.95
RETURN OF THE JEDI SPECIAL EDITION
Goodwin • Williamson
ISBN: 1-56971-235-2 $9.95
MANGA EDITIONS
Translated into English
RETURN OF THE JEDI
George Lucas • Shin-ichi Hiromoto
VOLUME 1
ISBN: 1-56971-394-4 $9.95
VOLUME 2
ISBN: 1-56971-395-2 $9.95
VOLUME 3
ISBN: 1-56971-396-0 $9.95
VOLUME 4
ISBN: 1-56971-397-9 $9.95

CLASSIC SPIN-OFF ERA — 5-25 YEARS AFTER STAR WARS: A NEW HOPE

MARA JADE
BY THE EMPEROR'S HAND
Zahn • Stackpole • Ezquerra
ISBN: 1-56971-401-0 $15.95
SHADOWS OF THE EMPIRE
EVOLUTION
Perry • Randall • Simmons
ISBN: 1-56971-441-X $14.95
X-WING ROGUE SQUADRON
THE PHANTOM AFFAIR
Stackpole • Macan • Biukovic
ISBN: 1-56971-251-4 $12.95
BATTLEGROUND: TATOOINE
Stackpole • Strnad • Nadeau • Ensign
ISBN: 1-56971-276-2 $12.95
THE WARRIOR PRINCESS
Stackpole • Tolson • Nadeau • Ensign
ISBN: 1-56971-330-8 $12.95
REQUIEM FOR A ROGUE
Stackpole • Strnad • Barr • Erskine
ISBN: 1-56971-331-6 $12.95

IN THE EMPIRE'S SERVICE
Stackpole • Nadeau • Ensign
ISBN: 1-56971-383-9 $12.95
BLOOD AND HONOR
Stackpole • Crespo • Hall • Martin
ISBN: 1-56971-387-1 $12.95
MASQUERADE
Stackpole • Johnson • Martin
ISBN: 1-56971-487-8 $12.95
MANDATORY RETIREMENT
Stackpole • Crespo • Nadeau
ISBN: 1-56971-492-4 $12.95
THE THRAWN TRILOGY
HEIR TO THE EMPIRE
Baron • Vatine • Blanchard
ISBN: 1-56971-202-6 $19.95
DARK FORCE RISING
Baron • Dodson • Nowlan
ISBN: 1-56971-269-7 $17.95
THE LAST COMMAND
Baron • Biukovic • Shanower
ISBN: 1-56971-378-2 $17.95
DARK EMPIRE
DARK EMPIRE
Veitch • Kennedy
ISBN: 1-56971-073-2 $17.95
DARK EMPIRE II
Veitch • Kennedy
ISBN: 1-56971-119-4 $17.95
EMPIRE'S END
Veitch • Baikie
ISBN: 1-56971-306-5 $5.95
BOBA FETT
DEATH, LIES, & TREACHERY
Wagner • Kennedy
ISBN: 1-56971-311-1 $12.95
CRIMSON EMPIRE
CRIMSON EMPIRE
Richardson • Stradley • Gulacy • Russell
ISBN: 1-56971-355-3 $17.95
COUNCIL OF BLOOD
Richardson • Stradley • Gulacy • Emberlin
ISBN: 1-56971-410-X $17.95
JEDI ACADEMY
LEVIATHAN
Anderson • Carrasco • Heike
ISBN: 1-56971-456-8 $11.95

THE NEW JEDI ORDER ERA — 25+ YEARS AFTER STAR WARS: A NEW HOPE

UNION
Stackpole • Teranishi • Chuckry
ISBN: 1-56971-464-9 $12.95
CHEWBACCA
Macan • Duursema • Others
ISBN: 1-56971-515-7 $12.95

INFINITIES — DOES NOT APPLY TO TIMELINE

*TALES VOLUME 1
Marz • Plunkett • Duursema • Others
ISBN: 1-56971-619-6 $19.95
**INFINITIES
A NEW HOPE*
Warner • Johnson • Snyder • Rio • Nelson
ISBN: 1-56971-648-X $12.95
**BATTLE OF THE BOUNTY HUNTERS
POP-UP COMIC BOOK**
Windham • Moeller
ISBN: 1-56971-129-1 $17.95
DARK FORCES
Prose novellas, heavily illustrated
SOLDIER FOR THE EMPIRE
Dietz • Williams
hardcover edition
ISBN: 1-56971-155-0 $24.95
paperback edition
ISBN: 1-56971-348-0 $14.95
REBEL AGENT
Dietz • Tucker
hardcover edition
ISBN: 1-56971-156-9 $24.95
paperback edition
ISBN: 1-56971-400-2 $14.95
JEDI KNIGHT
Dietz • Dorman
hardcover edition
ISBN: 1-56971-157-7 $24.95
paperback edition
ISBN: 1-56971-433-9 $14.95

SPANS MULTIPLE ERAS

BOUNTY HUNTERS
Truman • Schultz • Stradley • Mangels
ISBN: 1-56971-467-3 $12.95

* *New*
• *Prices and availability subject to change without notice*

6224

3 1170 00870 0522

Available from your local comics shop or bookstore!

To find a comics shop in your area, call 1-888-266-4226 • For more information or to order direct: •On the web: www.darkhorse.com • E-mail: mailorder@darkhorse.com
•Phone: 1-800-862-0052 or (503) 652-9701 • Mon.-Sat. 9 A.M. to 5 P.M. Pacific Time   *Prices and availability subject to change without notice